# BLUE Star GRIT

I dedicate this book to my first born Nic, the angel in the midst, who often sacrificed the connection he needed from his mother in loving support of his brother's short but full life. Nic played his heroic role which I'm sure Bart is eternally grateful.

ginnyluther@gmail.com

ISBN: 979-8-9875226-0-8 (paperback)
ISBN: 979-8-9875226-1-5 (ebook)
ISBN: 979-8-9875226-2-2 (hardcover)

Ordering Information:
Special discounts are available on quantity purchases by corporations, associations, and others. For details, contact ginnyluther@gmail.com, visit ginnyluther.com, or call (772) 486-5788.

Table of
CONTENTS

A MOTHER'S JOURNEY OF TRIUMPH AND TRAGEDY
RAISING A DEFIANT CHILD INTO AN EXCEPTIONAL LEADER

GINNY LUTHER

*Peace. It does not mean to be in a place where there is no noise, trouble, or hard work. It means to be in the midst of those things and still be calm in your heart.*

—*UNKNOWN*[1]

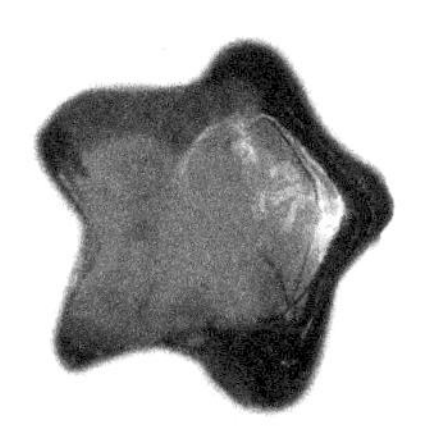

# PREFACE

I have been eager to write this book for 13 years—since shortly after my son, Bart, was murdered. I was in my fifties then—but a friend advised, "Don't write a book until you hit your sixties. That is when you'll *really* have the wisdom to know what to say." I didn't understand. The wisdom was there, but the block for me was that I hadn't attained a level of self-acceptance that allowed me to be my most vulnerable self in telling his story.

Vulnerability can be terrifying. I had to be willing to accept all the inadequacies I have been resisting throughout my life through blaming, avoiding, and hiding. The story I told myself was that making myself vulnerable would expose my weaknesses, leaving me a naked person in front of a clothed audience. Every possible *What if…?* flooded my head, from not feeling smart enough to fear of abandonment by those who are closest to me. But, as terrifying as it can be, one can find safety in vulnerability because, more often than not, opening yourself up to others creates a deeper connection.

The challenge for me was not to resist the terror, but to embrace it knowing the feelings and thoughts that are with me in those moments won't hurt me unless I choose to believe them as truth. By the time I had reached my early sixties, I understood what my friend had been telling me. I was finally ready to tell the truth, to dare tackling this writing journey.

Even so, writing this book is the scariest thing I have ever attempted. I had struggled in school, feeling I was given the clear message that I was not smart enough to succeed at anything. But as my writing progressed, and I contemplated not only Bart's life but also my own, I could no longer ignore the bigger voice from within that told me to share this story, the story of Bart and me. The struggle of raising a defiant child becomes personal growth when we recognize that examining the life of a child we birthed and raised affords us the opportunity to examine our own life and, with any luck, heal our own wounds. Thus, our children become our therapists.

Bart, my most profound teacher of my four children, was born wise, yet he suffered from an undeniable need to be understood. His incredibly inappropriate and disrespectful behavior forced me to pay attention to his cry for help. As a single mom, I vacillated between punishment and indulgence—as my energy level dictated—to discipline my children.

But even under the best of circumstances, Bart would have been a very difficult child to parent. He had an agenda for his life that rarely matched my own, or those of other adults. Temper tantrums and power struggles were our main form of communication when he was young until the threat of a wooden spoon sparked an epiphany: I couldn't change Bart's behavior, but I could change my own—and I needed to do that soon, or abuse would likely ensue.

And so began my journey toward becoming a more responsive, rather than reactive, parent. It took years of seeing him struggle and pursuing an in-depth awareness of how to shift my discipline from fear-based control to a love-based connection before I began to grasp the essence of "let go and let grow." I finally was able to let go, and he did grow to become an exceptional military leader. I changed my profession, creating my Peaceful Parenting business not only to teach other adults how to help children develop emotional intelligence, but also to help me to know how to use these skills to manage my own healing. Bart and I were definitely in this process together.

For the most part, this story excludes the journey of my life with my husband Jack, son Nic, and stepchildren Kristy and John. The deep love and many meaningful experiences they have shared with me over the years, individually and as a family, are what sustain me, but are not the focus of this book. This manuscript was created from a divine and urgent nudge intended to honor Bart's tragically shortened life.

Bart was a tenacious, intelligent man who lived a full life. His motto was *Go big or go home!* He lived intensely, from a deep love for his fiancée and family to his conviction that everyone has the right to be and live free.

Bart is gone, but he teaches me still. I have learned more about myself in the 13 years since he left this planet than I did my entire life leading up to that point. We brought out the best and worst in each other, but in doing so we helped each other grow up in our self-love, resiliency, tenacity, and desire to make a positive difference in the world.

If I had a dollar for every time someone has asked me, "How have you done it? How have you been able to get through so much with such strength?" I would be rich by now. But it is not strength alone that has given me the powers of love and forgiveness. It is the journey of seeing beyond the story to the gifts a story of struggle can bring.

What I want every reader to know is that you have more resiliency than you think. Don't resist the struggle. The struggle *is* the growth. When you find yourself saying, "I can't imagine…" know that is the story of unworthiness you tell yourself, the story that says you can't handle tough situations or grow from them. You *can* handle it. Believe me, you can. And you *will* grow.

I reveal myself to you with an intent to offer inspiration and hope so that perhaps you will come to recognize your own courage and admit that a hero lies within. We are in this together. Go big or go home!

*1st Lieutenant Robert Bartlett Fletcher*

# PART I

# BLINDSIDED

# Chapter 1
# THE SECOND BLINDSIDE

*You never realize how strong you are until being strong is the only choice you have.*
—Bob Marley[2]

*9:30 p.m. September 8, 2008*

"Don't fuck with me!" I screamed into the phone to Jerry, my ex of 20 years, while pacing back and forth from the living room to the dining room, trying not to hear what he was telling me. "It's true, Ginny. Bart is dead," his words came in gasps. He could barely get them out between sobs, as if wanting to retract every word before it slipped out. I heard his pain but couldn't acknowledge its cause.

I never mince words when I'm in fear or pain. What comes out of my mouth is unpredictably repugnant and scary at times. Expletives tumbled out of my mouth as if they had been sight words in my elementary school primer "This is *not* a joke, you asshole. I don't believe one fucking thing you're saying. Don't pull this shit on me."

Jerry handed off the phone to someone. I could hear them fumbling with it as it changed hands. An unfamiliar voice identified itself as an officer of the United States Army.

At that moment my doorbell rang. Panic gripped my throat. Jack, my husband of 18 years, flung open the door. As if on cue in what I mistakenly thought was Jerry's melodrama, two uniformed military officers stood on the threshold. The suddenness with which the door was opened threw them off their script. They looked at me, standing in the middle of the room with the phone in my hand, mascara smeared across my cheek, staring back at them as if they were aliens on my doorstep. They looked at Jack, his hand still on the doorknob. And then they looked at each other with dread. Obviously, the horrifying news they were there to deliver had preceded them.

I threw down the phone and began shrieking. Jack clutched me like an attendant on a psychiatric ward trying to contain an out-of-control patient.

"Breathe, sweetie, we're gonna get through this," he whispered in my ear.

"No, no. He can't be dead. He just got back from Iraq. No!" I screamed.

My world began to slow, the pace dragging and picking up again. What were those terrifying screams? Who were they coming from and where had I heard them before? I couldn't hear what the officers were saying. I could only read their body language and watch their lips slowly spell out the message I had dreaded for so long. My baby boy was gone…forever.

"On behalf of the President of the United States…"

He would never walk through that door again. I would never again see that beautiful smile that could light up a room in an instant.

"…and the Secretary of the United States Army…"

I would never be able to touch his precious face or feel the Mom-hug he demanded whenever he hadn't seen me in a while. I would never again listen to his laughter or be the recipient of his playful jokes that challenged my gullibility.

"…it is my unfortunate duty to inform you…"

We would never have another chat in the wee hours of the morning that defined the closeness and understanding we shared...

"...your son, First Lieutenant Robert Fletcher..."

We would never again be able to cook together during the holidays or engage in a lively political conversation.

"...was killed in the line of duty at 08:30 this morning."

In fact, his whole life passed through my mind in an instant as I continued to scream in denial of what was. I was only conscious of Jack's tight embrace as he whispered into my ear, "Keep breathing, honey. You are going to handle this. We're gonna get through this, sweetie. Keep breathing."

As my consciousness flickered in and out, flashes of my past emerged. I was crying for Bart, but I was 15. It wasn't Jack holding me; it was my oldest brother, Gordon, and there were no reassuring words. All he could offer was, "He's dead." My mind was flitting back and forth—fearing the past and denying the present. Bart. Dad. Jack. Gordon. At times it was hard to distinguish where I was, or who was there with me. I couldn't focus on anything around me. All I knew was that the place I was in felt very familiar; it felt like hell.

After 20 minutes of outright tantrum, my body began to settle into a surrendered, but numbed, state. Everything was surreal, as if it wasn't actually happening or I was making it up as I went along. I pinched myself to see if I could feel it. I could. "No," I moaned. This can't be happening again. What have I done to deserve this? I've worked so hard to bring peace to this world in all I do, work and play. It's my mission. I have tried all my life to be a child of God. I have worked hard to live by His rules, and this happens again? Why?

The army officers were pushing papers toward me to sign, but I waved them away. All I wanted to think about was how I was going to get my baby back.

My mind flooded with images of my other children. How were they going to handle this? Nic. Oh, Nic. Bart's older brother. He's alone. Who will be there for him? And John, my stepson, Bart's oldest brother. He at least has his girlfriend to hold and console him.

And Bart's fiancée, Katie, whom Jack and I had practically raised in her teens. She was all alone in Killeen, Texas, waiting for him to come home. By now he was very late. She would be worried. Would she find out about his death by watching the news? No! She had no one there to support her. My mind was distracted by all the drama that would ensue, the suffering.

As the officers were trying to explain the paperwork they wanted me to sign, a wave of nausea enveloped me. I ran to the bathroom and vomited into the toilet. There was a moment of hope that this violent purge would somehow make it all go away. When I was done, I rinsed my mouth and caught my reflection in the bathroom mirror. My face was ashen, eyes swollen, I couldn't recognize myself. Or maybe I just didn't want to. I desperately wanted to disappear, to not be the mother of a deceased child. Losing a child is every mother's greatest nightmare, and it was happening to *me*. Widow, orphan—these are labels that our culture can tolerate and accept in death. But there is no label for a parent who loses a child. Perhaps our culture isn't willing to accept it because we don't want to fathom ever being dragged down to that level of despair.

I found myself staring blankly into the mirror and I focused. I needed some answers. Everyone had told me all my life that I was strong, and I knew it was true. I had faced so many struggles, and my strength was the only thread of hope I had to keep me moving forward, choosing to face the fear rather than run from it.

*Ginny, you are strong. You are going to get through this. Just do it!*

This would be what I rehearsed in my head in the coming weeks, desperately trying to convince myself that it was even remotely possible.

Grudgingly I went back into the living room where the officers were still patiently waiting for me to sign the paperwork. Jack was on the phone making the dreaded calls to the kids.

"Who killed my son? Give me details. I want details."

"The only information we have, Ms. Luther, is that we know your son was shot by a specialist in his company who was suspected of criminally harboring some highly sensitive military equipment. The shooter committed suicide after killing your son."

I was shocked. "But what happened? How could this be? How does a member of the Band of Brothers do this to one of his own officers? How could this happen stateside? Bart was safer in Iraq, for God's sake!"

"We really can't answer any of your questions until there has been further investigation. But, ma'am, we need you to sign this paperwork."

Looking at their faces for the first time, I could tell this was a job they dreaded. My hands went through the motions of signing, but I will never remember what the paperwork was about. I suspect it was verification of receiving the news of Bart's death. Their compassionate persistence in getting me to help them complete their task was, I'm sure, an effort to get the hell out of my house and put this awful chore behind them. But imagining their own families receiving this same news endowed them with a particular gentleness and patience for which I was grateful.

Once the papers were signed, the officers told me that there would be a Casualty Assistance Officer who would be meeting me when I arrived at the army base in Fort Hood, Texas. He would be taking the lead in helping me with the processing of Bart's remains, funeral arrangements, and so forth.

I could barely focus. My priority was getting to Texas and holding my baby in my arms so that I could say goodbye. Wanting to make that last connection, I longed to feel that last touch and store it inside me forever as a loving memory. He needed to hear the soothing, maternal voice that would tell him that everything was okay. Momma is here. I hungered to hold his hand, no matter how cold, to let him know how much I love him, how much I would miss him; to kiss his sweet forehead as I did in my goodnight rituals with him in his childhood; to be the one that closed the coffin on his life, like the straightening of the bedclothes and the soft click of the bedside lamp before closing the bedroom door. As soon as I got to Texas, come hell or high water, I was determined to see my son.

Once the officers left, Jack and I had the daunting task of deciding our next steps.

"I should go, and you stay here to deal with everything on this end and arrange for his funeral," I said.

Jack, being the supportive partner he is, was more than agreeable. "You took that right out of my head."

We often shared thoughts, speaking them in unison at times.

My first order of business was to call my remaining children who at this point, I was sure, were in the depths of their own personal hells, each trying to process the news that would forever change their visions of the normal family life the six of us had created over the past 18 years. From now on there would be a new normal. Not knowing what it would look like, I was determined it would be nothing like the chaotic dysfunction I had lived after the first blindside.

There were no words to share with my children, just the pure, raw emotion that comes from complete shock, awe, and despair. No words were necessary. The emotional connection eventually soothed us. I just ached to hold and cradle each one of them until they could cry no more. If I could only turn the clock back and make all the hurt go away. Isn't that what mothers do? Make the boo-boos go away?

But at a deeper level, wisdom told me their grief was not mine to handle for them—that this was another time to let go and let grow. They were now faced with their first real blindside in life. My whole career as an early childhood educator had been centered on teaching children the skills necessary to cope with what life throws at them. My job now would be to model a grieving process for my own children that would inspire them to follow me through the healing. This would force me to hold on to that very fine thread of strength that would keep me from giving up, which at this moment I craved.

After connecting with my children, I knew I had to attend to my professional life. As a master instructor of Conscious Discipline® and public speaker in my Peaceful Parenting business, canceling my classes and speaking engagements for at least the next week was a no-brainer. I logged on to my computer and stared at the blank screen. What could I write to my colleagues that might lighten the burden of the news that was about to be dropped on them? One thing was certain: I did not want to be seen as a victim. That is what I have taught over and over from small, intimate parenting classes to hundreds of keynote speeches at early childhood conferences. Yes, I had been victimized, but I was not willing to call myself a victim. Being a victim—or not—is a choice. The latter was *my* choice. Experience had taught me that allowing myself to be carried away by a flood of pity would only lure me into the tempting, but toxic, depths of despair.

But telling everyone that all was well would be lying, because it clearly wasn't. I knew what I had to do. I needed to ask others to wish me well—to believe that I could and would handle this. If they could lend me their strength, it would be the bandage—albeit too small for such a deep wound—that would be enough to carry me for the short term. Absent was my ability to connect with the strength that lay deep within my soul. Asking for help was not my strong suit, since I was the one usually giving it. *Know in your hearts that all is well,* I wrote. *Please do not see me or my family as victims. Our strength in healing will come from how you see us handling this!*

The next order of business was to call two of my most valued friends who I knew could be there for me unconditionally. At this point there were no tears. Shock was setting in, so the phone calls were short and to the point.

Becky, my Conscious Discipline mentor and personal friend, would be there to keep me in the present, reminding me hour by hour to eat, breathe deeply, take a step forward, and know that I was safe.

"Bart's dead. He was killed by a solider at Fort Hood."

"Oh, no!" Becky whispered.

*Don't cry now, Ginny, or you won't be able to stop.*

"Listen, would you do me a favor and let our team of instructors know? All I really need is for you all to wish me well. Please don't see me as a victim, okay?"

"Okay. I'm here for you." A pause. "Ginny?"

"Yeah?"

"You got this. I'll be in touch soon."

My lifelong friend, Cathy, dropped her workload after getting my call and flew from Toronto to my home in Florida, where she would be waiting to take care of me when I returned home from Texas.

Next, I had to arrange the first flight I could get to Killeen. Once that was done, I realized I was going to need cash for the trip. My wallet was empty. Frantically I scoured the house for some cash. *The safe! I have some stashed in there.* When I dipped my hand in and pulled out an envelope, on it were the words *Katie & Bart's wedding*. This was the first moment I realized there would be no wedding.

Katie and Bart had been high school sweethearts and together for seven years. Love at first sight, and they never looked back. Bart had saved for more than a year to purchase the diamond ring that Katie fell in love with when they were shopping one day. He had just popped the question a few months earlier, and they planned to be married the next year after Bart returned from his second deployment.

"It's not fair," I screamed in despair, banging my fists on the metal door. The thought was a physical pain, as if someone had sliced open my belly and extracted all of my organs, leaving them on the cold, hard tile to wither and slowly die. I pounded the door with all my strength until I could no longer lift my arms.

It was midnight before the house fell silent and we made a pathetic attempt to sleep. It was an eerie silence, one in which I could not lie still. Jack and I lay spooned together, numb, anxious, and full of fear. The demons settled in my brain, chasing away the busyness of what needed to be done with heartbreaking images of what the future would look like without Bart. I didn't know what to say, how to feel, what to do. A miracle was all I could pray for, that my child would walk through my front door and I would feel his loving presence in my arms.

The void I felt in that moment was so overwhelming that I grabbed Jack, and we made desperate and urgent love. This, I knew as we clutched each other, would only temporarily fill the deep hole in my heart. I dreaded the empty moments to come. *Don't stop, Ginny. Just keep it going.*

But this distraction could not last forever. Staying in bed only increased the ruminating thoughts of what lay ahead. A wave of grief washed over my body. It would not be pretty, but giving myself permission to emote, alone, exactly as I pleased, without worrying Jack, would create the safety I needed to begin the grieving process. I did not want to be consoled, which would be the response of most people. Consolation would create an obligation for me to respond—more for their satisfaction than for mine—and it would only interfere with my grieving. I didn't need that pretense right now. Grief is ugly, but it's real and necessary. And at that moment I yearned to scream to the heavens above.

I slipped out to the back porch and wailed for hours. Wailing seemed to fill the place that sleep abandoned. I hoped it wouldn't wake the neighbors, but there was no holding back. Holding back only meant the healing would be deferred. I knew I had to face my pain by being present with it, not resisting it. Wailing felt productive to me. It gave significance to all the years I had spent raising this most difficult, but intensely close child. For the second time, I cursed God.

In between wails, I pleaded for Bart to reveal himself to me, one last time. I was desperate to connect with him. On some strange level, I felt closer to him. His celestial energy enveloped me while breathing in the warm, sticky breeze of the late-summer night. I could feel him when I opened my heart to a sky filled with crisp starlight. Every cloud passed with purpose. Every wisp of wind that swayed the palm fronds seemed intentional. He was with me, trying to send a message that was vague and unreachable. *Relax, Ginny. Let go. Listen.*

Suddenly clarity emerged with Bart whispering the very words I had written to him while he was in military readiness training, preparing for deployment to Iraq.

*What I want you to know is how proud I am of all the challenges that you continue to take on in your life. It is only with risk that we can fully experience life. If we all just played it safe, then we would watch life from a kaleidoscope rather than feel we had a part in it all. You, Mom, are a gift from God. You are here to make your mark in the world. I want you to know that I have always believed in you, no matter what the challenge. Any doubts about what you have done in the past are only doubts I have had in myself. You have always been one to live up to your tenets and the good of all people, no matter who has resisted or how you have stood in the face of others. Always, a leader must face the adversity of others' fears. Sometimes there were moments when I have questioned, just for the moment, whether I did the "right thing." It was only then that my trust and faith in God came to grips with all my questioning and self doubts of the past. You can do it, Mom, I know you will!*

For a precious few moments, I felt a deep sense of gratitude, lucky to have been the mother of this incredibly powerful young man. He had made his mark on the world in so many ways. It was his persistence that helped me understand that his agenda for life was one that required support, not control. He had helped me find the path for letting go and letting him grow to accomplish all that he wanted in his short life. It was a journey we had shared since he was two-and-a-half years old.

He taught me that his life was his journey, that his struggle was his growth. Who was I to deny him what he came here for? All his life he carried a deep drive within, and he had chosen me to be the unconditional, loving support to witness what he'd come here to achieve. In our journey, I learned that I was just like him in my passion for wanting to make the world a better place and my impatience with those who couldn't see the need for change. We were soul reflections of each other, which was made abundantly clear by *my* resistance to *his* resistance of my control. It took me awhile, but eventually I realized that I needed to step through the looking glass and be present with him to help him make sense of his world. My efforts at control only resulted in undermining his internal guidance and confidence. I came to understand that there is a greater power in all of life and that I must trust that all is well, no matter the outcome.

Bart had lived a short twenty-four years on this planet, fully and completely. He had felt deeply and accomplished more than most adults feel or accomplish in a lifetime. I knew in that instant that when the clouds lifted, something bigger and brighter would come. Bart would continue his legacy on this planet, even though I would never be able to experience the physical sensation of him again.

When the wave of wailing began to subside, and my body returned to reality, I checked my watch. *Shit! It's 3:30a.m. I better get moving.* It was time to take the next step on this surreal journey—get on a plane headed to uncharted territory. Jack would stay home to start making arrangements for a funeral. My job was to bring my baby home.

I threw clothes into a carry-on without much thought of what would be appropriate, knowing that I could not predict anything that was to happen in the next few days. I would be experiencing life like a two-year-old, entering each moment without any knowledge or forethought of what was to come, forced to live fully in the here and now, seeing and responding to only what was presented to me.

Turning to leave my bedroom, my eyes zoomed in on a blue glass star lying on the shelf in front of me. It matched the one I gave Bart shortly before he was deployed to Iraq. I scooped it up and slipped it into my pocket, not understanding why, but knowing I needed to take it with me.

# Chapter 2
# FORT HOOD

*Face it till you make it.*
—UNKNOWN[3]

As my plane took off from Palm Beach International Airport, I considered my destination. I have always detested the concept of war and everything related to it, so going to an army post filled with uniformed people who relate to and respect each other based primarily on an assessment of how they will perform in battle did not sit well with me. And I did not know what to expect in terms of how they would respond to me under the circumstances. What was clear to me, however, was my desperation to make a connection with Bart before they tore him to shreds in forensics.

Equally important, I wanted details. What exactly happened that could have triggered one of Bart's soldiers to want to kill an officer who was once his leader in combat? Was it revenge? Did Bart provoke him? Not likely since Bart had spoken of his soldiers with compassion and appreciation for their service to their country. He made a tireless commitment to keep every soldier under his command safe. He had sacrificed his own safety to make sure they each came home in one piece from Iraq. So, what happened?

As I faded in and out of consciousness during takeoff—my body's attempt to catch up on the sleep I had missed—another wave of sadness engulfed me. The plane soared upward through the dawn clouds and emerged into a stunning sunrise over the ocean. An ethereal connection with my precious baby enveloped me. I had flown a hundred times in my profession and often witnessed scenes like this, but this time was different. *This is what it must be like in heaven,* I thought. The tears streamed down my face. It was easy to be in this sadness. I could give in to my grief without triggering a barrage of sympathy from the other passengers who were blissfully unaware, thanks to the blessed muffling of my sobs by the hum of the jet engines. Leaning my head against the window, I cried, deep and long. Each time I came up for air, there would be a celestial scene outside my window—peace, light, beauty. *I hope this is where you are, Bart.*

When I arrived in Austin, Bart's commanding officer, Mike Doyle, was scheduled to pick me up at the airport to escort me to Killeen, about an hour's drive away, where Fort Hood is located. I was apprehensive about meeting him. Was he going to be one of those gung-ho army types who is full of himself? *One step at a time, Ginny. You can do this.*

As I exited through the doorway of the baggage claim area, a man dressed in civilian clothes got out his car abruptly and headed in my direction. His eyes were wide and his pace urgent. *This must be Captain Doyle.* He did not seem certain of how I might respond. Would I shriek with rage, screaming every obscenity in the book at him? Would I pound on his chest, imposing all blame on this man who was the one responsible for my son's safety?

He reached out to shake my hand. "Hi, you must be Lieutenant Bart's mom," he said with a quivering voice.

I couldn't deny the man my son so deeply admired. "You must be Captain Doyle. Nice to meet you."

"Oh, please, call me Mike," he insisted and took a deep breath. "Besides, Bart would not want it any other way."

"Bart spoke so highly of you as a captain and a friend."

Mike must have been relieved to see me keep my wits about me. He grabbed my bag and escorted me to the car. I was biding my time until I could start my interrogation. When we had settled into the drive to Killeen, Mike began the inevitable—the tragic story of my son's death.

Yesterday, Bart had gone to Specialist Jody Wirawan's apartment to reclaim some highly sensitive and expensive army equipment that Wirawan was suspected of stealing from the armory where he worked, Mike told me. They needed confirmation that he in fact had the equipment in his possession. Mike had called Wirawan several times to get him to return the items, but he did not respond. Wirawan had served two tours in Iraq and was scheduled to be discharged today. Mike had exactly one day to retrieve those items before his discharge.

It was a busy time for the Headquarters and Headquarters Company, or HHC as it was commonly called, as they were preparing for their next deployment to Iraq. Bart likely knew the stress his commanding officer was under, so he offered to go check on Wirawan and talk him into giving back the items if he indeed had them. The army wasn't interested in prosecuting Wirawan, Mike told me; it seemed insignificant considering all they had to do to prepare for the upcoming deployment and Wirawan's impending end-of-tour discharge. Besides, he explained, there wasn't enough time to get the paperwork together before his discharge. Why not take a shot at convincing him to return the items and get on with his life? Wirawan had been described as "not the soldiering type." The army wanted to let him go ASAP because he was not "in it for the right reasons."

Listening to Mike, I sensed a mentality of "We handle our own."

At the time, confronting Wirawan did not appear to be an impending threat. Someone just needed to go over to his apartment and talk to him.

Bart took Staff Sergeant Jones with him, as protocol dictated. The second-floor apartment was accessed by an open balcony, so they had no trouble finding Wirawan's front door. They knocked. No one answered. Mike had told Bart to get in touch with him if anything unusual were to occur or they ran into a dead end, so Bart took out his phone, called, and told Mike the windows were shaded but they were fairly sure Wirawan was in there. They were all wondering the same thing: if he was in there, why wasn't he responding to their knocking? Something wasn't right. Mike advised asking the apartment manager to unlock the door.

The apartment manager accompanied Bart back to Wirawan's door and attempted to unlock it, but the door was securely bolted from the inside. When Bart relayed this to Mike, Mike determined the situation was urgent and advised them to carefully remove a windowpane, if they could, to see what was going on inside.

Once they removed the kitchen window, they pulled the shade aside and scanned the apartment. On the table, scattered among empty liquor bottles, were a multitude of weapons and ammunition, Mike said. Staff Sergeant Jones spotted Wirawan coming out of the bedroom with a Glock in his hand. When Bart relayed this to Mike, he told Bart to hang up the phone and call 911 for assistance. The situation had just turned from a social call into a crime scene.

Bart called 911 and turned to Jones and the apartment manager and ordered them off the balcony.

They complied, while Bart stayed on the balcony. As Jones was going down the stairs, he saw Wirawan coming out of the apartment and slipping a gun into his pants pocket. He tried to signal to Bart, but Bart was preoccupied with the 911 dispatcher.

"Who are you talking to?" Wirawan demanded.

Bart ignored the question and tried to talk to him.

Wirawan yelled at him, "You better not be talking to the cops." He turned and stormed back into the apartment. Now would have been the time for Bart to leave. But he didn't.

Wirawan came back out of the apartment just as police sirens could be heard in the distance. Then the glass pane Bart and Jones had taken out of the window and left on the window ledge crashed to the ground.

Wirawan lost it, Mike said. "I told you not to call the cops!" He lunged forward; his gun pointed at Bart.

Bart had nowhere to go, nowhere to run. Wirawan fired his gun, killing Bart instantly.

By then the police had pulled onto the property and heard the shots. They exchanged gunfire with Wirawan, and Wirawan turned his gun on himself. The rest of the details were unclear as they could not get as much information as they were hoping for from Staff Sergeant Jones, who had suffered a mental breakdown after the incident.

Mike's voice had grown increasingly frantic as the story escalated, and the sudden silence startled me. His horrific tale had left me at a loss for words. But now I was shocked by the distress on his face. His next words shook me to the core.

"*I* was supposed to be the one," he agonized. "I was supposed to confront Wirawan. Bart took *my* place. I was the commanding officer. I was the one who was supposed to be shot." Mike fought hard to hold back tears of guilt and hopelessness.

In the silence that prevailed, I wanted to open the car door and run like hell. To be anywhere but here. Instead, I found myself consoling someone I subconsciously wished had followed through with the original plan. If Mike had gone to talk to Specialist Wirawan that day, my Bart would still be alive. And yet, if that had been the case, I would be sitting here consoling Bart and the hellish journey he would have to endure for the rest of his life—survivor's guilt.

This man had hand-picked Bart to be his executive officer. There was a bond between them. But he was an officer of the United States Army and would have to "suck it up" and pretend this was another casualty of war. But this wasn't war, was it? As far as the army was concerned, this was just some unfortunate accident, and Mike Doyle would have to live with that horrible truth every night of his life when the world went to sleep and he, unable to escape his guilt, would wrestle with his demons all night long.

For the moment, I could accept that Bart's death was a tragic and an unfortunate event, entirely out of my control. My journey would be an easy one compared to Mike Doyle's. For him, there would be no resolution, no calm.

When we got to Killeen, Mike drove us to the house of one of Bart's fellow officers. I was pleasantly surprised to see Katie there. Far from being devastated, as I expected her to be, she looked like I felt—numb. The two people on this Earth who had the deepest relationships with Bart embraced as if it were any other day, exchanging a brief hug.

"This sucks," Katie said.

There were several officers of various rank roaming around the house, chatting, and trying to keep things light, yet respectful. There was an eerie uneasiness in the place, like the feeling of a stifled truth. I couldn't put my finger on it, but everyone seemed uncomfortable.

Mike introduced me to the Casualty Assistance Officer who handles army protocol in Texas, helping families manage the deaths of fallen soldiers. Bart's major introduced himself, and soon after, Colonel Solomon arrived. They were solemn and cordial, but insisted they were open to all questions.

I didn't hesitate. "Where was he shot?"

You could hear a pin drop in the room. Every person in uniform stopped chatting and looked around, as if I had screamed the question. The tension in the room was palpable, creating a wall of disconnection. I wasn't like these people. We had only one thing in common—our shared passion in making the world a more peaceful place. The means by which each of us hoped to achieve this goal, however, were completely different.

At times disdain for what the military stood for welled inside me. Its mere existence intimidated me, like a teen with no athletic ability being thrown into a clique of jocks. It was a group I had no desire to be a part of. Unwilling to blindly follow their protocol of how a patriotic mother should respond to the loss of her son, I was reluctant to conform to what they thought I should be.

Colonel Solomon paused, then grinned, a perfect military grin. "You don't really want to know all the details," he assured me.

"Yes," I said calmly. "I do."

"As far as we know, he was shot in the chest."

*As far as you know?* I wasn't sure I could trust this guy.

"When can I see him?"

Deafening silence. Was paranoia prowling, or was there something they all knew that they had no intention of sharing with me? After an uncomfortable moment, the major took me by the elbow and explained that it wasn't protocol to allow the family to see the deceased's body. But he told me, he would do everything in his power to try to make it happen. He went on to say that it would be difficult, at best, because Bart's body was in Dallas for autopsy and forensics.

Sensing that I was getting a bullshit story, I pressed on. "I don't really care where he is or what they are doing. I just need to make closure. I need to see that it is really him. I don't have to see his whole body. I'm his mother." I gave the major my most ingratiating smile. "I can identify him by his hands, his toes, his thumb. All I need to see is his right thumb."

There were enough childhood scars on Bart's body that could only be identified by me. When Bart was 18 months old, we lived in an old apartment whose windows no longer stayed open without the assistance of sturdy dowels to hold up the heavy sashes. One day, while the boys were playing quietly in the playroom, I decided it was a prime opportunity to have some mommy time in the bathroom without an audience. As soon as my butt hit the cold toilet seat, I heard a thumping crash followed by a terrifying scream. Bart's curiosity had gotten the better of him. He had finally been able to pull the dowel out while I wasn't around to spoil his fun, but not fast enough to completely remove his hand. His right thumb was crushed between the window and sill. Miraculously, surgeons were able to reattach it, but the scar that remained gave it a distinctly odd look.

"We'll do everything in our power to make that happen, Ms. Fletcher. We'll get right on it."

*Sure, you'll get right on it.* I fumed. *Another line of bullshit!* I could feel with every cell of my body that he was lying to me, telling me what he thought I wanted to hear. *Why don't you get right on getting my name right?*

Suddenly I was overwhelmed by it all. There was no energy left to keep fighting a battle I knew I could not win. Days later I would discover my hunch was correct. In the meantime, they never followed through with granting my wish to make closure with Bart.

I asked Mike if he would step outside with me for a minute. I trusted Mike. Bart had always spoken highly of him. He seemed genuine, and I sensed he was being honest with me. It was clear his only mission right now was to protect me and my family, even if it was through the army's rigmarole.

When we were outside, I reached into my pocket and pulled out the blue glass star I had grabbed before leaving home. Cradling it in my palm, I looked him in the eye. "I need to tell you the story of this blue star.

"Just before Bart was deployed to Iraq last November, Jack and I flew him home so we could spend a few days with him before he left. I wanted to cook him some of his favorite meals, reminisce over his favorite stories, and have an opportunity to say to him all the things a mother needs to say before her child goes off to war.

"On the morning of his last day at home, I wondered what words of wisdom I could share with him before he left. I came up with nothing. I saw a blue glass star sitting on a shelf in my office. I immediately knew this was what I wanted to give him. He knew what it represented and what it meant between us. It was a way I could be with him.

"I'm pretty sure, Mike, that Bart always carried that star with him when in uniform. If he had it on him when he was killed, I'd like to know."

I placed the star in Mike's hand. "I can see this has been a horrendous experience for you too. I want you to have this star to remind you that Bart will always be with you, watching your back."

Mike could no longer hold back his tears. This tough soldier, who had been taught from the first day of boot camp to *Suck it up!*, knew the sacrifice Bart had made, and it tore him up. He promised he would do his best to find Bart's blue star.

"Thank you, Mike," I said, "because if I can't see my son one last time, I sure as hell want to get that star back."

"I understand," he whispered.

After two long days of dealing with the army's process for releasing a fallen soldier, Mike dropped me off at the Killeen airport. Reaching for the car door handle, I turned to thank him.

He had his hand out, balled in a fist. He smiled. "Hold out your hand."

I was too tired to guess what he might be up to. I sighed and held my hand out, palm up, as if we were playing a child's game. He dropped a blue glass star into my hand. I stared at it. "Is this Bart's star? Did he have it on him? *How* did you get it?"

He beamed. "I drove up to Dallas last night." And, in a playful whisper, "I had to break into the forensics lab."

"You broke into the lab?"

"I think I'd better keep the details to myself." He laughed.

I looked him in the eye. "Forgive me for asking, but this is Bart's, right?

You're not trying to make me feel better by giving me back the one I gave you yesterday?"

He leaned on his left hip and dug into his right pocket for a few seconds. He pulled out an identical blue star.

"You drove three hours up to Dallas, broke into a forensics lab, got Bart's star, and drove three hours back to Killeen?" I couldn't believe his compassion.

"Look, Ginny, I felt so bad that you didn't get to see Bart's body. It was terrible that you didn't have that closure."

"Mike, I have to ask. Where was it in his uniform?"

He looked down at his star and rubbed his thumb over the top of it. "It was in his shirt pocket."

"I thought that's where he kept it," I said, satisfied. "I don't know how I can possibly thank you for doing this. It means so much to me. You don't know." I looked him in the eye and shook his hand warmly. "I'll see you in Florida on Friday. Good luck escorting his body back home."

Mike lowered his eyes, "Uh, just thought I'd let you know, his body may not look like you expect it to. The air pressure from flying could distort it a bit."

I didn't know what to make of this statement. I knew the army was pressed to prepare his body quickly so it could be flown home before a major hurricane was forecast to hit Texas, but how bad could a bullet hole in the chest be? The tears began welling in my eyes, and I got out of the car.

My feet dragged as I entered the terminal, but my heart felt lighter than it had in days as I tucked Bart's star into my purse. *I may not be taking my son's body home, but I can carry his soul with me.* The star I had given him to remind him that I was always with him, was now a reminder to me that Bart would always be with me.

When I walked in through the front door of my home, my life would never be the same. Truth was, I knew nothing would ever be the same, but now I had Bart watching my back. *Keep breathing, Ginny,* I patted my purse. *You're going to handle this. All there is is now, so take another step and breathe again.*

I resigned myself to the fact that every moment from here on out would be different. I remembered that in the aftermath of my first tragic blindside, some of my friends abandoned me—not because they didn't know what to say or do, but because I was a constant reminder of the unpredictability of life and how devastating it can be. I wondered who would step up to the plate when my feet touched home base. Who would be there for me? Who would ignore my calls for support?

With two hours to kill before my flight, I was roaming aimlessly, not knowing how to still myself. I stopped at a newsstand to purchase a newspaper, wondering what had been printed in the local papers about the murder-suicide at Fort Hood. I picked up a copy of the Killeen Daily Herald, and there we were: Katie and I, front page center. A reporter had interviewed us the day before. *Kill*-een, I thought, *the place where my son was killed.* An uncontrollable urge to giggle at the irony of Bart being killed in Killeen, got the better of me. *Oh, Ginny*, I sighed, *you really are sleep-deprived.*

When I paid for the paper, the cashier looked at the front page and then back at me. She smiled in a way that was mostly a frown—a pity smile. It dawned on me that other people were looking at me as well. Killeen was a small town with a close relationship with the army post. Locals took these assaults on their community seriously. My face must have been imprinted in their memories from all the media coverage. Several seemed to know who I was. Some stared, some mustered the courage to approach me and say something, anything. It was usually one simple, disjointed phrase: "I'm sorry.... I can't imagine."

I found these eruptions of pity curious. Why would someone who had nothing to do with the incident say they are sorry? Sorry for what? They didn't do anything. Sorry for my loss? That phrase is so tired it doesn't mean anything to me anymore. Could they really mean, *I'm sorry for feeling grateful for my life when yours is so sad*? Or, *I'm sorry because I was fortunate enough to be spared from the private hell you are going through*?

This was going to be harder than I first thought. I had to get used to people coping with their pain of feeling sorry for me, pointing fingers at me, and whispering behind their hands, or just outright pivoting on the spot and walking away from me so they wouldn't have to look into my eyes and imagine the reality for themselves. Oh, the loneliness! I had forgotten how wretched the isolation could be. These ruminating thoughts were getting the best of me. Despite my body's resistance, I really did need to get some sleep.

After arriving at my gate, I sat silently, watching the people around me who didn't know—those who weren't offering condolences or stealing little glances my way. It was a relief, but then it started to irritate me. Part of me thought, *they should know*. The whole world should know of this crazy, horrible incident. But at the same time there was comfort in them not knowing. It meant the people sitting next to me would not scatter or shut down completely because they didn't know what to say or do. Not knowing meant I could have a conversation with them that was relatively normal.

Actually, a conversation would have been normal a week ago, but not now. Nothing was normal now. It all seemed foreign, but I derived some solace in revisiting normalcy in my imagination. I longed for normal, yet at the same time despised it. It was a toss-up of either screaming out at the atrocity of the offense or crawling into my cave of silence, alone and hopeless. Either choice did not have a good outcome. Tears flooded my eyes.

I snatched up my phone and called a close friend, someone I hadn't had time to connect with since Bart's death. Lisa would listen calmly while I vented, and I so needed to vent.

When she picked up the phone, there was an awkward pause.

"Ginny. Where are you?"

"I'm sure you've heard the news by now."

"I know. Oh, my God, Ginny. I'm so sorry! I can't imagine."

*There is that damn phrase again.* I took Lisa through the details of my current status—how pissed off I felt about the betrayal of the army and not being able to see Bart's body. It was the very least they could have done, an opportunity for closure that I never had after my father died. Lisa responded like many of the people I had encountered in the airport. Little mewings of pity and commiseration. The first calls with my closest friends would be no different. I knew they cared about me and what I was going through—

deeply—but no one knew what to say. Aside from little tut-tuts and other comfort noises, Lisa could say nothing that brought comfort—not that I'm sure anyone could have done any better—so I babbled on, trying to gloss over this moment even though I needed something more from her. I began to feel so depleted, I could hardly make sense of even the simplest conversation. Finally my flight was called, and I had an excuse to say goodbye.

Boarding the plane, I was delighted to discover my seat was in the first row by the window. Fortunately no one else was seated in my row and the bulkhead was in front of me, so I was protected from any passenger interference. But, sequestered comfortably in my safe little cocoon, I realized that was probably the plan. This was not the first time the airline had to deal with the bereaved family member of a veteran, and I was grateful for their forethought.

As it turned out, the airline knew exactly what they were doing. Once airborne, I was again engulfed in the heavenly clouds outside my window. And, as on the trip over, I felt an immediate connection with Bart. He was here, holding my hand and hugging my heart. The pain of what once was, again overwhelmed me, and I spent the remainder of the flight swaddled in a slow, steady wail, loud enough to cleanse my sorrow but blending perfectly with the pitch of the engines so that I was not disturbing the other passengers.

One man across the aisle, however, had noticed me sobbing. He looked at me, concerned, like he was considering asking me if I was all right but didn't want to intrude. I picked up the copy of the newspaper that was sitting on the seat next to me and acknowledged his concern by pointing to the front page. The flight attendant noticed him looking at me and went to explain. She handled it quietly and graciously. Yet, as comforting as her attempts were, part of me once again could not escape the isolation of grief.

What is it about our culture that we go to such effort to avoid the subject of death? Death is such an integral part of life. If we would just learn to accept it, deal with it, so people can provide comfort without feeling the fear of how to offer it.

Once the plane landed back on my home turf, anticipation of what I had to face in the next few days hounded me. *God, help me! Every minute feels like hours.*

As I was preparing to disembark, an attendant approached me. "A Casualty Assistant Officer will be meeting you at the gate when you get off the plane, Ms. Luther."

*Thank God! Now I don't have to think about what to do next.*

When I emerged from the jetway into the gate area, a man in uniform stepped forward, his hand extended. "Ms. Luther, I'm Colonel Maddox. I'll be helping you over the next few days as your liaison with the US Army."

The moment I shook hands with him, relief flowed through me. Someone to hold my hand and help me navigate the perplexing world of the US Military. My ability to maintain the facade of strength was waning. Home was where I wanted to be—with my family. He took my arm and gallantly escorted me down the escalator to baggage claim.

Unfortunately, being escorted through the airport by a uniformed officer sparked much curiosity from the other passengers disembarking from the plane. Once they saw his hand compassionately tucked under my elbow, they instantly made the connection. Bart's murder had become national news; the local news stations, especially, were having a field day with the story. One of their own, a fallen soldier, a story that never gets old for any patriotic American.

"I'm sorry for your loss."

"Thank you for your service to our country."

"You should be proud."

Everyone wanted to reach out to me, but their words fell flat. I was not even close to feeling proud of what happened. Disgusted, anxious, disappointed, angry, exhausted are how I was feeling. But, for the sake of patriotism, I pasted a plastic smile on my face and responded graciously, thanking each person who approached me. *Home, please take me home,* were the words circulating in my head, but more than that, I wanted Bart to be home. I yearned to walk through the front door of my home and collapse into the waiting arms of my family, my *whole* family.

When I arrived home, I did collapse into the arms of my first-born, Nic, who was waiting by the door to be the first to greet me. As we embraced, we sobbed. Our biological threesome—Nic, Bart, and me—was forever broken. I thought of all we had been through together in my years as a single mom before Jack came into our lives. Nic, the one who afforded me the happiest day of my life on the day he was born. Nic, the "good one," whose maternal attention was eclipsed by the birth of his younger, more challenging baby brother. Nic, who became his brother's protector out of necessity, if for no other reason than to keep Bart from burning the house down before he left home. Now we were two. In that moment it resonated in me how much I needed Nic. I hugged him even tighter.

Over the next few days, I experienced some of the most honorable and touching tributes to my son, courtesy of the United States Army. Never did I imagine there could be such an outpouring of honor to a soldier who gave his life in service to his country. And yet, inside, I was holding back a silent scream. I was torn between being completely grateful to the army for its efforts and feeling angry with them for ever having allowed this to happen.

The very core of me had always hated war. Hated guns. Hated the false pretense of security that oozed out of everything the military stood for. It seemed pointless to me—worse than pointless, over-glorified, violent, and dangerous. Fight for freedom? What an oxymoron! How do you impose democracy on another country? Freedom requires taking responsibility for your own choices, not those forced upon you. Force is not choice.

I was captivated by it all with a desire to see my son recognized for his contributions, but on the inside I struggled. *What a sham!* Yet I played my part. I would look like a selfish, unpatriotic bitch if I didn't. And my acting role fit right into the surreal nightmare that was my life. One day I would pinch myself and wake up in the world I had—the world that included Bart. But as day followed day, the pinches only served to deepen the bruise.

## Chapter 3

# PATRIOTIC TEARS

*How lucky I am to have something that makes saying goodbye so hard.*
—A. A. Milne[4]

When I got home from Fort Hood, the house was in complete upheaval. Jack was busy with funeral arrangements, and there were so many people coming and going it was difficult to maintain any sense of order. Things were scattered everywhere. Before I got the news of Bart's death, I had been in the middle of creating a scrapbook of his childhood years as I had done for both John, my stepson, and Nic. There had been neatly organized piles of photos and craft materials on every surface in the living room. Now it was all in total disarray, thrown into a large suitcase presumably to keep me from having to deal with it—or to prevent me from sitting and reminiscing over memories of Bart.

It would take hours to reorganize everything again, and the thought of it sucked what was left of any energy out of my body. I knew the mess was just a sign of the turmoil we would be living with for a while, but having a clean house soothes my soul, and my soul needed soothing right then. *Just tell everyone to get out so you can clean up this mess.* But under the circumstances that wasn't feasible, so I let it go and apologized for my dirty house to every person who walked in and out of our front door.

I was grateful my friend Cathy was here because I knew she would pick up the slack by cooking meals, keeping me moving, and generally keeping the whole family organized. Someone needed to tell me what to do. Every moment of my existence seemed like an episode of watching myself in a dream—never a part of it, just observing from the sidelines like an actor sitting in the audience. If my reality was just a horrific nightmare, then I could wake up and feel the relief from knowing it wasn't real. This daze I was in must be due in part to my sleep deprivation. I had not slept since receiving the news of Bart's death, and I had been stumbling through five days of a nightmare that had nothing to do with sleep.

From my fog I heard the doorbell ring. When I opened the door, a close former colleague, Lena, was standing on the doorstep. She didn't need to say much; the meeting of our eyes told me everything. She was uncomfortable staying for any length of time. She was feeling that all-too-familiar awkwardness that most mothers feel around me, praying that what had happened to me would never happen to them.

"Ginny, I know you, and I am sure you haven't slept. So here, I hope these will help." She reached out her hand. A Ziploc bag containing five little white pills dangled from the end of it.

"What are these?"

"Xanax. They should help you get through this."

I had never taken Xanax before. One of my friends referred to it as "the happy pill." I could use "happy" right then, but what I really needed was sleep. When Lena left, I showed them to Cathy who gently took my arm and dragged me away from everyone and into my bedroom.

"I want you to take a Xanax and lie down. It will help you relax. I'm going to give you a foot massage while you listen to some quiet music. Then you are going to try to get some sleep. Forget about what is going on out there. We'll handle it." In that moment, as in so many moments of my life, I felt extremely grateful for Cathy being in my life. I slept like a baby for a couple of hours.

There were so many people stopping by the house to offer condolences that Jack and I rarely had time to be alone together. We hadn't yet talked about what funeral arrangements he had made and what was going to happen next. Colonel Maddox, the Casualty Assistant Officer, had told us that the following day my baby boy's body was scheduled to arrive from Dallas at Fort Lauderdale airport. Katie and her mom would be on the same plane, along with Captain Doyle and Claude Hoffman, the company chaplain who was a close friend of Bart's.

"There's only one problem," Maddox told us. "For security reasons the airport limits the number of family members who can attend to four."

In addition to our sons John and Nic, Jack's daughter Kristy was with us. "Crap, that means two of us can't go," I said. Cathy my true-blue sister, was hoping to go but knew she would be the first to be denied.

"Ginny, I'll stay," Kristy graciously offered. "Nic and John need to be there. I haven't lived with you all for a long time. They were much closer to Bart than I was."

Instinctively I hugged her. "You're no less a member of this family, you know, and thank you. You will be missed. You and Cathy will be with us in spirit."

Like a child anticipating a day at Disney, I was eager to receive Bart. Even if his body was in a casket, I would be closer to him here. That mommy-instinct of wanting to kiss away all his hurts and have him close by was a comfort to me. With great relief, we learned the plane carrying Bart home had made it out of Texas. Hurricane Ike was rapidly bearing down on the state, and for a while the departure of the plane had been touch and go.

The colonel continued. "There's a bit of protocol to receiving Bart's casket that we want you to be a part of. There will be a small ceremony on the tarmac at the airport, and we need to get you all cleared to take you out there. Bart is due to arrive at noon. You need to be at the American Airlines terminal by ten o'clock so we can get all the paperwork squared away. Any questions?"

When I woke the next day, I was feeling a little more ambivalent about the day ahead. The excitement of finally being able to be close to Bart was kiboshed by the reality that this was the end of life with Bart as I knew it. Done, over, kaput—a nightmare I could never wake up from. Until now, there was a part of me that held on to the hope that maybe it hadn't really happened. After all, I hadn't seen his body; I hadn't even seen a casket. Would I—could I—handle the fact that all of this wasn't just a bad dream?

When we arrived at the airport, we were greeted by Colonel Maddox and escorted to an area behind baggage claim that the general public rarely sees. We were brought into a small reception area that was beautifully decorated with flowers. On a table lay a small feast. Was this courtesy of American Airlines or the United States Army? I didn't know. Regardless, we felt like royalty, as they intended. We were truly honored, but eating was not on my radar as my hunger signals vanish when I am subjected to this kind of overwhelming stress. But I managed to fill a small plate and nibble at it to show my appreciation.

Ten minutes before Bart's plane was due to arrive, we were escorted outside to the tarmac. The colonel took us to a space between two boarding gates so that we could observe the ceremony for Bart's return. Off to the side, waiting in limbo, was a hearse with six US Army honor guards standing at attention. They were as still as a frozen movie frame; not even the slightest movement could be detected. A thousand feet beyond the gate were two firetrucks parked on opposite sides of the path that led from the taxiway to the terminal.

The background noise of jets coming and going on the tarmac made conversation difficult. Jack tapped me on the shoulder and pointed to the terminal above us and at the gate below where Bart's plane was to dock. The tarmac was lined with American Airlines' and airport employees awaiting the plane. Passengers in the terminal were lined up at the windows with noses pressed to the glass. All anticipated the spectacle that was about to unfold. I tapped Colonel Maddox's shoulder and pointed at all the people.

"They shut down the terminal for this occasion," he shouted in my ear.

My eyes teared, and I looked away.

Then Colonel Maddox tapped me on the shoulder and yelled, "Here's his plane now."

As the plane turned from the taxiway toward the gate, the hoses on both firetrucks suddenly opened at full capacity forming an arc of water over the plane as it passed through. I glanced at the people standing at the windows in the terminal and at those standing on the tarmac. They were all saluting.

"Do you know why they're spraying water?"

I shook my head, speechless.

"The water represents the tears that are shed for a fallen hero killed in the line of duty."

It was hard to contain my emotions in that moment. I was in awe of all the patriotic tears being shed for my son. Then I realized that tears were streaming down my cheeks—tears of sadness and tears of honor—acknowledging that Bart had accomplished his biggest dream. Since he was a young child, all he had wanted to do was serve his country with honor and respect. The high regard in which this airline, the military, and all these people held for my son gave me great pride. Bart was being honored in a way he would have done—he had done—for others. I hoped he was watching and smiling down on this from the heavens above.

When the plane came to a stop at the jetway, the engines shut down and there was an eerie silence. In the quiet we could hear the voice of the plane's captain addressing his passengers.

"Ladies and gentlemen, we have a fallen hero on board. We ask that you remain seated until the family disembarks and retrieves the remains of their loved one. We thank First Lieutenant Robert B. Fletcher for his service and sacrifice."

As Katie and her mother, Linda, proceeded down the aisle to the exit, the entire body of passengers applauded and offered gestures of sympathy and gratitude. "We're so sorry for your loss," and "Thank you for his service." Captain Doyle and Chaplain Hoffman were then requested to exit; they received a similar response.

Katie, Linda, Mike, and Claude joined us on the tarmac as the airport personnel open the plane's cargo door. The honor guard that had been standing at attention for at least 15 minutes in the September heat performed their meticulous march over to the open cargo bay and formed two lines to receive the casket. It seemed to take forever to prepare the casket for delivery, but the American Airlines and army personnel in the cargo bay wanted to make sure the flag was placed perfectly on the casket before its public viewing.

Finally, the casket crept slowly down the conveyor belt. The honor guard executed their duty flawlessly, to my untrained eye anyway. At the very least, it was precise and sobering; at best, respectful and moving. In absolute silence the guards, with ever-so-small marching steps, carried the casket to the hearse. The only sounds that could be heard were the occasional sniffles and sobs of the bystanders.

In front of the hearse, several men on motorbikes were starting to congregate. Later we learned they were Patriot Guard Riders, a voluntary group of citizens formed in 2005 to protect grieving families of fallen soldiers against protesters.[5] They were ready to escort our small procession—the hearse and our cars—on the hour-and-a-half drive back to the funeral home. We would see them again, a few days later, during the funeral. Once Bart was secured in the hearse, the ceremony was over.

We were told we would be escorted back to our cars, then would meet up with the Patriot Guard and the hearse. Our car, driven by Jack, followed the hearse. Maddox, Doyle, and Hoffman followed behind us. I couldn't imagine how this caravan was going to stay together on one of the most congested sections of I-95 in the state of Florida.

It was obvious Jack was nervous by the way he was tailgating the hearse.

I was backseat driving from the passenger seat. "Back off, Jack," I cautioned. "You're too close. If that hearse has to slam on its brakes, we'll be one big dead family."

"I don't want to lose him. And I don't want anyone to get in front of me."

John and Nic were in the backseat. "Oh, so better off dead than lost?" John winced.

Nic piped in, "Dad, you're making me nervous. It's not going to help if we all end up in Bart's casket."

None of this deterred Jack. He was not going to let anyone get between him and his Bart. It was a white-knuckle ride all the way to our exit ramp.

I was never more relieved to see the exit sign until I saw lights flashing from several police cars at the end of the ramp. From a distance I could barely make out what looked like a blue SUV waiting on the shoulder of the ramp next to the police cars. *Oh, no! Now what's happened? When will this shit ever end?*

"Hey, that's our Honda," Nic pointed out.

We realized that the police were stopping traffic so our procession could drive through. And then they signaled for the waiting Honda, with Kristy and Cathy inside, to join us. Thank God—and Colonel Maddox—they both got to be a part of this day after all.

## Chapter 4

# THE FUNERAL

*Death is nothing at all.*
*It does not count.*
*I have only slipped away into the next room.*
*Nothing has happened.*

*... Whatever we were to each other, that we are still.*
—HENRY SCOTT-HOLLAND[6]

As the day of the funeral approached, I could only focus on one thing: creating a masterpiece slideshow of Bart that could be shared with everyone attending the memorial service. It had to be something that would truly capture his spirit and remain forever in their hearts. I've never been known to do anything half-assed, so, true to form, I locked myself in my bedroom and obsessed over it day and night.

During the years I was raising my children, I chose to focus on my profession rather than be a more balanced mom, a choice that both my biological sons complained about for years. My guilt was the catalyst for my obsession with creating the perfect tribute to Bart. But catharsis played a pleasant secondary role. It was my way of touching, hugging, holding, and inhaling him for the last time.

Outside my bedroom door were so many well-wishers who had come to pay their respects and offer condolences. They meant well and I loved them for it, but I couldn't stand the thought of rehashing the details of the tragedy anymore. No matter how rude it may have seemed to the consolers who went out of their way to visit us, I needed to be alone with Bart in a way that kept me connected to him. Others were left to explain the details of his death, funeral plans, and my truancy. Lack of sleep for five days helped me prioritize. My number one priority right then was myself, and my focus was on that slideshow.

I was fine-tuning it the day before the funeral when a thought struck me like a brick. If I was going through the horror of Bart's death, how was Jody Wirawan's mother feeling? For a brief moment I was grateful that I was not in her shoes. How does a mother cope with the knowledge that her child has murdered someone and then, in the worst kind of death imaginable, taken his own life? How could anyone cope with that without wanting to crawl into a hole and die?

I picked up the phone to call her. *Wait a minute, Ginny, you don't even know her name, much less her phone number.* I paused only for a second before calling Captain Mike at his hotel.

"Are you kidding?" Mike almost shouted into the phone. "Ginny, why do you want to call Jody's mom? What could you possibly have to say to her?"

"I want to wish her well."

"But, Ginny, her son killed *your* son. Why in God's name would you want to wish *her* well?"

I didn't hesitate for a second; to me it was obvious. "Mike, I know what *I* am going through. I can't imagine it being any harder than this, and yet she suffered a double blow. *She* had nothing to do with it except that *she* was his mom. She was his *mother*! Don't you get it, Mike? There is nothing that stops a mother from loving her child."

"All I get is that she deserves nothing from you."

"I understand that's how you feel, Mike, but I need to do this for me. Please?"

He hesitated, and I could feel his resistance in the midst of pending silence. But he acquiesced. "If you're sure you want to do this, Ginny, I'll see if I can get the number. But I have to get approval."

"Okay. Thank you so much, Mike!"

"And she may not want to talk to you. From what we've heard, she's been getting a lot of threatening phone calls—some death threats—which is not surprising."

"Hello. Is this Susan, Jody Wirawan's mother?"

"Who's asking? Is this another crank call? Who are you?" The voice sounded nervous and frazzled.

"This is Ginny Luther, the mother of Lieutenant Bart Fletcher who died in the tragedy with your son, Jody." There was an uncomfortable pause, like a blanket of thick smoke rolling in, tickling the back of my throat. I was afraid Susan would hang up if I couldn't find my voice, but I couldn't catch my breath.

"What do you want?" she demanded, but there wasn't much fight in it. Her voice seemed to come from the bottom of a deep, dank pit.

"I know this seems odd, calling you, but I just had to talk to you. This was a terrible tragedy, and I've been thinking of you the last few days. I don't know where you live, and I don't know your situation, but I feel a connection to you. I just want you to know that I am wishing you well. This whole thing hasn't sunk in yet, and I'm thinking you must feel numb like me. I just wanted you to know I am wishing you the best."

A heavy silence hung between us. I didn't know what to expect, how receptive she would be.

Finally, "You know, they never told me? I was waiting at the airport for Jody to come home. We were goin' on vacation together like we always did when he had leave. Only this time he was comin' home for good. He sent all his belongings to a storage place where he lived in Alaska. He was going to meet me here in Washington for our trip before going home. He was gonna start a new business. When his flight came in and he wasn't on the plane, I asked the airline lady what happened. She said he wasn't on the flight and to wait for the next plane. I waited and waited. He wasn't on that flight neither. This time the flight lady made some phone calls to Dallas. They told her he never made the flight to Dallas from Killeen. She told me to go home and call the Killeen police station. I drove back home and went on the computer to find the phone number, and there it was."

"What? There *what* was?" My heart was pounding.

"The news. I saw the news about a soldier being killed in Killeen. And there was my son's apartment building. I was looking at a picture of it. I got real scared and called the police. When I told them who I was and asked what happened, they told me Jody murdered a soldier and then killed himself. Then they started yelling at me and blaming me for what happened. Like it was *my* fault.

"I'll tell you what I think. I think it was all a conspiracy. They killed him on purpose. No offense to you, but I think that soldier that went there was setting him up. He shouldn't have gone up there the way he did. They shoulda known Jody doesn't like anybody in his territory. They knew he was gonna get mad. It's all the army's fault, and your son should never have done that. I'm not done with this. They're not going to get away with this."

The hair on the back of my neck stood at attention. Chills ran down my spine. The mother-bear in me was preparing to attack. *How dare she blame Bart for this?* But I hesitated just long enough to realize that Susan was suffering a deeper horror than I could ever imagine. She was suffering the loss of her child while coming to terms with the fact that he had murdered another human being, *and* she was being blamed for it all. Now *I* was the one thinking, *I can't imagine.* Defending Bart and his actions was not going to help either Susan or me heal. But I also knew I couldn't listen anymore.

"Susan, I can hear how hard this is for you, and I want you to know that I feel pain too for my loss. I just wanted to call you and let you know that I am wishing you well in the months to come. That is the only reason I called." I hoped this was enough. I quickly said goodbye before abruptly hanging up the phone.

Tears streamed down my cheeks. I had failed to make a connection with the one person I was sure would understand my pain. My protests came alive. "We've both suffered through the same damn tragedy. Why? Why, does life have to be so fucking hard?"

I dried my tears, took a deep breath, put on my pseudo-happy face, and went to greet the barrage of visitors at my kitchen table waiting to give me their condolences. "Oh Ginny, I can't imagine. I am so sorry." Blah, blah, blah, blah, blah!

The day of the funeral finally arrived. *It's almost over,* I kept repeating to myself. This day was sure to be long and hard, but it would be over soon. *Just do it and get through it* was my motto for the day.

It was a day to both mourn and celebrate, not a concept that made much sense to me in the moment. Part of me was anxious about the sadness to come, while the rest of me, strange as it sounds, was excited. Finally, I would make contact with my baby boy. There would be a private viewing of the body at the funeral home for family before the public was welcomed to express condolences.

The anticipation of seeing Bart was like the suspense that comes on Christmas Eve. I never knew what Santa would bring, and I was always thrilled at the excitement of it. But, of course, there was always the anxiety associated with the possibility of a disappointing outcome. "If you're not good, Santa will put coal in your stocking. And there won't be anything under the tree for you either, so you'd better behave," my parents never failed to remind me.

I was excited to see Bart one last time, for one last kiss, one last hug, and one last moment of connection. But what if he feels too cold to touch, too ashen to kiss, too dead to make any connection? Would I get the closure I so desperately needed and never had in the first blindside of my life?

As the family ran from room to room, frantically working on logistics for the day ahead and trying to get dressed for the funeral, my focus was on the final touches of Bart's slideshow and what to wear. Jack was trying to find shoes that matched. John was trying to get a spot off his suit at the kitchen sink, and Katie was in the bathroom working her magic with her makeup. To add to the pandemonium, the doorbell rang.

"What now?" I was struggling to synchronize music and photos on my computer while simultaneously trying on earrings. I glanced at the clock—again. Two hours until the limo picked us up. How was I going to get everything done in two hours? "Who could this possibly be?" No one moved toward the door, so I reluctantly dropped what I was doing to answer it.

Standing on my doorstep was my friend, Rabe, who worked with me almost two decades earlier when I first moved to Florida. We had crossed paths many times in our common mission of serving children. Both of us were now immersed in our own businesses, but we occasionally saw each other at social functions over the years.

"Hi, Ginny." She stepped into the house and hugged me. "I'm so sorry for your loss." Her eyes watered and she blinked back tears.

In my frenetic state, all I could think was that this was *really* bad timing for a visit.

"Rabe! Thank you for coming. But I need to tell you that we're getting ready for the funeral. You're welcome to come in, but I don't think I have time to sit and chat right now. I'm so sorry."

"Oh, no," she assured me, "I didn't come here to chat. I came here to be of support. I won't talk to you. I am just going to sit here," she gestured toward the living room couch, "and whenever you need something I'm here at your service. Now go, do your thing. I'll sit quietly on the couch until you need me. Just say 'go,' and I'm here for you."

My initial thought was, *How odd!* but I didn't argue. I didn't have time.

Lo and behold, as the time for the event drew nearer, everyone's stress levels shot up with last-minute tasks we had each forgotten.

"Do you all have tissues?" Rabe suggested.

"Oh, crap. I forgot tissues!"

Rabe popped up from the couch and ran to the store to return with individual packages of tissues. She polished shoes, reinforced loose buttons, pinned corsages, and so much more. I don't even know everything she did, I was so caught up in my own chaos, but every time I saw her she was bustling around the house helping someone. When it came time for us to go, I gave her a hug and thanked her profusely. Now it was my turn to get teary-eyed. She smiled a warm, sympathetic smile and drifted out the door.

"Who was that?" John asked as he came out of the bedroom.

"An angel," I said softly, as I pondered the strength of character that she had to show up at an inopportune time and gently insist on helping us. The angel in our midst had given us a gift of love that I will never forget.

It was a sultry 93 degrees outside, and the morbid, black limo that picked us up at the house only added to the heaviness of the day. As we approached the funeral home a full hour before the scheduled public visitation, a line was already forming at the door and trickling down the street. I was shocked. Those people were there, an hour early, to make sure they got in to pay their respects to Bart and his family. It was so important to them to honor this fallen soldier that they chose to stand in Florida's intense September heat to be able to grieve with us. If only I could invite each and every one of them in out of the heat. But when I stepped into the funeral home I realized it would be impossible. There just wasn't enough room to shelter them all.

Why is it that funeral homes always look like a cross between a movie theater and a brothel? The few windows were draped with heavy velvet to block any rays of happiness from getting through, and there was an overpowering shade of red to every room in the building in a vain attempt to happy-up a venue that had no hope of ever achieving any adjective other than [illegible]. The only effort that managed to lift the human spirit was the flowers. If it wasn't for the stream of photos of Bart flipping across a monitor in our designated viewing room, I would have felt no connection to that place. There was nothing else there to offer me solace.

As soon as I stepped into the foyer, I was all business. If I slowed down and allowed myself to think, I would completely fall apart. It was important for me to be there for my husband, my kids, and the hundreds of people waiting to pay their respects. If I fell apart, they would too, and Bart would not want to be celebrated in that way.

The funeral director asked me to join Chaplain Claude and Captain Mike in a conference room off the foyer. She had laid out several catalogs on the table, and I was asked to decide which casket I wanted for the cremation. I was confused. "He already has a casket. Why would we need another one?"

Claude explained that you can't cremate a body in a metal casket.

I became indignant. "What the hell? Why didn't someone point that out when I was choosing the one in Fort Hood?"

No one could give me a clear answer, and there was a lot of shoe-examining and bottom-shifting in chairs. More than the aggravation of now having to choose a wooden casket at the taxpayers' expense, was my offense at the military's waste of a perfectly good casket.

"What are they going to do with the metal casket?"

"It will be discarded properly," replied the funeral director.

"Can't they recycle it? Seems a shame to throw away a perfectly good casket just because it's been used for a couple of days." Silence, with discreet smirks all around. They didn't think I was serious! I didn't have time for this, I decided. Hundreds of people were standing in line out in the heat, and we hadn't even had the private viewing yet. I scanned the catalog closest to me. "That one," I declared while pointing at a simple, wooden casket and turned to leave the room.

The time had come for Jack, Nic, and me to view the body. John and Katie were given the option but declined. They waited in the foyer with some of Bart's army buddies. John had no desire to replace his current memories of Bart with nightmares that would haunt him for the rest of his life. And pre-med Katie, as much as she loved Bart, knew all too well that the Bart she would see now was not her Bart.

The room was deathly silent. Several family members and close friends sat in chairs lined in rows in the back of the room, quietly waiting for Jack, Nic, and me to view Bart's body first. I could hear nothing but the distant, soft ticking of a clock in the far corner of the room. We moved toward the half-opened casket draped with an American flag. Our footsteps on the thick, crimson carpet were in sync with the ticking of the clock, which seemed to grow ominously louder with each step. The excitement of finally being able to see my son fluttered in my stomach, but I gripped Nic and Jack tighter, digging my fingernails into their arms to communicate the fear that also gripped my heart. A few feet from the casket, we peered inside. Sheer panic ensued.

"What the fuck?" The raw words flew from my mouth, bearing neither glory nor shame, just real in-the-moment horror.

Nic stood by the casket stunned, his face frozen.

"Wait a minute!" Jack bellowed. "That's not Bart!"

The family members in the room rushed forward to see for themselves.

"It's a conspiracy," yelled my twin brother, John, who had flown with his family from New Jersey to support us and pay respect to his nephew, Nic. "What did they do with his body? This is fucked up. Where's Bart?"

I stood motionless, staring in disbelief. Another blindside! *Can nothing go right for me?*

My friend, Cathy, rushed forward and put her arm around me.

"How could they do this to me?" I cried. "They wouldn't let me see him in Texas. And now, what is this? Captain Mike warned me that Bart might look different than what we expected. The hurricane was closing in on Texas, and they'd had to prepare the body quickly to get him out of Dallas in time. He had said the air pressure on the flight could make him look different, but this? What the hell happened to him? He looks horrible. There is nothing on that body that resembles my son. Nothing!"

I looked around frantically for someone to explain this, but no one was there who could answer my questions. I persisted. "Is this the best they could do? He was shot in the chest, for God's sake, not the head! This looks like someone else's body!"

"Hold on, Ginny," Cathy said calmly. "Look at me."

I turned to look in her eyes.

"We are going to find out what happened, but right now you, me, and Nic are going over to this body to see if we can find something—anything—that identifies him."

Cathy moved quickly to pull the casket away from the wall so we could view every angle of his face to find something that told us this was our Bart, not some contrived corpse. While scanning his face I noticed his ear. There was a small asymmetrical protrusion on the upper ridge of Bart's left ear. "There. That's his ear. I'm sure of it. Nic, Nic, look. See? See the bump? That's his ear, isn't it?"

Nic studied the body's ear carefully and nodded his confirmation.

The tears flowed down my face. *Finally, my baby boy is here.* I would be able to say goodbye after all.

In the meantime, Jack was conducting his own examination. He traced Bart's hairline and stopped behind his right ear. He stood up and came around the casket to me, whispering in my ear. "Gin, there's what looks like a bullet hole behind his ear. Come look. See? This isn't right. We need some answers."

I simultaneously felt surrender and resistance. My whole body wanted to collapse, just fold up and sink to the floor. But something was not right, and I couldn't give up yet. If my son was shot in the chest, why was there a bullet hole behind his ear? Heads were going to roll until I found out the truth about what happened to my baby, but until then I had hundreds of mourners to greet and a funeral to get through.

With a huge lump in my throat, I went to the other side of the coffin and reluctantly caressed the bright, white glove that encased my son's strong, but gentle, right hand. I was dying to take that glove off so I could see Bart's unique, scarred thumb. But his hand felt oddly skeletal—cold, hard, and spindly—when I grasped it, and I was too afraid to look. Scarred thumb or not, it was not the hand I had held so many times in the past. Not the hand I had examined, counting all the tiny fingers over and over in the first few hours of his life, marveling at the difference they would make in the world. Not the one I had held in safety, crossing the street with him when he was a small boy. Nor the hand that I held walking in celebration at his college graduation. I felt cold and sad on the inside, a sadness that could never be soothed. This was reality, his life was over. I would never hold his hand again. Hugging it now was depressing, as it destroyed the illusion of a loving goodbye. This was no longer my son—just a cold, empty corpse.

The funeral director had come into the room and tugged at my black-lace sleeve. "I know you need more time with this," she whispered, "but there is a line of people a mile down the road wanting to pay their respects to you and your family."

I snapped out of my sadness and beamed a stellar smile, one of hope, faith, and gratitude. I would be the one to console the mourners passing through the family receiving line situated before the casket. I took a deep breath, determined to be the strong one for every mother that walked through that door. *Be the person you want them to be, if this ever happens to them. Step up Ginny. You can do this.* Oh, if only it were possible to fast-forward five years and bypass all the pain that was ahead of me.

The casket was closed, and the family quickly gathered in front of it to accept the good graces of the community. People paraded through for what seemed like hours, people I hadn't seen in lifetimes.

The funeral director politely interrupted again by whispering in my ear. "You need to let people know it's time to leave. The army needs to get Bart's body to the church so the service can start on time."

"But there are still people waiting to come in," I said, "lots of people! What am I supposed to tell them?"

I turned to Jack. "Sweet Jesus," I hissed. "She wants us to tell them they have to leave. Why us? Isn't that her job?" We would find out later that this had been the largest attended viewing in the history of this small-community funeral home. They had been significantly unprepared for the crowd.

I turned back to the director to tell her I had no intention of asking these people to leave, when Jack piped up and addressed the line of people who had taken the time and braved the heat to be there. "Excuse us! Excuse us, everyone! Can I have your attention, please? For the people who have so graciously waited to pay their respects, we have been told that we must stop receiving people now so Bart won't be late to his own funeral."

Thank God for Jack! The laughter that followed lightened a very awkward situation. He continued, "We are happy to continue this line at the church. Please join us there as we are eager to connect with you."

And they did.

The sanctuary of the church was filled with hundreds of flowers positioned in every possible nook and corner, but I barely noticed. I also didn't attend to all the servicemen scattered about the room who had traveled from afar to pay their respects to my son. They had known Bart in some way or another, from college to Iraq, throughout his short but active career. For a moment I glanced at the life-size poster of the proud, uniformed soldier next to the casket. Such a handsome man, so dedicated and happy in his chosen career. He did not have that serious, stoic expression that so many soldiers present to the public. No, Bart's eyes positively glowed with glory and pride.

It was hard for me to take it all in. I vacillated from deep sadness and anxiety to gratitude for the love and support of the people who knew my son and his family, and also, for those who didn't know us at all but yearned to mourn with us for the tragic loss of a devoted soldier. I hoped to remember every detail, from the humorous stories people shared to the somber silence before the 21-gun salute. The doors of the sanctuary had been opened to the outdoors, and each report of the guns made me jump as it split the air, no matter how hard I tried to prepare myself for each one. I studied each of Bart's fellow soldiers as they folded the flag from his casket, helping to lay a brother to rest while knowing that this also could have been them. And finally, accepting the flag that was presented to me, the fallen soldier's mother, in thanks for giving him life.

As Colonel Maddox spoke, I fought impending tears. "The President of the United States and a grateful nation present this flag to you in remembrance of your son's service." Grief overcame me. I could no longer bear the pain. I surrendered with subdued sobs that shot pain through the heart of every person in that sanctuary. You could feel the tension in the air as throats tightened, eyes filled with tears, and noses began to run. Not a sound was heard but my weeping. Everyone present, if they hadn't before this moment, now comprehended beyond a shadow of a doubt the pain of a mother who has lost a child.

Bart's life, the acknowledgements of my contributions as his mother, the love and support given so freely by everyone who had been a part of this day—it was all over. And now we, Bart's loved ones, were expected to go home and pick up the pieces, to try to resume some semblance of our normal lives. *The party's over,* I thought, *and yet a part of me is still missing—will be missing for the rest of my life.*

With the lifeless flag in my lap, all I saw was a symbol of death. I knew the Stars and Stripes meant a great deal to Bart, but for him they would fly no more. All it was to me was a poor substitute for my child. All of whatever Bart could have been was in that flag—everything I had envisioned for his future. It was Bart standing beside Katie at their wedding. It was me, holding their newborn child as I, without the worries of taking care of its daily needs, planned to love and spoil it. It was Bart, years later on the phone, venting to me about his struggles with parenting, with the sound of bickering children in the background. It was the holiday traditions that meant so much to him that he would pass on to his children and grandchildren—that we would enjoy together for years to come. It was Bart holding my hand at my bedside as he helped me transition to my next life, as he and I had done for my mother. None of this would I ever know with Bart.

With this flag, I had lost the ability to have the future I imagined, and that was more than I could bear.

*South Florida National Cemetery*

# Chapter 5
# THE FIRST BLINDSIDE

*We are not given a good life or a bad life. We are given a life.*
*It's up to us to make it good or bad.*
—DEVIKA FERNANDO[7]

It was a sunny Connecticut day in early April 1970, one of those glorious spring days when the streaming rays of sunlight felt warm for the first time since autumn. Winter was melting into patches of slippery mud-ice as I carefully picked my way through the minefield of slushy water and muck, enjoying the tender caress of the sun on my face. It was a week after my 15th birthday, and I was walking home from my best friend Cathy's house where I had spent the night. The contentment of spending the weekend in the cocoon of Cathy's friendship was quickly fading into resentment, uncertainty, and dread as I contemplated what lay ahead of me at home on this Sunday afternoon.

Sunday meant that Monday was just around the corner, and Monday meant school and chores. As the only girl in my family, I did the lion's share of the chores. Chores were considered "women's work" in my family. My brothers were not expected to contribute to the same degree. They shared one chore among the three of them, taking out the garbage. They took full advantage of their freedom by describing in detail the plots of television shows they watched while I slaved over a sink of dirty dinner dishes, or teasing me as I vacuumed around their reclining bodies. I knew, deep down in my core, that I loved my family; I just didn't enjoy spending time with them.

But the greater part of my dread and uncertainty came from something that had happened two days earlier, as I was getting ready to leave for school on Friday. Despite the chauvinistic views toward chores in our family—and most of America in the late 60s and early 70s, truth be told—my father was the parent who took on the task of feeding four teenagers breakfast every morning before school. He was committed to getting us up and out the door with schoolwork in hand and food of some sort in our bellies. He always had an Ovaltine milkshake and a multi-vitamin ready to shove into our hands if whatever hot breakfast he had prepared toggled the power-struggle switch toward rejection.

"I'm not hungry," we'd protest, as if we were awake enough to have figured that out yet. We each managed to drink the Ovaltine at least, which gave him some sense of parental consolation and relief.

After chugging down my shake on Friday, I grabbed my schoolbooks and turned to give Dad my ritual goodbye peck on the cheek. When I saw his face, I froze. He looked like he had aged 10 years overnight. It was hard for him to make eye contact. He seemed lost, stranded in a world where evil lurked around every corner. His face wilted, and I thought he was about to cry. Something was wrong—very wrong.

"Dad, are you mad at me?" I asked.

He responded by grabbing me and hugging me tighter than he'd ever done before. It was desperate, confining, and absent of any comfort.

Awkwardly I told him I loved him, pulled away, and scooted out the door as fast as I could. I hesitated in the front yard, trying to put a name to my uneasiness. His response was confusing at best. I wanted to run back into the house and ask him if he was all right, but I was afraid he would reproach me to cover his distress. He often showed anger when he was scared. I knew he'd insist everything was fine, just fine. He was going away for the weekend to our farm in Vermont. Maybe he just needed some time away to work in the fresh air in his place of refuge.

I tried to forget my dad's odd behavior by immersing myself in my plans to spend the weekend at Cathy's house. We'd probably watch some TV, eating whatever junk food we could find, inspect our pimples and blemishes in the bathroom mirror for at least a couple of hours, and then spend the rest of the night talking into the wee hours of the morning. We'd wake up in the early afternoon, eat something, and repeat. There was nothing better than hanging out with my friends. But all good things must come to an end, so they say, and now I was wondering with trepidation what I was going home to.

The house was eerily quiet when I stepped through the door. No dog greeted me. No bellowing of the TV came from the playroom. No brothers playing pool. No Dad home from Vermont yet. I found my mother reading a book in the living room, her go-to place to get a break from the family.

"Hi, Mom. I'm home. When's Dad coming home? I thought he would be home by now."

"I did too," she said. "I've tried calling both the big house and the little house, but he's not answering. He must be on his way now." Our 350-acre dairy farm in Vermont was our year-round getaway. In the summer, when we kids weren't in school, we settled into the bigger farmhouse, but in the winter, when we spent less time up there, we used a smaller cottage on the property. It was less costly to heat the cottage than that big old house.

Staring out the living room picture window, I studied the canvas of pink and white dogwoods flowering on both sides of our long, winding driveway, marveling at how nature could reproduce this awe-inspiring burst of color every year without any help from mankind. On another day I could have stared at them for hours, realizing that in a few precious weeks the blooms would be gone for another year, but today an underlying anxiety was eating away at me. I couldn't stop thinking about my dad's unusual behavior before he left on Friday. Something wasn't right. My mom's concern made me worry more, so I went in search of our dog, Gus, for some much needed love and [illegible]

I found him in "his room," the laundry room, a place he was often sent to when visitors came to the door. His instinctive need to protect, more often than not, resulted in aggressive greetings that intimidated even the most dog-loving visitor. It was unusual for him to be in the laundry room of his own accord. He was lying curled up with a forlorn look on his face. His normally happy-go-lucky tail didn't wag as usual but thumped heavily on the floor once or twice as if he knew what he should be doing but just couldn't bring himself to carry it through. It dawned on me that he too knew something wasn't right. Gus and Dad were best buddies, and I knew Gus sensed something was off.

I lay with him on the floor and asked him, "Is Dad gonna be all right?" Gus's head lay still on the carpet; his eyebrows lifted, and his big, sorrowful eyes blinked at me anxiously.

It was like waiting for a dreaded hurricane coming our way. You never know if it is going to hit, but you prepare and pray with some sense of faith that everything will be all right. You pace around trying to distract yourself from the uncertainty of where it will hit and how hard. You know at your core that you have no control, even though you have done everything in your power to convince yourself you have. You ruminate incessantly about what you might have forgotten to do, or question what more you could do to keep yourself safe, mostly because you have nothing else to do but sit and wait. One thing for certain, it's impossible to sit still.

"You'll just have to wait, Ginny," I told myself. But wait for what? A phone call? For him to pop through the front door all smiles and happy greetings? Was he lost in the woods, or maybe killed by a bear? There were so many possibilities.

Dusk was turning to dark when I returned to the living room where my mother still sat, her book now closed on her lap and a stiff drink in hand.

"Mom, where's Dad?"

She could sense my agitation. "I don't know. I'm really starting to get worried. I called the Burlesons an hour ago."

The Burlesons were our next-door neighbors in Vermont. They lived a half-mile down the dirt road in that remote and rural community. They rented property from us to farm and run their dairy business.

"I asked if they would go check the big house to see if Dad was still there. They said the lights were all on, but Dad was not there. They were going to look around and get back to me. I haven't heard back yet."

After another hour Gus started barking frantically, announcing visitors at the door. As I grabbed him and dragged him to his room, my parents' best friends, Whit and Shirley, hurried into the house. Their eyes were swollen and red, as if they had been crying. In that moment, I knew my life would never be the same. The storm had made landfall. The only word I heard was "dead." No more information was needed. My father was gone.

The sound that came out of my body was not of this Earth. It wasn't so much a cry as a wail so profound and steeped in heartbreak that it could make the hair on your arms stand up and your skin ripple like gooseflesh. People can't tolerate the sound because it doesn't sound human. It conjures up subliminal, imprinted memories of feral beasts in the darkness when there is nothing between you and them but a small flame.

My oldest brother, Gordon, came around the corner and pulled me into him. At 18, his paternal instincts kicked in instantly and he held me, trying to comfort me. But I was impossible to console, screaming in denial of the truth. It took an hour for me to calm down long enough to ask for details.

Shirley sat me down and pulled me closer, her arm securely around my shoulders. "Your father was found dead on the ground on top of the Merry-Go-Round field," she explained. The Merry-Go-Round was an area of rolling hills that lay behind our big farmhouse.

"How? How did he die?" I asked. "Did something kill him? A bear or something?"

Shirley hesitated to find the right words to explain. Words that would cut me to the core; stabbing words that would change my life forever. "He shot himself with a gun, sweetie. He must have felt very desperate to do this and leave you like this. That is all we know right now."

The wailing boiled up inside me again. "Why, why, why?" I screamed. There was no soothing response. My family and friends were as much at a loss as I was. I was in the middle of a nightmare, confused and angry and not knowing how to wake up. Answers were what I wanted, but there were none. All I could do was sob until someone answered my questions.

After such a devastating loss, you might envision, as a young teen, that your family would come together to grieve and console each other in the pain they share. Our family did exactly the opposite. In fact, after my father disappeared from our lives, we would never again be in the same room together as a family, except for the socially required appearance of the family unit at my dad's memorial service. But on that first night of our shared grief, we separated and went to our respective spaces to grieve. With no other place to go for comfort, I somehow made it upstairs to my bedroom. I could not stand to listen to my mother's cries or bear witness to the decay of our family. I lay on my bed, alone in my dark room, and cried myself to sleep that night and for many nights to come, until there were no more tears to cry.

The following day we learned that my father had taken his life because of financial ruin. He had inherited a substantial amount of money seven years earlier when his father died. Dad came from a wealthy family. His great-grandfather had made his fortune in the railroad industry in Toledo, Ohio. Each succeeding generation had reaped the financial benefits of the family fortune as it was passed down, but none, sadly, had the financial savvy to sustain it. The fortune had dwindled.

Dad was a musician at heart, but his father pressured him to seek a business career. Dad pretended—and struggled—until the inheritance dropped into his lap. It had seemed like a gold mine to him at the time, the answer to his financial prayers. He had suddenly moved up in the world. He bought the farm in Vermont first, and a few years later moved our family to a more affluent community where we could live a more privileged life.

Unfortunately, like his grandfather and father before him, Dad wasn't very good with money. Within a short period of time, he had gambled it away. He borrowed money over a period of three years, rotating between three banks until it became obvious that the loans would never be paid off and the banks discontinued his lines of credit. His last-ditch effort was to gamble away the funds from his wife's and children's personal savings accounts to recoup his losses.

Whenever my mother had tried to talk to him about finances over the years, it turned into an argument, so she began to avoid the subject. She knew something was wrong with Dad in his last few years. She thought he might be having an affair but didn't want to broach the subject for fear of finding it was true. She loved him too much to lose him. She had no idea how bad our financial situation was until he took his life. My father committed suicide so that the life insurance policy he had taken out months before would bail us out of debt.

Getting through the next days proved to be as challenging as taking in the news itself. We each received a personal letter from my father that he had written just before taking his life. At best it was sad and confusing, at least to my teenaged mind. He was trying to justify the reasons for his decision. He was cautioning us about the trials and tribulations of the world and advising us as to what we needed to do to avoid the obstacles that would impede our successes. *Whatever you do,* he counseled, *don't do this or don't do that. I'm doing this to save the family from the consequences of my choices. Just remember that I love you more than you could ever know.*

My only response was to rant my anger and rave my guilt. How could he say that he was doing this for our benefit? How is leaving us like this supposed to make us happier? This is how he loved us? That is so fucked up. But then feelings of guilt nudged aside the anger. I was responsible for his happiness. I was his little girl, the one who always brought a smile to his face. If I hadn't pulled away from him on Friday morning, maybe he would still be alive. I should have gone back and made him tell me what was wrong. If I had done more to make him happy, he would have chosen to live. If I had been smarter, would he have stayed?

My father was the core of our family. The fun parent. The one who loved to do things with us. He seemed to have lived his entire life for us. Most of my friends had a crush on him because he was so "cool." In the winter he would spend entire days with us building iced toboggan trails that went on for what seemed like a mile. He was the proclaimed driver for anywhere we wanted to go with our friends. In the summer, he would take us on long hikes in the woods on our property in Vermont. During our winter vacations in the cottage, he would dance with us to the latest Beatles songs. He taught us a slew of card games that we played for hours by the warmth of the fireplace on dark, chilly nights. He was the one who was always there for us. And now this?

After reading the letter two more times I threw it in the garbage in sheer disgust. I couldn't connect with the man in that letter because that man was not the father I knew. One thought kept running through my brain: *If you loved us so much, Dad, how could you do this to us?*

By the end of the first few days, I was exhausted from no sleep, yet feeling antsy to see my friends. We hadn't been to school since our father's death, so I hadn't seen anyone outside of my family. None of my friends had reached out yet, and I was desperate to connect with them. I'm sure they didn't know what to say to me, and I didn't know what to say to them either. When I told my mom I wanted to see my friends before the memorial service, she sat each of us down individually for what I thought was going to be some parental guidance on how to talk to our friends about our grief.

"It is very important that we keep the way he died a secret," she told me. To even mutter the word "suicide" was too much shame for my mother to bear. "You can't tell your friends about it or we'll have problems with the insurance company."

"You mean, you want us to lie?" I asked, dumbfounded.

"Yes, you have to."

I was raised in an affluent town in Connecticut where this kind of tragedy was hushed before it became common knowledge, and genuine concern was replaced with pretentious smiles, as if nothing unexpected had happened. When I was a young child of five or six years, I couldn't label it as disingenuous, but I could read their nonverbal messages and feel the negative energy of their intent like a hot cigarette held too closely to my cheek. The disconnect and emptiness left me feeling scared and anxious because I knew I would never be able to trust what these people were saying or thinking. I would always hold them at arm's length.

So, per my mother's order, my family swept this nugget under the rug where it continued to fester and swell. We would have to tell everyone Dad died of a heart attack so the family wouldn't have to bear the brunt of their judgment. His secret gambling habit had left us destitute. Another skeleton to bury in the closet of New England shame. If anyone in the community knew the truth about my father's death, no one ever spoke of it for fear their own closet doors might be thrown wide open.

I had to consider what my mother was saying. The insurance money was important, but I didn't know if I'd be able to pull off the lie. The depth of connection I had with my friends was based on honesty and trust and being able to talk about anything. They knew me inside and out. They'd be able to tell I was lying. There was no way I'd jeopardize the relationships that were most important to me. Lying to my parents was much easier because if they found out, the worst repercussion would be a long lecture. Unlike my friends, they couldn't give up on me until I was an adult—although now, that notion was debatable. But if my friends found out I lied to them I could lose their friendship, which was much more devastating to me than risking some insurance money for our family.

My mother must have sensed my hesitation because she continued to talk about our dire circumstances and family loyalty. She finally left me alone to think about it. Eventually I concluded that lying was a necessary risk. It was deceptive, yet I shuddered to think what would happen to our family otherwise. If we didn't get the insurance money, we'd probably have to sell our house and move, and I could lose my friends anyway. Protecting the family became the priority. I would have to deal with the guilt and pain of lying to my friends and the loneliness of losing our connections of trust.

The only thing I could count on from here on out was that my life would no longer be normal. Normal was gone with what in hindsight seemed like the snap of a finger. When I was six years old and I prayed to God to make me special, unique, something better than boring old normal, I never expected this. It was like living in a foreign land, in a culture I didn't understand and with a language I didn't speak, scrambling to find a way to be accepted and maintain a sense of belonging. Belonging felt impossible because my friends and community would never truly understand what I was going through, simply because I couldn't tell them. Some would try to offer sympathy for my loss. Some would treat me as if it never happened, and that might even have been better than sympathy because I could pretend that this cyclone had not just destroyed everything in my world worth living for.

# Chapter 6
# THERAPY

*But darling...in the end, you've got to be your own hero because everyone's busy trying to save themselves.*
—UNKNOWN[8]

With the memorial service for my father behind us, my mother had to sort out what she was going to do with her life. First and foremost was how she was going to support four teenagers for the remainder of our time at home and in our college years when she had a large debt to repay and no financial resources. Throughout her marriage to my father, my mother wasn't employed, not because she wanted to enjoy a life of leisure but because my father thought it was socially unacceptable. What would the denizens of our affluent community think about his ability to provide for his family if his wife was working? He wouldn't subject his family to that kind of embarrassment.

Mom, a very intelligent and resourceful woman, had always wanted to work if only for the intellectual stimulation and personal gratification of having a career. Come to find out, Dad could have used some financial assistance, public opinion be damned. It would have literally saved his life. But Mom, unaware of Dad's gambling attempts to save our family fortune, complied with Dad's wishes. If she had known, would she have insisted that he let her work? We will never know, and now she was left holding the proverbial bag of shit my dad left behind.

Mom took a real estate course and easily passed the exam to earn her realtor's license, all while parenting four grieving teenagers. When Dad was alive, he had gladly taken on the primary care of us kids, and he was a natural. Mom was anything but natural at parenting, but now she had no choice but to take on the role. Adolescent mood swings are difficult to deal with under the best of circumstances, but after our family tragedy they ran rampant. Mom was not the type to nurture or comfort. She had a job to do and accomplished it with tenacity. She was the breadwinner, paid the bills, bought the groceries, and we were essentially left to muddle through the rest of life on our own. There were two crucial tenets she managed to drill into me in her own dispassionate way, however, and I've never forgotten them: Never trust anyone to take care of you, and get an education; it's something no one can ever take away from you.

Despite my mother's best efforts to maintain a stable home life, she was overwhelmed by anger, shock, and fear—oh-so-much anger. Most nights she drank herself into oblivion trying to manage the pain of it all. She drank alone, asserting her rage through repeated rants of what she wanted to say to my father for doing what he did—but never got the chance to say. Like my father, she was determined to maintain a facade for the community that the Hannah family was doing just fine. There was no one, not even her closest friends, to whom she could pour out her heart, and the truth and fear gripped her. Eventually I became Mom's surrogate confidante, someone who would listen to her and whom she could trust not to expose the truth.

"Ginny, come sit with me. We can have a glass of wine together," was always how the nights began. The offer was enticing to a 15-year-old. Acting like an adult made me feel important. Oddly, it allowed me to connect with my mother on a deeper level than ever before. But I struggled in this role and was ambivalent to take it on. On the one hand, I liked playing adult—but with my friends, not my mother. Gone was the innocence of adolescence. I was too young to be acting this old. To be a normal teen was no longer possible for the mere fact that this was *not normal* behavior. Weariness enveloped me, spending evenings with my mother in this way as she attempted to drink away her sorrows and cry out her grief. I longed to take refuge in my room and do homework while talking to my friends on the phone. The relatively boring life I used to have was no more. Without it, I lost my sense of connection to my friends, and the isolation left me depressed. The tears I shed were boundless, like a river overflowing the boundaries of a levee and intruding on regions meant to be dry.

Even though my mother was immersed in her own issues, she couldn't ignore the fact that no one in the family was coping well. She appealed to the minister of our local church for advice. We weren't members, but I had attended services many times with friends who were members, and the minister knew me. He advised her, and any of us kids who were willing, to seek therapy to help manage our grief.

My brothers declined, but Mom and I went to therapy with different therapists. Therapy lasted all of two sessions before my mother inexplicably cut it off. I knew something had happened when we got into the car to return home after the second session.

"We're not going anymore," my mother announced.

"Why?"

She wouldn't answer me but gripped the steering wheel and fumed silently all the way home. I didn't care because therapy felt weird to me. They had placed me in a group of my peers, most of whom were experiencing major mental health issues that required medication. Their experiences were not at all related to what I was going through. One of the teens in my group had non-stop tremors in her hands. Her face bore a lost expression, and she never engaged with the group. Later I was told these were side effects of the lithium she was taking.

I wondered how the others viewed me, what they were reading on *my* face. I was not on any medication, so I hoped I wouldn't be seen as a misfit because on the inside I surely thought I was. It was difficult to relate to any of these people, and the sessions were doing nothing for me. Surrendering therapy was easy, if for no other reason than I could go back to my normal friends.

Later that night, when my mother had enough vodka in her to inhibit her social filters, she revealed to me that the psychiatrist came on to her, pressuring her to have sex with him. Whenever my mom was scared, her eyes opened as wide as an owl's. I could tell she was traumatized. And I knew this wasn't the first time.

My mother was born in Indonesia and raised in the Netherlands. She was 18 years old when Hitler invaded in May of 1940. Her father, my opa Nicolaas Tierie, was a colonel in the Royal Dutch Army at the time. During the first week of the Nazi occupation, he abruptly disappeared. It was all very hush-hush. Someone claiming to be a government official had phoned the house and spoken with my mother, instructing her to pack some of her father's underwear, pajamas, and toiletries in a small suitcase and deliver it to a specific address. There was no explanation. The only communication the family received that indicated he was still alive were random messages relayed by strangers saying "Aunt Nicolein" was well. There was no Aunt Nicolein in the family, but my mother and her siblings understood that their father was reaching out to let them know he was safe. He returned home to The Hague five years after disappearing. By then his marriage to Oma was all but over.

In the first few years of the Nazi occupation, my oma and her five children continued to live in The Hague, and life was relatively normal except for the absence of my opa Nicolaas. The children attended school and summer camp as usual. But as the Nazis extended their reach into the western Netherlands, everything changed. In the winter of 1943, my mother's family was forced to evacuate their home. Oma took the three youngest children to a small holiday cottage she rented near the town of Ede, some 70 miles inland. There was no room in the small cottage for the two oldest girls: my mother, Cora, and her younger sister Matsy. My mother, 21 by this time, found a two-room apartment in The Hague and continued her post-secondary studies in art. Matsy, 19, had finished secondary school as well and had secured a job as an au pair in nearby Delft. She would often visit my mother when she had time off in the afternoons. One day in early 1945, my mother returned to her apartment to find nothing but rubble. Sifting through the bombed-out building, all she found was a tin of cleansing powder. She had lost everything but her life.

With no place to live, my mother was forced to give up her studies in The Hague and go to Ede where she found her mother and her three siblings barely surviving. Food had become increasingly scarce as the war progressed. Vouchers were required for all purchases and were hard to come by. Often, she resorted to digging up tulip bulbs from the frozen ground as a source of nourishment. There was no electricity, and wood for the stove—for cooking and heating—was almost non-existent. My mother became a surrogate parent to her three youngest siblings, finding them warm places to stay with relatives or sympathetic strangers and scrounging up food to feed them. At times she had to steal provisions from under the noses of Nazi soldiers. That winter she trekked almost 2,000 miles all over the Netherlands trying to keep her siblings safe and fed. At one point she took her sister Erna, age 14, and brother Robbie, age 12, from Ede north to Friesland by bicycle, a journey of about 100 miles. The rubber tires on the bicycles had quickly disintegrated, so they rode along icy roads on nothing but metal rims. By sheer persistence, and lots of slipping and falling, they managed to get to Friesland in three days.

My mother and her family suffered immensely at the hands of the Nazis. She spent her early twenties living in survival mode. As a beautiful young woman, she drew unwelcome attention from both Nazi and Allied soldiers, often avoiding their less-than-honorable advances through sheer wits or defiance, risking her life—at least once at gunpoint—by doing so. To this day her siblings call her a hero, and so do I.

My mother survived the war, but collateral damage ensued. Shortly after the war ended, she married a man she had met during the war. I don't know much about my mother's first husband. No one in the family ever discussed the marriage, but my mother told me that she was physically abused by him. She refused to put up with it, so she left him. A few years later she met and married my father, and he brought her to America.

The cost of what my mother had endured during the war—and then afterward, with an abusive husband—was the difficulty of finding a place for joy in her life again. She had fallen in love with my father and then been blindsided by his dishonesty and death. She had lost so much trust in men, and now was being propositioned by her therapist when she was at her most vulnerable. But she was tough, and I knew that she was not going to buckle. I'm sure she told the therapist, in her own indomitable way, to fuck off. And then she canceled therapy for both of us.

We were left to ourselves to manage our own emotional chaos.

## Chapter 7

# SETTING MY FIRST BOUNDARY

*The things that torment us thrive on our hushed fears and insecurities and they are made powerless by a resilient voice: An inner voice that says... "No More!"*

—*Jason Versey,* A Walk with Prudence[9]

By age 16 my role of dutiful confidante to my mother had grown old, very old. Mom needed my presence and sympathetic ear almost every night as she drunkenly rehashed her woes. The burden was an anchor dragging me ever downward. I was becoming increasingly concerned that she was growing too dependent on her nightly pity sessions. If I didn't make a break for it, this could go on for the rest of my life.

One night, amid her ritual purge, I decided to head upstairs to bed before my mother was done for the night. I had tried several times before to make the break from this unhealthy interplay without success. She was in the middle of a poor-me story that I had heard a zillion times.

I stood up. "I'm going to bed, Mom."

She pleaded with me. "Please don't go yet, Ginny. It's still early. Have another glass of wine."

"I'm already sleepy. I'm going to bed."

Mom's tone stretched toward indignant. "You are my daughter, Ginny, and I need you now."

When my expression didn't change, she switched tactics. "You're all I have, Ginny," she slurred.

Guilt hit me like a spear on fire. "Mom, I really want to go to bed."

"Please. *Please!*" I hated the begging especially. The pleas disarmed me, and I wanted to cave in.

Holding firm, I tried one more time. "Mom, please? I really want to go to bed."

Her eyes grew hard. "If you don't stay down here with me, I'll do what Dad did. I can't take the loneliness anymore."

My heart leaped in sheer panic. "Okay, okay, Mom. It's okay. I'll stay with you. Just don't say that. That's a horrible thought!"

My mother had won. "Just stay for another half-hour or so, please?"

As much as I was sure it was only a threat, it succeeded in stopping me from leaving her. But what if I was wrong? What if she really would go through with it? If she's as lonely as she says, and she doesn't have me to keep her company…then I would be responsible for both my parents' suicides.

Encouraged by her success, Mom continued with her new ploy over the next several months, increasing the frequency of her threats. One night I couldn't take it anymore. I was still stuck in that same boat, only now the stakes were higher; water was coming in over the sides. I pondered my options all night long.

Two days later I ran away from home.

I was a popular babysitter in our neighborhood. From my very first job at 11 I loved to my core the children I watched. The day before I left, I dropped in at the home of one of the families I worked for. I was 16 and had been a mother's helper for them on and off—long enough for them to know the struggles I was having at home. I explained to the mother in very vague terms what had transpired the night before. She offered me a more permanent mother's helper job in exchange for room and board.

My mother was devastated. She was in regular consult with the minister of the church we rarely attended. He helped her accept the choice I had made by telling her he knew the family I was with and that she had nothing to worry about. It took 18 months before I was ready to return home, but first I had to establish boundaries that I swore myself to live by.

The first night back at home my mother began her old ritual. My brothers were off on their own, each struggling to find their way in this tragedy with some semblance of success. She opened a bottle of wine and took out two glasses. My hands started shaking and my heart pounded so hard I had difficulty breathing. *Now's the time, Ginny, don't back down. You promised yourself that you would only come home under one condition.*

"Mom," my voice quavered. Our eyes met. I took a deep breath, then walked over and hugged her.

She smiled at me. "I'm so glad you're back," she said. "I've missed you. Let me pour you a glass of wine."

For a moment I felt guilt consume me, tugging me back toward the trap I had escaped 18 months earlier. My heart started racing again. The words were stuck in my throat, holding onto the walls of my larynx for dear life. "No, Ma, I think I'm going to head upstairs to bed."

"What do you mean? I have to sit here all alone?" She fixed a hard gaze on me. "You know your father did this to me…put me in this position. How could you do the same thing?"

"I'm gonna head upstairs, Ma."

"You can't go," she insisted. "If you do, I'm gonna kill myself, just like him. I'll take a knife out of the drawer and kill myself. I swear I will."

She'd said it.

With a huge lump in my throat and a calm belying my fear, I replied, "If that's what you need to do, then go ahead. It's not my problem."

Leaving the room abruptly, I ran up the stairs to my bedroom.

My heart was still pounding hard in my chest as I thought about what I had just done. For the first time in my life, I was able to set a boundary with my mother. I had not known it was an option until I left home and then considered my return. I knew I could never live with her again unless the complicit drinking binges stopped. As I paced my bedroom my heart began to slow down.

The dread kept pace with me as I crossed the room. *Will she do it? Oh, Mom, please don't. Please, please, please don't do it, Mom.* My ears strained to hear what was going on downstairs. The silence was unbearable. Then I heard Mom in the kitchen, slamming drawers.

*Oh, my God! She's going to do it. Shit!*

An eerie silence prevailed for what seemed like hours. In reality, I'm sure it was only a few minutes, but I was petrified. Was this all an act to make me go running back downstairs? Deep down in my soul I was certain it was—all those pointless threats of suicide since my dad had passed nearly two years earlier—but how could I be sure? Maybe this time I went too far. The silence gripped me while waiting for something, anything, to happen. The "what-ifs" screamed in my head. Which was worse: the evil, menacing silence of waiting or those piercing, deafening screams of my anguish?

I heard my mother slam her bedroom door, yelling obscenities at me from within her room. A rush of relief flooded my body, making me light-headed. I'm not sure why, but at that moment I knew beyond a shadow of a doubt that my mother was not going to follow through with her suicide threat.

The authentic me emerged like a butterfly sliding its last wing from the chrysalis, exercising those amazing appendages for the first time, and instinctively taking flight—free from the confinement of guilt that had been imposed on me. I had spun a protective cocoon around me, a barrier against my mother's dysfunction, and for this moment I was a completely transformed magical creature. Finally, I had moved forward in our relationship empowered by choice, rather than fear.

I kept my distance from my mother, knowing if I opened a door of sympathy she would barge in, dragging me into that pool of guilt in which I would eventually drown. It would take me another 30 years to understand that sympathy was just an immature form of empathy. With nothing but good intentions, the naïve enable their loved ones to the point of victimization. If I had realized this at the time, I might have helped my mother to see the best in herself and accept her frailties with understanding and compassion. Sympathy did not serve her or me. Its lovely wrapper had enticed me to try to help her fix what I didn't understand and couldn't possibly achieve, and in the process I had made her worse.

My mother was a gift to me in many ways, despite my entanglement in her web of sorrow. She taught me that I could be or do anything I wanted in my life. She was so incredibly angry at the world because her choices had been stripped from her. Saddled with four essentially orphaned siblings as a teenager, then a family of her own that was larger than she felt emotionally capable of dealing with, it was too late for her to do what she had wanted with her life. So she tried to live vicariously through me, her only daughter. Truth is, her persistence in reminding me of what she would have done differently served me well. In the struggle that was my teen years, we finally connected. And I heard her.

## *Chapter 8*

# ILLUSIONS OF A HAPPY FAMILY

*No matter how bad things are, you can always make things worse.*
—*Randy Pausch*[10]

My first husband, Jerry, and I met when I was in my early twenties and a senior in college, majoring in speech pathology. Interning as a student clinician in the college's speech pathology clinic, I had developed a close relationship with my professors and the staff, and at times socialized with them on weekends. The secretary at the front desk knew Jerry and matched us up on a blind date. I remember he brought me a bouquet of flowers on our first date. No one had ever given me flowers, so I was quite charmed by him. He seemed like a perfect fit, both romantically and socially; he was sweet and his connection with my college professors impressed me. I found myself falling in love.

Amid my budding relationship, I graduated from college. All spring I had agonized over what my next step would be, wanting to get a master's degree in the Midwest where some of the best post-graduate speech pathology programs were, but I was too apprehensive to go solo. My new relationship became an unintended excuse to avoid confronting my fears. Afraid to fail without someone to hold me up, I chose to stay in New York where I could pursue my master's degree in the safety of my current surroundings. On the surface I pretended to be confident, acting as if staying was what I originally planned. But inside, I gave in to the fear that was so familiar it was comforting. By staying in New York I was committing to my relationship with Jerry on a deeper level, but was I also fearful where our relationship would end up? I was. An inner voice expressed doubts to me early on about the chances of this relationship ever becoming a viable marriage. But I assured the voice that even if it didn't work out, I would just divorce him and move on. In hindsight, having developed such a casual Plan B so early in the game meant only one thing: We didn't stand a chance. But my dreams of creating a happy family shushed my fears, and we were married the following spring.

Jerry and I had many talks about our ideals and values before we got married. He had assured me at the time of our engagement that he wanted children just as much as I did, but as time passed he seemed to be changing his mind. Every time I brought it up, he shut me down with a not-now attitude. It seemed there was never a good time to discuss the subject.

Jerry was deep into the party life. It consumed him. So, rather than be shut out of his world, I joined him hoping that at some point he would come around and we could have that baby conversation. Partying became the focal point of our marriage, the primary way we spent time together. But after a couple of years, I found myself growing tired of it. The time we spent with our friends as a couple was becoming devoid of intimacy. Having a good time—all the time—eventually numbs you to the point where you don't know what a good time is anymore, you're just going through the motions. Getting high becomes a thing you do out of habit, not for joy. I started to wonder if that was all there was to life, and believing that left me feeling empty and unfulfilled. Surely there had to be more from life than this mindless, pointless diversion. I longed for deeper, more meaningful connections. It was time for me to grow up and put this immature lifestyle aside.

At the time, I had completed my master's degree and was working full time at a state psychiatric center, employed in the children and youth department. Jerry and I were three years into our marriage, and my maternal clock was wound so tightly I could think of little else. My body and soul were on fire with the desire to have a child. By badgering and begging, I finally convinced Jerry that it was time to move forward with our family plan. Sensing he was not fully on board, I was confident that once he set eyes on our first child, he would fall head over heels and embrace his role as a parent. Surely then he would recognize that raising a child was infinitely more satisfying than this artificial party world.

Early one April morning I stepped out of the bathroom and knocked lightly on the bedroom door where Jerry still lay asleep. "Guess what," I whispered, waving the pregnancy test stick in the air like a magic wand. "We're pregnant!"

"Great," he said with a hint of sarcasm, pulling the bedsheets over his head.

My heart sank. I expected the positive news would stir some indication of paternal excitement, but his response confirmed that his heart was not in it. Hopefully the idea would grow on him. But the next nine months were a constant struggle to get him to share or, at the very least, support me in my rapture. I tried to involve him in setting up the baby's nursery. The best location for it was the bedroom closest to ours, Jerry's office, a room he rarely used. But he resisted every step of the way. After months of begging and pleading, I was finally able to convince him to slap a coat of yellow paint on the walls. His acquiescence had to be partly due to my nagging and was a way to shut me up. I was desperate to share in this joyous time with him, yet I felt so alone. My hope could have been restored if he had put one-tenth the energy into this endeavor that he put into the bathroom he had recently renovated. With each rejection, my sadness and disconnection deepened. Why? Was he afraid of the responsibility? Perhaps he never really wanted kids in the first place and was too afraid to tell me the truth for fear that he would lose me. Maybe he wanted out of the marriage and didn't want to complicate things by throwing a child into the mix. My doubts covered the full spectrum of possibilities. If Jerry wouldn't talk to me, my only option was to guess what his thoughts were.

During my pregnancy I talked incessantly about staying home with the baby after it was born. Jerry knew that if I left my job, he would at least have to match my not-so-paltry income. His current job in his father's piano repair business wouldn't provide what we needed. He struggled with what kind of profession to go into, feeling like he wasn't qualified to do anything that paid enough.

One day Jerry confided to me that his only gift, the only skill he felt proficient at, was selling drugs. *Selling drugs?* I did not see that coming. My mind scrambled to keep up. Clearly drugs were a part of his party world, but selling them? Apparently, he had learned the "trade" in Ohio before I met him and decided that any job he'd get with a college degree would be less profitable. But eventually he had given it up and returned to his hometown in New York to work with his father.

How could I not know this about him? I knew he loved to party, so why was it so difficult to imagine that he would cross the line and start selling? I may have been naïve, but I felt Jerry had been deceitful. Maybe he hadn't lied outright, but until now he had neglected to tell me about this rather significant part of his life. If he had been hiding this truth for so long, what other things had he kept from me? My world was turned upside down, and my dreams, like furniture in an overturned dollhouse, lay broken on the ground. My hope was to stay home and raise my child in the warmth of a loving family, but that didn't quite jibe with Jerry's proposed choice for providing for us. Rather than sweep up the rubble, I walked right over it, refusing to acknowledge it was there. I chose to ignore Jerry's confession in hopes that he, with my encouragement, would come to his senses and realize how preposterous this suggestion was. But my intuition told me that Jerry had already decided: If he were to be the primary breadwinner, he would have to make his living the only way he knew how. He wouldn't change. As always, I would be the one who would have to change and surrender my dream.

When Nic was born, I fell in love in a way that was completely different from any love I had ever experienced before. When the nurses placed him on my chest with the umbilical cord still pulsing, I marveled at the perfection of human creation. "Ten fingers and ten toes. He's perfect!" I announced to the world as he was belting out his first cries with outstretched limbs, just begging for his first human embrace. Nic brought great joy and purpose to my life. He gave me the opportunity to feel love again, and I was going to give him all the love and connection that I yearned for as a child. He was the joy that replaced the pain, guilt, sorrow, uncertainty, and insecurity that was eating away at my soul. My love for him became the distraction that kept me from facing the dysfunction of my marriage.

Jerry, although not much involved in Nic's daily care, was a proud daddy. But he was diving deeper into the depths of his social life inundated with drugs. I had started removing myself from it when Jerry agreed to start a family, and our paths had grown farther apart since. It seemed the more I tried to convince him to participate in our family life, the more he ran from it. I thought I had fallen in love with a lifelong companion, but what I had really fallen in love with was an illusion of a happy family. My dream was to create a safe, secure, and happy family like those in *Leave It to Beaver* or *Father Knows Best*, two of my favorite shows as a child. I had been certain I could make it happen, but Jerry had other plans.

In the months following Nic's birth, I rode a wave of resentment, anger, and fear. We never discussed the illegal activity Jerry engaged in after Nic was born because he had told me once, "The less you know, the better—for your own sake." In reality though, I was as guilty as he was by the complicity of my silence. I was losing sleep worrying. It was only a matter of time before the shit hit the fan, and the thought of losing my precious son to state foster care terrified me. Yet still I did nothing. The Scarlett O'Hara in me was at it again.

When Nic was five months old, my fear finally overrode my denial. I told Jerry that I was returning to work so that we could stop the insanity. There was a cost and a payoff with this decision. The cost was giving up my precious time with Nic, and the payoff was the relief from the worry that was dragging me down. Losing my son was not an option. I blamed Jerry for forcing me to make this decision. Mentally, he was another child I was caring for, minus the reciprocal love and adoration. My husband and our marriage were becoming a burden. The constant bickering and dysfunction made me happy to get out of the house.

When Nic was 18 months old, I discovered to my shock and mortification, that I was pregnant again. How could this be? I was using birth control, and Jerry and I had essentially no physical relationship. Yet a couple of months previously I had, in a desperate moment of wanting to reach through the numbness, succumbed to sex with him. The desire to feel something, anything, was enough to shut out all the anger of the past couple of years for a short while, yet it left me feeling emptier than before. And now, here I was. Pregnant. The thought of having another child under the current conditions was unimaginable. Legal separation from Jerry was something I had recently considered. Taking my child to split, leave, run as far away as possible was something I contemplated daily. In my mind, it was a done deal. Emotionally, I had already made the separation. Now what was I going to do?

It took an incredible amount of courage to tell Jerry about this unplanned pregnancy. Of all the possible scenarios I conjured up of his reaction to the news, never in my wildest dreams did I imagine the one I got.

"You might as well get an abortion because it can't be mine." Jerry's calm denial was shocking. It was as if he didn't even have to consider my culpability; it was a foregone conclusion. My mind reeled. However improbable it was, the fact remained that he *was* the father, and I had hoped to be able to have a conversation with him about our future predicated on that fact. He had pulled the rug out from under me by throwing it all in my lap, and I didn't know how to respond.

In hindsight I realized that the thought of this added responsibility must have been too much for him to take in at the time. He too must have been grappling with how to move forward, with or without me. He knew his attempts to appease me and pursue a legitimate profession were not working, and never would. He had started selling real estate several months earlier and hadn't come close to selling a house yet. His heart just wasn't in it. Later I would discover that his real estate job was actually a front for the drug business he was hiding from me.

This unexpected response from Jerry jolted me into actually considering abortion as an option. I was pissed to the point of calling his bluff. But it only took a day for me to recognize that I wasn't capable. In my heart I knew that no matter how dire our circumstances were, I would never be able to live with the guilt. It would eat away at me until there was nothing left of my already fragile self. And I couldn't bear the thought of giving my child up for adoption. Going through with the pregnancy and keeping the baby meant that life was going to be unimaginably challenging for me. Jerry would not be there—in any capacity—to support me.

In my heart, my marriage was over. Jerry and I went to marriage counseling when I was seven months into the pregnancy. It was our last-ditch effort to repair the disconnect, but we were only going through the motions to be able to justify the inevitable end. Jerry was spending more nights away from home doing God-knows-what. When I pleaded with him to come home and be the father and husband I pressured him to be, he just became more remote. I expressed my frustration through blame, thinking it was possible to make him change if I just heaped on enough guilt. I installed myself as the martyr in the relationship, reasoning that the more I did to keep our home together and functioning, doing all the things *he* should be doing, the sooner he would see it my way.

Seven months pregnant, I was mowing up and down the grassy hills of our acre-and-a-half while Jerry watched from the comfort of a lawn chair. A real estate colleague of his had stopped by to talk to him and watched in agitation while I struggled to push the mower. When he saw that Jerry wasn't going to do anything, he rescued me by finishing the job himself, dressed in a suit and tie no less. It had no visible impact on Jerry. And all the "*I* have to do everything" I hurled at him wasn't enough to bring him back. Every time I blamed, I rendered myself more helpless. The more I pushed to prove I was right, the more disconnected we became. I was feeding what little power I had left to the lions, and they were devouring it greedily while I watched in horror.

I discovered—too late—that the only person I can change is myself. My choices were mine to own, not Jerry's, and I opted to blame him for the outcomes of my behavior rather than owning my contribution to the dysfunction. It was more important for me to be right than to be connected.

Choosing to stay with Jerry through the pregnancy while hating my situation left me fighting depression and anxiety daily. I had no idea how I was going to handle the stress of raising two babies while financially supporting the family. How would I keep it all together with an absent, unsupportive husband? I would have to figure it out as I went along. It seemed the only choice I could live with. I wanted this baby.

In May 1954 another mother—my mother—faced the same decision that I had just made. Appalled by yet another pregnancy, she considered her options. She had aborted her first pregnancy in Mexico—before she and Dad decided to get married—to save the family from social disgrace. Silent and secret could be kept in the closet; only she would have to bear the pain of her choice.

After they married, there would be more pregnancies. First, my brother Gordon—not planned, but by now socially acceptable at least. Then my brother, Mark, planned and decidedly loved. But then, with a three-year-old and an infant, my mother was confronted with another unplanned pregnancy. She wasn't sure she had the strength to see it through. It was a difficult decision, but she chose life. Little did she know that she was choosing *lives*, plural. Two of them, because hiding in baby John's shadow in her womb was little Ginny—his twin. Would this knowledge have changed the outcome? It's difficult to say. Thankfully she didn't know until she was on the delivery table.

I didn't want to be responsible for making decisions like these. I would put the choice in God's hands. I would have this baby, and God would choose his path.

# PART II

# BART

## Chapter 9

# CHRISTMAS TREE DELIGHT

*Genius is one percent talent and 99 percent hard work.*
—Attributed to *Thomas Edison*[11]

Extracting myself from an unhealthy marriage was not as much of a relief as I had hoped it would be. Being the single mother of a two-and-a-half-year-old and a five-month-old was demanding. My professional work at the psych center was difficult. Getting the kids to childcare every day was challenging, and then having to rev up the energy on our return home to take care of their needs for the remainder of the evening was especially onerous. My feelings of guilt for not being a better parent—not spending more time at home watching them grow and attending to their needs with more patience and compassion—only added to the stress. I was bone-tired and could barely tolerate myself. At times I harbored fantasies of having a whole year to myself—no children, no husband, no friends; just me—to put my life into order and learn to like myself again.

Those who knew me told me I was strong, especially those who knew the challenges I had overcome in my childhood and young adulthood. But the truth was, I felt like a fraud. All my life I had adored children and longed for my own someday, and here I was fantasizing about getting away from them. I was an early childhood professional on an interdisciplinary team dealing with some of the most physically and emotionally abused children in a large, rural county, yet I could barely manage my own children without losing control. Far from being the most joyful time of my life, motherhood was drudgery. I hated doing it alone, always having to be "on," making every decision myself, never getting a chance to say, "You decide. I just don't care right now."

Thankfully, my best friend, Cathy, was still in my life. She lived in Toronto and we saw each other as often as we could. When the first Christmas I faced as a single mom was approaching, I longed for it to be a special time for the kids. I didn't want to sacrifice any of the traditions and rituals that were so important to me; passing them down could help keep cherished memories alive in my children's adult lives. But the added stress of buying-wrapping-decorating-baking, on top of working full time and all the other daily to-dos, left me barely keeping my head above water, groping for a life raft that was just out of reach. My stress was directly driven by that movie in my brain of what a perfect Christmas should look like, but I wasn't willing to let it go. I called Cathy to vent. She always made me feel so much better.

"Ginny, let me come down and help."

She didn't need to ask twice.

One evening Cathy and I were baking in the kitchen, singing along to Christmas music playing on the stereo. Nic was absorbed in putting together a puzzle in the living room, and Bart was cruising around the house in his walker. I heard the Nic alarm go off.

"Uh-oh, Mommy, Bart!" Nic was an extremely dependable warning device. He was truly concerned for Bart's safety and had proven himself an attentive steward of Bart's welfare many times in the short seven months of his brother's life.

Both Cathy and I rushed into the living room to find the Christmas tree bent over at a 45-degree angle, begging to be relieved of its tension and allowed to snap and crash to the floor. Incredulous, we both looked to see what was causing the tree such distress. From the mid-section of the tree ran a taut string of lights, extending like a clothesline across the living room and disappearing into my bedroom. *How in the…?* We followed the string into the bedroom, through that room, and into the nursery. At the end of the string was Bart, gleefully pushing himself backwards in his walker, arms outstretched, and grasping the end of the string in his tight little baby-fists. His expression was one of pure delight, not because of his accomplishment per se as much as his realization of his newfound power. With every step backward, his face lit up brighter.

A sensation initiating from deep inside my core began to materialize in my consciousness. *Uh-oh!* Minuscule alarm bells pinged inside me. Watching Bart's face, I saw no remorse or fear, nor reading of my face to see if this new action was safe or going to trigger reprimand from me. He had tasted power and there was no going back. He was so emboldened by the rush of it that he had no concern for anyone else's response. This child's life from this moment forward would be focused on exercising his power and how to get more of it.

At the time, I was not consciously aware of what this behavior signaled for the future. I passed it off as cute and funny—a story to share with him when he was older, something we would repeat and laugh over when we reminisced. But inside was an uneasiness I chose to ignore. Passing it off was the healthiest thing I could do for the time being because if I ruminated on it, I might convince myself that I would never be able to handle this path given this child's tenacious spirit. I had to play the cards of parenting one hand at a time.

# Chapter 10
# GEORGE

*Never lose hope. Storms make people stronger and never last forever.*
—ROY T. BENNET[12]

Bart's precocious nature only fueled his tenacity. He began to walk and talk at 10 months and maintain conversations with adults at 18 months. Not little conversations, but reciprocal, articulate conversations.

"Okay, Bart, we are going to the grocery store," I'd start.

"We are going to the grocery store? Why?" he'd return.

"To get some food, so we can eat and be healthy."

"To get some food so we can eat and be healthy? Why?"

"So we can be strong and do all the things we want to with our brains and bodies."

"So we can be strong and do all the things we want to with our brains and bodies? Why?"

He was obviously learning the social rules of reciprocity in conversation, but he was also comprehending everything I said to him. You never know when information he gleaned was going to come back to you in a different context. This back and forth would go on for hours if I allowed it. Honestly, sometimes I just had to stop talking. It was the only way to shut it down and maintain my sense of sanity. As a speech pathologist working with young children, I was astonished at his ability. He was exhibiting language skills of a four-year-old. In the grocery store, people would turn their heads looking for the four-year-old who was talking.

"Who said that?"

I would point to Bart.

"He is so smart. Wow! Is he ever bright!"

On his second birthday, he received birthday cards from people congratulating him on turning three.

Bart's persistence challenged me regularly. Pick a day, any day, and it started with 45-minute tantrums when I didn't give in to his requests for candy at breakfast. And these weren't collapsing-on-the-floor-in-tears tantrums. The tantrums were violent. Papers and pictures stuck on the fridge were ripped down and thrown across the kitchen. Chairs were pushed on their sides and toys flew off the shelves. It always ended with an intensely chaotic goodbye as I dropped him and Nic off at childcare.

Nic, my "good boy," always gave me hope. But sadly, there was a cost to being good. He succumbed to the fact that he would never get the attention he needed and deserved because of his brother's behavior. Nic was a naturally compliant and easy-going child, but I'm sure he realized at an early age that by being extra good he wouldn't contribute to my stress from dealing with Bart. He was the peacekeeper, and he would loyally follow me to the door while I physically carried his brother, still in full tantrum, into the sitters' house. This is the way I began each workday. Despite the regularity of this scene, each morning I woke clinging to the hope that maybe today, by the grace of God, I would miraculously get a break. I don't know where I got the optimism.

One of the wonders of my life is the balance that tends to prevail, even when it seems like the cards are stacked against me. For every choice I make, there is a cost, but also a payoff. For every struggle there is always a rainbow in the waiting, angels always lurking on the sidelines of my life, ready to come to my rescue when needed. With all the dysfunction I experienced in my family of origin, there were people not blood-related who swooped in to give me the security, encouragement, and hope I needed.

Bea and Carl, my sitters, were two of those angels, and they just happened to live no more than a stone's throw from my apartment. They had been in the childcare business for 30 years and were highly regarded by the community. But more importantly, they loved my boys and me as if we were their own. They became surrogate grandparents to Nic and Bart, and that security gave me the confidence I needed to handle the stress of being Bart's single parent. Their love for Bart allowed them to deal with his tirades. Of course, Bart was never as challenging for them as he was for me, but they agreed he was not easy to discipline.

Because of their kindness, I was able to extend my childcare hours to get errands done without the kids on my way home from work. Bart was impossible on our outings. When he was with me, I rarely got through a shopping trip without having to abandon a cart full of items in the middle of the store. All too often I had to carry him out screaming at the top of his lungs. Jerry's commitment to visitation was sporadic at best, and Bea and Carl's support allowed me to catch a break occasionally with an evening out with a girlfriend or sometimes even a weekend away. They were my saving grace, and any sanity I still possess is in large part due to them.

Even with moments of respite, however, there were days when, for whatever reason, I felt I was at my breaking point. A stressful or tiring day at work, a whirlwind trip through a long list of errands, or a bad night's sleep can cause anyone to be short tempered. One day I came home to kids who were demanding attention I was too overwhelmed to give. Both boys were pulling on my pant legs, talking at me simultaneously and in voices much too loud for that time of day. They were making ridiculous demands, the kind my brain was telling me any good parent would easily say no to a couple of hours before bedtime.

"Mommy, can we go get ice cream?"

"Can I watch *The Gremlins*?"

"Can we go see Bea?"

In my exhaustion I often questioned myself: *Do I give in just this one time so I can have a little peace and quiet, or do I stick to my principles?* This time was different though. I just wanted them to be quiet—right that moment—and give me five minutes to put the groceries away.

"That's it! I AM NOT YOUR MOTHER ANYMORE. From now on, my name is George. GEORGE! That is who I am!" I was now watching the whole thing as if it were playing on a screen—watching myself go crazy, watching my kids go quiet, and watching their shocked little faces. My only recourse and resource in that moment was to get away from them. I needed to be alone, somewhere quiet where I could think. Stomping upstairs to my bedroom and slamming the door, I threw myself on the bed and began to weep. Immersed in self-pity, I just wanted to disappear.

I heard the pitter-patter of little footsteps steps coming up the stairs. *Oh, no! Here we go again. I can't get one minute to myself.*

Nic whimpered as he climbed the stairs in pursuit. On the other side of the door he desperately pleaded, "Mommy, please! You have to be my mommy. You can't be George. Please be my mommy." Guilt clouded my brain. Nic, the precious one who so needed me and now thought I was abandoning him.

Bart's footsteps marched up the stairs and to my bedroom door. He rapped on the door; his pacifier pushed to the corner of his mouth so he could talk. "George! Hey, George! Get out here. We need you!"

I couldn't stop myself. I burst into laughter—hysterical laughter—until I felt like I was going to pee in my pants. I opened the door, knelt on the floor, opened my arms, and hugged my kids with wild delight, tears of relief streaming down my face. "I will never stop being your mommy." In that moment, I knew everything was going to be all right and they did too. I would never give up on my kids and they would never give up on me either—no matter what my name was. We were all we had, and that was enough.

## Chapter 11

# THE WOODEN SPOON

*I believe that every single event in life happens in an opportunity to choose love over fear.*
—OPRAH WINFREY[13]

My most challenging times as a parent began when Bart was two and Nic was four. One afternoon, on a typically frantic day, Bart decided to defy me by jumping on the couch and repeatedly switching the lamp on and off for what felt like 2,000 times, triggering me into emotional craziness. It was that moment every parent experiences at one time or another, when instinct kicks in and the "music" starts playing without you ever having to press the play button.

"I have had it with you, mister! You are jumping on my last nerve. You're driving me nuts. You are not going to get away with this." Blah, blah, blah.

He flashed me a taunting look.

Like the undertow of a seemingly innocuous wave, a nagging pull started in my core. Before I realized it the shore was but a hazy line in the distance. Bart had pulled me under again, and I knew what was coming next.

The wave of irrationality broke over my head, and I watched myself stomp into the kitchen, snatch a wooden spoon from the utensil drawer, and bound toward Bart like a snorting bull. I was about to violate every rule in my playbook about the negative effects of corporal punishment, yet I was helpless to stop myself. In slow motion, I saw myself slip into a rage, screaming while wagging the spoon in Bart's face.

"If you do that again, this spoon is going on your bottom. Do you hear me?" I froze, glaring at him, just waiting for fear to wipe that grin off his face.

Nic saw what was coming and retreated to where he could find safety, the storage space under the stairs—his go-to place when Bart pushed Momma over the edge. This was not going to be pretty.

With grin intact, Bart turned his back on me and bent over, sticking his butt out. "Go ahead and spank me, Mommy," he taunted. "I want you to spank me." On his face was a textbook picture of a shit-eating grin.

I was puzzled. Perhaps it was his way of saying "Let's just get this punishment over with." Maybe it was an unconventional expression of fear. Kids have a funny way of managing fear sometimes. They can turn it into a game which sometimes triggers the parent even more. An abundance of emotions surged through me as I stood there, stunned, with the spoon poised in mid-air. I was confused, then intensely angry, then immobilized by my own fear. Blood drained from my face to my feet. I knew in that moment that I was not going to spank him, which was a blessing, not only because it was the wrong thing to do but because if I did, I was sure I would seriously hurt him.

A string of visions of Bart's future life flooded my brain. I visualized him failing school, racing a car recklessly down the road at a hundred miles per hour, putting himself and others in danger. I had him pegged as a serial killer by the time he was 16. I was afraid—afraid of what would happen to him in the future. What if I could not get this child under control? The wooden spoon was my last offensive straw, and I had been sure the threat of it would do the trick. Now I was faced with a child who was controlling me—and the whole family. Without any other strategy up my sleeve, what was I going to do?

Then came the wave of shame at my failure to know better and that familiar feeling that I was a fraud. I was the professional. I should know how to handle this. Yet I had displayed only a minor fraction of the patience I would have shown to the children I cared for at the psychiatric center. But my deepest shame was wrapped around my feelings of abject drudgery at being his mother. I was angry—at myself, and at God for giving me this child. How was I going to get Bart to comply and give me back my power as a parent? How was I going to motivate him to listen and be respectful?

Every attempt in the proverbial book of traditional discipline had failed. I tried sticker charts with a goal of going to McDonald's when successfully completed. McDonald's was something I didn't condone, but the kids loved it and I would use it for an occasional celebration. The sticker chart didn't work. He wasn't patient enough to wait a week to earn his reward, and I wasn't willing to shorten his trial period and reward him with unhealthy food on a daily basis. I tried threats of throwing toys away. That didn't work. He only threw longer, more violent tantrums. At times I was so afraid he would hurt himself, I had to physically restrain him. I tried using guilt to coerce, manipulate, and bribe him into compliance. Nothing worked. How was I going to control this child? After all, that was my job. Wasn't it?

The epiphany hit me the moment the word "control" entered my brain. *Maybe the problem was not with Bart but with me.* He was, after all, watching and learning about the world from me. Maybe my out-of-control responses were impacting his behavior. Maybe his tantrums were him mirroring my behavior toward him. I can't imagine what I must have looked like, standing there with that spoon two inches from his nose, my face a mirror image of the Wicked Witch of the West. He couldn't possibly feel safe when I threatened him like this. Toughest of all for me to accept was that maybe, before I worked on Bart's behavior, I needed to work on myself. All these questions, but I was very sure of one thing: I would need to find a better way and it had to start with me.

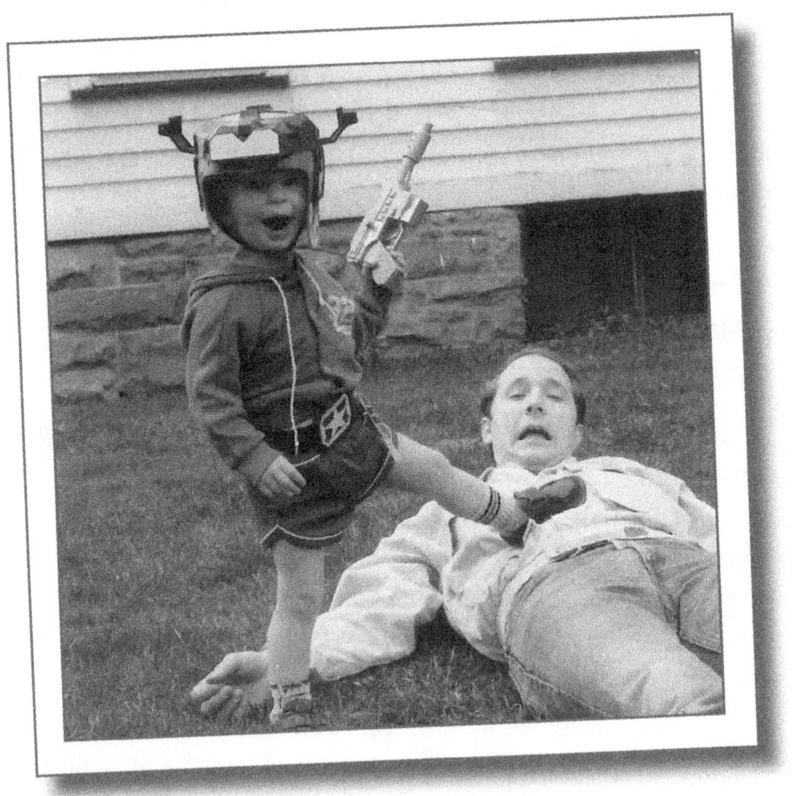

*Bart age 2 with his Uncle John*

## Chapter 12
# CENTREVILLE AMUSEMENT PARK

*When one reaches the end of his rope, he should tie a knot in it and hang on.*
—*Unknown*[14]

Later that year we traveled to Toronto to visit Cathy for a weekend of fun and relaxation. One day the four of us took a ferry to the Toronto Islands on Lake Ontario to walk, picnic, and enjoy Centreville Amusement Park.

At one point in our stroll, we came upon a kiddie-boat ride on a small pond. For only two bucks the boys could steer a motorized boat shaped like a swan around the pond for 10 minutes. Both boys were beyond excited about getting in a boat they could "drive" themselves. There was a catch though: You had to be four years or older to drive the boat. Both Cathy and I clearly explained the rule to the boys.

"Nic is the one who will drive because he is four, and Bart, you can ride in the boat if you sit next to Nic," we explained. "You may not drive the boat, Bart, because you are not four years old. You just sit next to Nic, okay? When the man blows his horn, that means it is time to come back.

Do you understand?"

Both boys nodded with delight.

The tender captain transported the boys to the boat and helped them get situated, giving the swan boat a gentle shove into the middle of the pond to get them started. I got my camera out and started clicking away, marveling at the cuteness of it all. Cathy and I giggled at the sight of them, but with some trepidation. Would they be able to handle it? We both were hesitant about Bart, knowing his potential to blow up if he didn't get his way.

They were calm and cooperative, until the tender captain blew his horn and instructed them to return to the tender. Then all hell broke loose. Nic started to turn the boat in the direction of the tender when Bart decided that it was not going to happen until he got a turn to drive. He started to tantrum and fight with Nic, grabbing the steering wheel.

"Gimme a turn," Bart shouted in Nic's face while fighting for control of the steering wheel. Nic said nothing as he was only interested in maintaining his job at the helm as the adults had expected of him. The more Nic held firm his position, the louder Bart got and the more the boat became unstable, wobbling from side to side.

This was one time that Nic would not give in to Bart's tirade because he was afraid of getting in trouble with the tender captain. Nic was a rule-follower, as first-borns tend to be, and he was not going to allow Bart to bend the rules.

"Boys!" I screamed. "Get in here now. Nic take the wheel and come back."

Nic tried, but come hell or high water, Bart was not going to come back until he got a turn.

The tender captain kept calling to them to bring the boat back, and Bart kept resisting with a loud and persistent, "No!"

The more Nic fought Bart's coup, the louder Bart became. The louder Bart became, the more people on the banks of the pond stopped to watch the commotion on the water. By now the tender captain realized that the boys would not be returning under their own recognizance and was attempting to tow them back to the dock.

With each defiant cry, fear's claws gripped me tighter. *Oh, shit! Am I going to be able to handle this one?*

Cathy watched us as I helped the angry tender captain struggle to secure the wobbling boat to the dock.

At this point Bart was in full-fledged tantrum, and I struggled to get him out of the boat and onto the lawn. Those in the park who didn't have a front row seat to this spectacle must have thought that someone was beating the poor child. This was one of those moments as a parent when I questioned why I ever thought I wanted to be one.

By now those who could see what was going on were all in agreement, I'm sure, that this spoiled-rotten little brat needed to be punished. I too wanted to lash out and let him know how disrespectful his behavior was. If he would only stop, I could feel better about the throng of judging adults closing in on us. I wanted this commotion to evaporate so the spectators would mind their own business and move on. I knew that spanking was not the answer, not only because I was familiar with the early childhood studies that proved the negative impact of corporal punishment on children, but also because I knew Bart. Punishment would only escalate his resistance. Imposing guilt and shame on Bart would only fire him up. The level of intensity we were witnessing now would be nothing compared to where he would go if I tried to control him through punishment. I didn't spank because, plain and simple, it would not work.

I did the only thing I could think of to disarm him. Cathy, Nic, and I left Bart, writhing, and screaming, in the middle of that beautifully manicured lawn. We walked about fifty feet away and sat on a bench, chatting away as if we didn't know this unruly child. Nervous laughter peppered our conversation as we waited and watched, never taking our eyes from him. We pleaded with the Universe to hurry it up so bystanders would stop wondering where the delinquent mother was. I could only hope at least some of them had the heart to be sympathetic to my situation, thinking *That poor mother! I wish her well. I'm just glad it's not me.*

After 45 minutes Bart was too exhausted to keep it going. When he was calm enough to pick himself up, I was there to take his hand and continue our day. I did not say anything about what had just occurred. I knew if I tried to admonish him he would likely go right back to full tantrum. Silence was golden.

Later I reflected, *Oh, the will of this child! Am I ever going to be the mom I want to be with him? Is he ever going to see me as the mother he wants me to be?*

One thing I knew was that Bart would never stop pursuing what it was he wanted. He had a drive and a passion that were undeniable. But how was I going to help him learn compromise and accommodation? How could I teach him that aggression, especially toward those people closest to him, would only drive them away and push his goal of demanding that things go *his way* farther out of reach? When—oh, when—would a better way present itself to me?

# *Chapter 13*
# NIGHT NIGHT, SLEEP TIGHT

*The only person you can make change is yourself.*
—DR. BECKY BAILEY[45]

One of the most challenging aspects of single parenting is the mental and physical stress that goes along with it. There is no one to help make daily decisions or share in the physical work. On the downside, I rarely got a break. On the upside, I didn't have to negotiate decisions I thought best met the needs of my children.

There was a constant buzz in my head that centered on guilt. Guilt for my failed marriage. Guilt that there were not enough hours in the day for me to give my children the attention they needed. Guilt for wanting to pawn them off on someone else so I could get a few hours to myself. And worse, guilt for feeling guilty. My brain crackled and sputtered with guilt, my stress at a high-static level. The incessant noise of it threatened to send me over the edge at times.

Night time—the witching hour of parenting—was often the most difficult. I was so done with the day after giving it my all at work. If I could just get a scrap of cooperation during the bedtime routine, it would give me some sense of sanity. As the time neared when I could watch the boys drift off to peaceful sleep, a quiet desperation would creep into my veins. All I could think about was the moment I would plop myself, exhausted, on the couch with a glass of wine. There would be no desperate calls from upstairs, no more demands for my attention. I yearned for silence—sweet, golden silence.

Nic was easy. After the hustle and bustle of baths and bedtime stories, we ended our nighttime routine with kisses and lights out. Not a peep came out of him. But, of course, that was not the case with Bart.

"Come on now," I'd say to him as he started to use diversion tactics to delay the process. "Let's get into bed. No dilly-dally. Come on. Come on. Just put your head down. Come on." There was a sense of urgency to my command and Bart could sniff it from a mile away. I'm not sure what he made of it, but he didn't like it. He was hell-bent on keeping me from disappearing downstairs.

Every night I read a few books, did my loving rituals with him, gave him kisses and then turned lights out. Five minutes later he would get up and call down to me that there were monsters in his room. On a good night, my normal response would be to help him relieve his stress, going through his room to identify all the monsters, have a tea party with them, and then escort each monster out the front door. When I wasn't stressed, this usually worked.

But there was one night when I'd had a long day and I was determined not to play Bart's games. I had to be firm but loving and stand my ground. *No matter what, I'm not going to let my guilt get the better of me.* When he came out of his room, I quietly picked him up and placed him back in his bed while engaging as little as possible. I did not talk to him, sit with him, or allow him to draw me in. *Just gently guide him back to bed, Ginny. Stay cool.* Giving in was not an option, no matter how long it took. If I had to give up my sacred time on the couch, so be it; I would go back as many times as necessary until Bart got the message that I was not going to engage. Hopefully we could put these prolonged bedtime routines behind us. This time *I* would rule. Let the power struggle begin.

After my tenth time climbing the stairs to put him back in his bed, I decided it would be easier if I just plopped my fanny down on the top stair so I didn't have to keep going up and down. I may have moved my command post closer, but I was not going to give up on my strategy.

Two-and-a-half hours later I was at my breaking point. *Oh my God, child! Will you ever give up?* The more I frothed at the bit, the worse he became. He upped the ante by coming out of his room more frequently and persistently, asking for things like water, another story—any of his usual tricks.

My dam finally burst. "That's it! I've had enough of this. Now you go to bed and stay in that bed. Do you hear me?"

"Can you rock me, Mommy?" came the sweet, plaintive voice.

I caved, *caved*! I picked him up and stomped into my room where the rocking chair was.

"This is it, Bart. After this, you will stay in your bed. Do you hear me?"

"Yesh," slid past his Binky.

As I rocked him, I started to sing *Hush, Little Baby*, his favorite. As I sang, his little hand patted my back in time to the music as if to say, "It's okay, Mommy. You'll be all right." He didn't stop patting until the song was done.

I had an aha moment: Bart had been soothing *me*.

In an instant, I switched from anger to calm. In my calm I was able to look at the situation more clearly. From the very beginning he had just needed a bonding moment, and for two-and-a-half hours I had passively resisted him. What I interpreted as his manipulation to be able to stay up later was actually anxiety at my urgency to separate from him. I was unable to see beyond my disciplinary strategy to the truth because it was more important for me to be right than to see that he was just asking for me to connect with him.

Thinking back to other nights of drawn-out bedtime routines, I discovered that they tended to occur when I wasn't present and mindful and my urgency to meet my needs was more imperative than his need for connection. At those times, my repeated visits to his bedroom became the only connection—however negative—he could get. But when I chose to move from control to connection, he was able to fall asleep, content that I was at peace and secure in the thought that I was there for him.

I tucked Bart into his bed, turned off the light, and in my calm I gazed at his sweet face on the pillow and saw him for the little angel he truly was.

## Chapter 14

# AVALANCHE!

*Real courage is…when you know you're licked before you begin, but you begin anyway and see it through no matter what.*
—*Harper Lee,* To Kill a Mockingbird[16]

On one rare occasion, Jerry committed to taking the boys for a weekend. I was behind schedule getting them there. The day before, we had had a huge storm that dumped two feet of snow on us. I had to shovel the walkway and driveway around my car before I could get out to the street. My car was blanketed as well. I scraped off the hood of the car and windows so that I could drive safely. After I got the boys into their snowsuits and their baggage packed into the car, I realized I had forgotten something in the house.

"Sit tight, guys. I'll be right back."

While I was in the house, Nic came flying through the door. "Uh-oh, Mom. Bart's in trouble." The Nic alarm. Nic, ever the scout master for Bart's wayside merit badges, would never rat on his brother to get him in trouble. He alerted me because he knew the situation rapidly unfolding was not safe. I never questioned. I ran out the door.

When I got to the car, both front seats, the console, and the gear shift were covered in a heap of snow. I had not cleaned the snow off the roof of the car, and somehow two-year-old Bart had managed to wrangle out of his car seat, squeeze between the front bucket seats, and push the button to activate the sunroof. I can imagine that for a brief moment the ceiling of snow had lain smooth as sheetrock above the car interior while both boys sat mesmerized, staring in awe at the sunlight shining through the snow, turning it iceberg blue. Then, as the sun warmed it, instant avalanche! What followed ranks as one of the Top Five most humiliating moments of my parenting.

"That's it, you little shit! I've had it!" I pulled Bart out of the front seat and heaved him into a deep snowbank along the side of the driveway.

His head popped up out of the pile and he laughed.

I cried. I cried from sheer exhaustion at Bart's unceasing tenacity and from the deep disgrace of not being able to maintain my composure. I was becoming exhausted with myself and my inability to let go of control.

*Chapter 15*

# GI JOE AND THE TEA SET

*A leader is one who knows the way, goes the way, and shows the way.*
—*John C. Maxwell*[17]

There are many moments in parenting young children that can give you a sneak peek into their future. What play they choose to engage in can often provide the first clues of a future career path. Every child is different, and every parent who has more than one child knows this; one child likes the baby swing and another hates it. One sleeps soundly when you turn the lights out; the other can't seem to settle, begging you to lie down with them. One loves to be cuddled and rocked; the other can't sit still on your lap, too eager is he to jump up and explore the world.

Because children have distinct and very personal interactions with their worlds, parents will develop different relationships with each of their children. And if our relationship with each is different, then our love for each is different. The *depth* of our love for each can be the same, but the *way* we love each is unique to that child and impacts the way we respond to them. To be fair and just we may try to love and discipline them the same, but in reality, we cannot.

When my boys were very young, I realized that if I took the time to stop, to see and be in their energy without influencing their behavior, I could discern unique character traits that were developing in each child and thus speculate what was to come. Nic was enthralled with two-hundred-piece puzzles when he was two years old. He could play with Legos by himself for hours, manipulating the bricks into an infinite number of original designs. When he was introduced to computers, he was fascinated with learning how to use them. I could have projected that he would become a software engineer in his adult life. The writing was on the wall.

Bart, on the other hand, was tenacious and exhausting. I spent so much time trying to calm his tantrums that it was hard to be present in his play. My focus was on anticipating the next conflictive strike and racking my brain to offer him constructive choices. I didn't often have the luxury of observing his play without interacting. But one occasion in particular stands out in my memory, and I recall wondering, *What is this child's path?*

I loved the Christmas holidays in my kids' early years. Santa was their reality, and the idea of him delivering an abundance of presents to the house once a year, for no discernible reason, brought them tremendous delight. As soon as one Christmas was over, anticipation of the next would begin. To a child, anticipation is what dreams are made of.

For Bart's fourth Christmas, he told me that all he wanted was a GI Joe uniform...and a tea set. *Really?* At three-and-a-half, children are just becoming aware of the wide world and all the toys that exist in it. They see toys at childcare, toys at their friends' homes, and toys in the stores, which opens a world of opportunity and "I wants." Yet all Bart wanted was a GI Joe uniform and a tea set. Of course, Santa couldn't stop there and brought him more than his two simple requests, but after opening these two prized items Bart had little interest in the others.

He immediately put on his GI Joe uniform—over his pajamas—and started to prepare "tea" as if he were expecting royalty. I had to smile as I watched him blend these two roles. How did these two disparate interests become intertwined in his mind? It didn't become clear until 17 years later. When Bart was in college, he enrolled in army ROTC while majoring in international relations. His dream was to be a diplomat—the perfect blend of military acuity and international protocol. They say that intelligent children often decide their careers at a very young age. Obviously both boys had determined their paths by the age of three.

*Christmas morning 1987*

# Chapter 16

# BYE BYE BINKY

*I relax, let go, release and surrender.*
—KAREN DRUCKER[18]

When Bart was on the edge of turning four, his pediatrician advised me to take away his pacifier, his beloved Binky, since it was affecting his dental alignment. I knew it was going to be a battle regardless of how we attacked the issue because of his dependency on it, so I opted for all-out control.

"No more Binky."

The next week was hell. The tantrums increased in number and severity. Oh, God, what was I thinking? This was a battle I was sure to lose. How would I convince him to give it up? I pulled out all my traditional approaches that worked for most children, but, of course, not for Bart. From bribery to threats, none of it worked. If I could only find the magic touch to enlighten him. I was growing impatient with myself because I didn't know what to do, but I had to do *something* different. Control would not work for now, so I shelved it.

I decided to return his Binky, but with a caveat: Binky must stay in his room. If he felt like he needed it, he could go to his room, stay as long as he needed to, and then come out when he was done. The only time it would come out of his room was on family vacation trips. His sitter also kept some at her house—for emergencies. In hindsight it was clear that his Binky was the soothing mechanism Bart relied on when I was unavailable to him.

After Bart turned four, he told me he wanted to stop using his Binky. His friends at childcare were teasing him about still having it—in my mind, a beneficial consequence of peer pressure. I was excited for him because he was choosing to let it go on his own. He threw it in the garbage, and we went about our day. That night, while putting him to bed, I saw a Binky in his mouth. He had found a spare one lying around the house somewhere. The temptation was too much.

"What happened? I thought you wanted to get rid of your Binky."

"I think I'll wait till I'm five," he said, matter-of-factly. He turned over to go to sleep.

A few weeks later peer pressure got the better of him, and he wanted to try again. This time we planned a goodbye ceremony so he could let it go with intention.

"Okay, Bart, this time when it goes in the garbage it's going to stay there. Mommy's not going to take it out. Do you understand?" I hugged him. "You can do this."

He nodded resolutely. After he threw it in the garbage, we celebrated with dancing, clapping, and a special treat.

That night, while putting him to bed, I acknowledged his courage. "I am so proud of you, Bart. You did it! You were able to throw your Binky away for good."

"I want it back, Mommy," he moaned.

"I know you do, sweetheart. It is so hard to give it up. It takes so much courage to let it go, but I know you can do this, Bart."

That night I lay with him until he fell asleep. He never asked for his Binky again.

Bart had learned a valuable lesson. Letting go of his comfort object would allow him to grow into the big boy and young man he was to become, on his own merit. And I learned a valuable lesson as well: trying something different was better than doing the same thing over and over and expecting a different result. I had a mindful moment and reached for a strategy of understanding versus demanding. Shifting from control to connection gave us the outcome we both wanted. This did not mean that I would forever abandon control as a means of discipling my children, however. My mind is deeply wired for control as my first line of defense. But it was a step—a baby step—in a more peaceful direction.

## Chapter 17

# FOR THE LOVE OF GUNS

*Instead of trying to shrink this part of my child, I will try to grow this part of my child.*
—*Dr. Becky Bailey*

When Bart was 11 months old, he fashioned a gun from a piece of toast—or at least that's the way it looked to me. I was futzing around in the kitchen. He was in his highchair eating toast, or so I thought, when I heard sounds that mimicked a gun firing. I turned to him. His toast was pointed right at me, and shooting noises were coming out of his mouth. I stood there, dumbfounded. What would possess an 11-month-old child to do that? Where had he ever seen a gun before, and how did he ever conceive of making one of his own? Children that age do not plan. This wasn't thought out in advance; it seemed intuitive. But what alarmed me the most was the look in his eyes—a look of elation, the same look I had seen on my father's face when he was around guns. *Oh shit! Could this be in his DNA?*

"Oh, sweetheart, no, no, no. It's not nice to shoot guns."

It was hard for me to believe he knew what he was doing at that age, but I felt compelled to correct him. Guns were not allowed in play in our home, and I avoided any kind of exposure to violence or guns on TV. I detested them, especially because of my dad's suicide. Nic was not interested in them, so Bart couldn't have picked this up from him. Maybe he was mimicking someone at the sitter's house, or perhaps he had seen something on TV there that had sparked his interest. I ran it by Bea, his childcare provider, but she couldn't remember Bart being exposed to anything like that at her house either. Regardless, the undeniable knowingness of guns in the eyes of an 11-month-old was unnerving.

From that day forward, there was no stopping Bart's obvious passion for guns. If he were to pick a toy out of the toy box at a friend's house or from the shelves at Toys R Us, he would go right for the guns. A power struggle would ensue as he not only demanded that I buy him one, but also insisted on the most authentic looking one in the store. Each time, I went through the embarrassment of a major temper tantrum and would eventually have to leave, asking myself, *Where is this coming from?*

When he was four, I made concessions with him on his birthday and holidays to prevent the tantrums in advance. I agreed to buy, or allow Santa to bring, some toy guns, but only the ones that don't look real.

"Santa doesn't believe that real guns are safe for children. You can ask for space guns or water guns or crazy-looking, colored guns. But no guns that look real. It's either toy guns that *look* like toys, or *no* guns; that's your choice."

This wasn't a choice that empowered Bart particularly; it was, in my mind, more of a necessary consequence of his passion for guns. In order to keep Bart safe, I found it important to introduce the idea that guns were dangerous.

As the boys grew older, it became a holiday tradition to watch *A Christmas Story* together, a movie about a nine-year-old boy, Ralphie, who dreams of getting a Red Rider BB gun for Christmas. He plans various schemes and manipulations to convince his parents and Santa that it's imperative that he have one. Each scheme results in some adult preaching, "You'll shoot your eye out."[19] When we watched the movie, Bart would remark, "Man, I wish I could get a BB gun." Each time my response was an emphatic *No!* I knew Bart was not ready. My gut told me he liked guns a little too much. No good would come of it.

The year Bart turned nine, Jack approached me with a twinkle in his eye after watching the movie. "I think we should surprise Bart with a BB gun for Christmas. We can hide it behind the tree, just like in the movie."

"No! No! No! No! No! He's not ready. You see how out of control he gets with his anger. You really think he's going to use it responsibly? Besides," I said, unable to help myself, "he'll shoot someone's eye out!"

"I think he'll be responsible if we give him some strict and clear rules around it."

"The rules won't stick, Jack. *I* know it and *you* know it. Are you really willing to take the risk of him hurting someone after it's been in his hands for five minutes?"

"It's an opportunity for learning. Isn't that what you always say? I think he can do it. I think he can be responsible."

With an apprehensive sigh, I conceded. I wanted to believe that Jack was right. "Okay, but one little incident and the gun is gone for good. No second chances."

Christmas morning arrived, and after all the presents were opened Jack nudged Bart. "Bart, go look and see if there's one more."

Bart's last present was hidden behind the tree. The movie was playing out right before my eyes, only instead of a round-faced Ralphie with glasses, the nine-year-old was Bart.

"What?" He tore the paper off. "Oh, my God! Yes, yes, *yes*! Thank you, Mom and Dad! Thank you, thank you! Can I go outside and shoot it?"

I put myself between Bart and the door with the palm of my hand extended. "Stop right there. We are going to sit down and talk about the rules around using the gun."

In our family we had weekly family meetings where we would discuss and negotiate things like bedtimes, curfews, and when homework and chores would be accomplished. Our meetings were an integral part of the family decision making. Agreements and consequences for not abiding by those agreements were decided by consensus. Sometimes we would brainstorm ideas for an hour before coming to an agreement. If nothing else, it modeled a democratic process for solving problems. The rules and consequences for this BB gun, however, were non-negotiable. Bart had no input. If he wanted to use the gun, he had to follow our rules.

"The rules are as follows," I began. "You may only shoot at the paper target. You may not point or shoot the gun at any person or animal. You may never take the gun outside without our permission. You may not allow anyone else to use it. You, and only you, are the user of this gun. The moment you break any of these rules, the gun is gone. You don't get it back, period. Do you understand?"

"Yes, Mom. Now can I go?" He was so eager to get outside and shoot the gun that I couldn't help but think of the look of delight on his face when he was a baby in his walker, pulling the string of Christmas tree lights through the house. And I had the same misgivings about Bart's perceived sense of power with that gun in his hands.

I sighed. "Yes, once Dad shows you where and how to shoot it."

"I know how to shoot it."

"I know you know, but Dad and I want to know what you know."

"Okay, Mom."

Jack escorted Bart out the door and gave him a shooting lesson before returning inside and leaving him to it. My stomach was in knots. I wanted to trust him, but I couldn't. I wanted to supervise, but I couldn't. Bad memories of my father's death triggered anxiety, fear, and dread as they always do when I'm around guns.

"Let's just see how well he does," Jack said as he put his arm around me. He knew exactly what was going through my head.

I counted on my hands the number of minutes that passed before Nic came rushing into the house. "Mom, Bart is pointing the gun at John Donovan and telling him he's gonna shoot him!" John was a friend who lived next door.

Jack raced out the door and grabbed the gun from Bart before anything could happen.

"But Dad, I was only kidding," Bart said. "I wasn't going to shoot him. I was just goofing around."

In less than 10 minutes, Bart had lost the BB gun. Just one lick of the lollipop. That's all he got. He ran to his room and slammed the door, but he never said another word about it. No tantrums, no persistent arguments, no pleading. He knew I was not going to give in, and I think there was a part of him that also realized he was not responsible enough yet, no matter how much he loved guns.

The BB gun remained on the top shelf of our bedroom closet, never again to be touched by Bart. On the day he left for deployment to Iraq, Jack gave Bart a letter telling him of his pride in Bart's achievements and his immense respect for his talents and accomplishments. He ended the letter with:

> *From one GI to another, I want you to know that I salute you because you deserve it.*
>
> *I love you and wish you well...Dad*
>
> *P.S. I've decided that when you come home from Iraq, you can have your BB gun back!*

## Chapter 18

# A PASSION FOR LOVE

*Nothing can bring you peace but yourself.*
—Ralph Waldo Emerson[20]

Bart's passion for love, as it turns out, was every bit as intense as his enthusiasm for guns. When he was 12, he fell head over heels in love for the first time. What was, in my mind, a clear case of puppy love was in his mind so much more.

I returned home from work one day to find Bart in his room with the lights out, sobbing on his bed. When I asked him what was wrong, he could barely get his words out. "Sandra broke up with me."

I rubbed his back. *How sweet,* was my first thought. I didn't want to downplay his grief, but surely, he knew that any "love" relationship at this age was going to end sooner rather than later. But I was touched by how deeply this affected him. Better a broken heart than a callous dismissal and on to the next girl who flirted with him.

"I just want to die, Mom."

My hand froze. Why had he chosen those words? Visions of my dad popped into my head. I sat beside him in silence for a minute, grappling with the right words to say. "You are not really serious about that, are you Bart?" I was hoping this was just a 12-year-old's melodrama; nevertheless, I was searching for any clue that might indicate he was genuinely that upset.

"I don't know, Mom. I feel like I want to die. I can't go on without her."

I honestly did not know what to say, but I was positive about what *not* to say. There were no words to convince him that his feelings would pass with time. This sensation of a broken heart was so intense that I knew his pain could not be ignored. Holding his hand, I just sat with him and thought about his words. For the first time in Bart's life, I was truly scared for him and worried about his safety. I was afraid to take his words too seriously, but even more afraid not to take them seriously enough. My gut told me not to leave his side. He needed to be watched carefully. There was no way I would let him return to school until I was sure he was over this hump.

"Bart, I can see this is so hard for you, and I want you to know I am here for you. You are not well enough to go to school tomorrow. I want you to come to school with me. I could use your help with the play my class is putting on for the school. Are you willing?"

Bart nodded reluctantly. "Okay."

Thank God he agreed because I wasn't sure what I would have done if he had refused.

The next day, Bart joined me for a very busy day with preschoolers who had varying exceptionalities. Frankly, I did need his help because it was not a routine day for my students. They would require much more guidance and direction than usual. They'd need help getting their costumes on and off, getting up and down from the stage, staying calm and feeling safe in the unfamiliar chaos. Bart was so busy there was little time for him to dwell on his situation, yet I still found him weeping in a corner or in the closet of my classroom several times. When he calmed himself, I would gently pull him back into the activity of helping with the kids.

After our busy morning, we fed the kids and put them down for rest time. Each child needed help to settle on a floor mat and hopefully nap. This was a routine the children were used to, and Bart was a helpful extra hand to rub backs and assist in transitioning them to dreamland.

When the last child was settled and asleep, Bart squatted quietly in the tiny preschool chair massaging his hands periodically, stopping to explore the lines on his palm. But underneath his actions I could see his mind was focused on contemplation of his situation. I watched him from the sidelines while prepping for the next day. He seemed more settled than I had seen him in the last 18 hours. There was no doubt that his helping with the children contributed to his finding his own calm around his romantic predicament, and I was grateful the idea had come to me.

At one point I made eye contact with him—no words, just a connection that asked, *You okay? You gonna make it?*

Bart gave me a smidgeon of a smile and flipped his thumb up, indicating *I've got this.*

A surge of relief enveloped me. It was over. His body language signaled to me that he was going to make it; he could handle the devastation of his first broken heart.

I didn't fully realize the depth of Bart's passion until I got a phone call from his guidance counselor at the middle school later that afternoon. "Hi, Ms. Luther. I'm calling to check on Bart."

*Hmm. That's odd.* The school had never called me before to check on a child who had only been absent for one day. "Yes, he's fine. He's home sick today." Revealing anything more might cross Bart's boundaries of sharing personal information.

"Well, that's good to hear. We got reports from several of his friends that they were concerned about him. He had told them yesterday that he was going to kill himself."

In this moment I was grateful to his friends for listening to him and telling a responsible adult. I was glad for following my gut and taking the actions I did in response to Bart's devastation. It was clear to me that his passion for love was going to be a force to be reckoned with as he grew older, much like his love for guns. Bart's passion for life was remarkable and, coupled with his tenacity, led him to love as deeply as he did. But the cost of loving that deeply can result in an avalanche of devastation that seems impossible to manage. What I learned is that as fierce as Bart's passion was, he *could* be resilient no matter the obstacle. He was learning to self-regulate his intense emotions and accept the consequences of failure. With this emerging resiliency I knew he would overcome the hardest of challenges.

## Chapter 19

# DELUXE TUX

*The way kids learn to make good decisions is by making decisions, not by following directions.*
—*Alphie Kohn*[21]

Jack and I decided to give the kids a monthly allowance when they were in their young teens so they would learn fiscal responsibility. At the beginning of each month we would give them their allowance with the reminder, "You are free to manage your budget on your own, however, if you run out of money to buy things that are to be paid for from your allowance, do not ask for more money. It will be given on the first day of each month and no sooner. You are resourceful; you'll figure it out." Their allowances were intended to cover school lunches, school supplies, clothes, and general spending money. We agreed to pay for things required for special events or school projects.

The hardest thing to do as a parent is to sit back and watch your kids struggle until they get the hang of something, much like taking the training wheels off the bike. As you push them off for the first time, you watch and wait knowing there is no way to rescue them if they fall. They wiggle and wobble until they learn to synchronize their movements into a smooth ride. We watched without judgment and without interference as they learned to budget their money—or not. With each child we watched the successes and failures that became opportunities for learning.

Nic was the thriftiest of our three boys. At the end of every school year he had a surplus of money. He could make the clothes and one pair of shoes he bought at the beginning of the school year last a whole year without additional purchases. At one point, he requested to do his own laundry to avoid the risk of his stepdad unintentionally ruining his clothes with bleach. John spent his money on a few expensive items but learned quickly that his money would not last with those kinds of purchases and adjusted his strategy.

Bart had his money spent before it hit his hot little hands. Remarkably, he spent as little as possible on himself. The majority of his money was spent on others, mostly his girlfriends. He would shop for his shoes at Payless, make his own school lunches, and ask for clothes for Christmas. But it was a plan that seemed to work well for him, until the time came for his first prom at the end of eighth grade.

Since prom was a special event, I offered to pay for his tux. One Saturday we drove to the formal clothing store in the mall to rent the baseline tux, the one that most 14-year-olds wear on their first prom date.

"We'll take the standard," I told the salesman.

"No, Mom! I don't want that one," Bart interjected. "I want this one." He pointed to a deluxe tux adorning a mannequin strategically placed by the entrance to the store. Bart would no doubt stand out in such a fine suit, but it cost enough to outfit him and another of his friends.

"No, Bart. I'm sorry, but that's too much."

"But, Mom, pleeeeeeease!" This was not a typical teenage plea I was hearing. I could sniff the beginning of a childhood tantrum in the making.

"Bart, I am not willing to pay for that tux. I am willing to pay for the standard tux that we agreed to before we came here."

"You are so mean. It's not fair! Why do you get to buy what you want, but I never get to buy what I want? You *have* to buy this, Mom." He crossed his arms and shot me that same defiant look he gave me when he was two and the world was not going his way.

I knew this was not going to go well because once Bart chose his path, there was nothing that could change his mind. He glared at me as if to say, *You wanna play this game? Come on, try me.* Visions of the wooden spoon incident replayed in my mind: Bart turning his backside to me, wriggling his little bottom and challenging me, "Go ahead and spank me, Mommy." It did not concern him in the least that his growing temper was drawing the curious looks of mall shoppers.

I was not going to give in to public embarrassment or guilt. I knew better. Giving in would only set a precedent for the next tussle which could be longer and harder. "What part of 'no' do you not understand, Bart? I am willing to pay the 75 dollars I committed to you. If you want the deluxe tux, you will need to use your own money to pay the difference. Did you bring your money?"

Bart's face confirmed what I suspected: He didn't have the funds to support this desire. This scene was not going to have a pretty ending.

"Why won't you buy this for me, Mom? Why? Because you are mean. All the other kids' moms do so much more for them than you do for me. They drive them everywhere. They give them cellphones. You never do anything for me. *Please?* I promise I'll pay you back."

"How much money do you have at home? You'll need another 75 dollars."

The answer was clear as day without him speaking a word.

It took all of my courage to politely tell the salesman we were not ready to rent a tux and walk gracefully out the door, while Bart was taunting me with his obnoxious demands.

"I'm not coming until you buy this for me, Mom. You're just going to have to leave without me."

I said nothing as I headed toward the mall exit and the parking lot. He chased me while continuing his tantrum. He was like a yapping terrier nipping at my heels, barking out his grievances and attracting the attention of the appalled onlookers I studiously ignored.

*Keep going, Ginny. Say nothing. Just get to the car as fast as you can.*

I couldn't get out of that mall fast enough. I would have willingly mowed down anything that dared to cross my path. Bart was nowhere in sight when I got in the car. I started the engine, ready to leave with or without him. I figured if he could be that rude and defiant to me in front of crowds of people, he certainly wouldn't allow anyone to kidnap him. If I left him behind, surely, he had the internal resources and fortitude to handle any conflict coming his way—or at least to wear them down trying.

Just before backing out of my parking space, I heard a knock on the passenger window. Bart signaled me to unlock the door and let him in. He slouched into the front passenger seat, a burning glare of disappointment covering his face. We left the parking lot and headed home.

"I know you're upset that you're not getting the tux you wanted. You have a choice. You can come up with the extra money to pay for the one you want, or you can go with my original offer."

Silence. "Okay, okay, I'll get the boring one."

"Does that mean you are ready to go back to the mall now and get it?"

Bart gave a slight nod of concession.

"Great! Let's do it."

Bart did not get his way that day. This time I had the strength not to give in to my discomfort with his anger, or the embarrassment and guilt I felt because of it. Those were my issues to deal with, not his, and I overcame them by sticking to my principles. It was difficult to hear the blame that Bart had thrown at me in his anger, but I was able to resist getting drawn into his drama by not taking it personally.

Some days I was stronger than on others. But driven by this opportunity to teach Bart the harsh reality of delayed gratification, I knew that he was mature enough now to be able to manage his disappointment and develop his flexibility, something that would serve him well in the future. It was becoming ever more apparent to me that Bart had the resources to do great things someday, but he needed assistance in honing those skills and practice using them.

*Chapter 20*

# LETTING GO AND LETTING GROW

*When I was a boy of 14, my father was so ignorant I could hardly stand to have the old man around. But when I got to be 21, I was astonished at how much the old man had learned in seven years.*

—ATTRIBUTED TO *MARK TWAIN*.[22]

As a parent of three adolescents, it was a requirement that I modify parenting tactics. I realized it was time to challenge the boys to take more responsibility to fill their developmental need to be more independent. They were becoming more in charge of their choices and their paths for life. My ability to set boundaries changed from imposing limits on their day-to-day lives to help them navigate to focusing on boundaries that pertained to *my* physical and emotional safety. I could no longer tell them who they could choose to be their friends, how to hang out with them, or rules of engagement regarding their personal responsibilities such as homework and personal hygiene. When I did try—with good intentions—to set limits around their personal responsibilities it always backfired, which might challenge them to go behind my back and entice them to engage in risky behavior that could end badly for everyone.

"You need a haircut." I might say. "So I made an appointment for Saturday afternoon."

"I'm not going. It's my hair, and I like my hair. You never asked *me.*"

These were signals to back off, for if I persisted it could lead them to come home from the barber with a shaved head or a multicolored mohawk. They were willing to risk mistakes to exercise their new sense of autonomy. Essentially, my attempts to protect them from making mistakes—using the same techniques I did when they were young—was not working. I had to shift and learn to set boundaries that pertained to me. If they wanted to stay up into the late night and play loud music, then I could set a limit about the noise level because it was affecting me personally, but I could not *make* them go to bed. They were responsible for their exhaustion if they did not get enough sleep.

Whether I liked it or not, they had the independence and gumption to do anything they set their minds to. My job was to provide limits that kept them safe but allowed me to guide them in their choices versus dictating to them. My intention was to let go of trying to prevent failure so their mistakes could provide them an opportunity to grow.

One example in our house was Bart's bedroom. Bart was not known for his concern for cleanliness. In fact, he was a slob. I would open his bedroom door, shocked to find that an F3 tornado had hit his room and miraculously spared the rest of the house. It was a daily struggle to help him choose to take responsibility for cleaning it.

"Bart, this room looks like a tornado hit it. For the life of me I don't know how you can find anything. God knows what's crawling underneath these piles. I want it cleaned by Friday."

"It's my room. I know exactly where everything is in here. It's perfectly fine. But I will. I will. Just chill. It'll get done." Only it never got done.

I finally realized his disaster of a bedroom was his manifestation of typical adolescent autonomy. He was choosing not to conform to the way things were done in the rest of the house by using his room as a canvas on which to express his ambivalence, absent-mindedness, and internal chaos.

I could not force Bart to clean his room, so I created my own limits. The boundaries I chose to set for myself were based on visual assault on my peace and calm, vermin control in my home, and respect for my property. Boundary #1: His bedroom door was to be kept closed at all times. Boundary #2: No food was allowed in his room. Boundary #3: Some semblance of cleanliness and order must be maintained to preserve the integrity of my house. If Bart refused to clean his room himself, he would have to pay me or someone else to do it. Suffice it to say, there were several times he had to pay up.

There were times when I established a boundary but found it difficult to enforce. I had always told my children that they were responsible for remembering things that were important to them. Bart was particularly forgetful about remembering to take things he needed to school and would often call me and ask me to drop them off for him. Usually I wouldn't comply, gently reminding him of his responsibility.

Bart had decided to make his lunches at home, in lieu of buying school lunches, so he could save his allowance for other things. His extravagant lunches included much more than slapping together a peanut butter sandwich. He'd make egg salad with all the fixings, cut up cheese cubes, and throw in his favorite snacks. It was enough to feed me lunch twice. The problem was he often forgot to take them to school and then would call me at work pleading with me to bring him his lunch. Not wanting him to go hungry, I would rush home the moment I had a planning break, snatch up his lunch, drive it to the middle school, and then return to my job seething with resentment. One part of me felt like the valiant mother who went to the ends of the Earth to ensure that her child was well fed. The other part of me wanted to wring his neck for adding this major inconvenience to my day. I struggled with my own concept of "the good mother" and my choice of giving up a boundary I had set to instill responsibility. Rescuing Bart was my choice, and it wasn't working for me.

A mentor once taught me, "What we overprotect, we make weak." Homework is the teen's responsibility. If they fail, it is theirs to handle. Friendships are theirs to choose. If they get hurt in an unhealthy relationship, it's their job to reflect on what values in a friendship they really want. Keeping their bodies clean and healthy is theirs to manage. If they choose to engage in unhealthy consumption or not get enough sleep, it's theirs to reflect on the outcome. It was necessary I talk to Bart in an attempt to reinforce my boundaries.

I knocked on his bedroom door. "Bart, I'd like to talk to you about something. Is now a good time?" I was modeling to Bart how to respect me by the way I respected him.

"Sure. Come in."

I entered, trying to ignore the piles of clothes, schoolbooks, and papers scattered about the room—and what might lie beneath. *Refocus, Ginny. Focus on what you want to accomplish with him right now.*

"Bart, I noticed you are choosing to make these amazing lunches for school on your own, and a couple of times last week you forgot to take them with you. I took them to school for you because your nutrition is important to me and because I don't want you to feel disappointed after putting all that hard work into making them. But today when I brought you your lunch, I felt really frustrated because it is a huge inconvenience for me to leave my job to get it to you, and it is not my responsibility to rescue you when you forget your lunch. Your lunch is *your* responsibility, so you need to know that I am no longer willing to take your lunches to school."

"Okay. I won't forget again. Don't worry." A lickety-split response to get me out of his room so he could get back to whatever he was doing. I had every reason to doubt his sincerity.

"You know, if you do forget you will have to either buy your lunch with your monthly allowance or wait till you get home to eat. How do you want me to support you remembering your lunch? Do you want me to remind you before I leave for work?"

He rolled his eyes at me. "Chill, Mom. Don't worry about it, okay?"

"Okay, let me know if you need support remembering." That was that. I did not hear another word about it from him.

No sooner had I set this boundary than he forgot his lunch again. I fumed silently when I saw it sitting on the counter. *Did we not just have this conversation?* I had planned to take a duly deserved day off of work and offered to drop Bart off at school on my way to a fitness class. He was already in the car, waiting for me. I contemplated saying something to him before we left. He had made it clear me to *chill* and not to remind him. I wasn't sure how this would play out, but it was time for me to stand my ground and live up to my end of the agreement.

It took tremendous effort for me to keep my mouth shut as we pulled out of the driveway. We were well out of the neighborhood before Bart realized he had forgotten his lunch.

"Mom, after you drop me off, can you go back home and get my lunch and bring it to school? *Please*?"

"I told you I was not going to bring forgotten lunches to school anymore."

"But you're taking the day off. It's not fair! You can do what you want for yourself, but you won't do anything for me. All my friends' moms would do it. This sucks. It's not fair! We're going on a field trip today, and I'm not going to have anything to eat. You want me to starve?"

The guilt buttons were being jabbed so quickly I was afraid my circuit would overload. I felt an ever-so-slight urge to acquiesce. I took a deep breath. "I know this is hard for you, but one thing I know about you is that you are very resourceful. You will figure it out."

We pulled into the car line at school and Bart got out. I wanted him out of the car as fast as possible. If he continued to work on me, I would cave.

"Please, Mom. I'm going to have to watch everyone else eat while I have *nothing*. You are so mean." He slammed the car door.

*Whew! I barely made it through that. Now all I have to do is deal with this nagging guilt for the rest of the day, begging me to take Bart's lunch to school.*

My worry was that he would make this into something much bigger than it was. I questioned if I had done the right thing, afraid the school would call me requesting I bring him a lunch for the field trip. In that case, I would have to eat crow for my parental neglect. Would I get a call from the nurse saying he passed out because he didn't have anything to eat or drink? So many possible scenarios ran through my head, all of them proving me wrong.

Bart returned home from school while I was busy in the kitchen. He seemed fine, but he said nothing. I was too curious. "So?"

"So, what?" as if nothing unusual had happened that day.

"Did you figure it out?"

"Lunch? Yeah, you'll never believe it. I told everybody on the bus I didn't have a lunch, and they all felt so bad for me that they gave me all their good stuff. The stuff *you* never buy for us: Ring Dings, chips, Cheetos. I got it all."

I could feel the sting he was trying to impose. I bit my tongue. "What did I tell you, Bart. You are resourceful and you handled it. I am so glad you figured it out."

Nothing more needed to be said. It had been a learning opportunity for us both. I had set a boundary for myself, knowing that I could not control how he felt about it. Bart had turned his disappointment about making a mistake into something he handled with resilience and resolution. And he'd learned that laying a guilt trip on me would not work. At bright moments like this I had a hunch we might all actually make it through his adolescence after all.

## *Chapter 21*

# LOSING IT IS EASY TO DO

*Imperfections are not inadequacies; they are reminders that we're all in this together.*
—*Brené Brown*[23]

In my personal growth, I looked for healthier ways of managing the daily stress of being a full-time teacher by day, parenting instructor at night, wife, and mother of adolescents. Exercise along with a healthier diet became my Binky and part of my daily regimen. I found it easy to master the discipline of exercise if I changed up the routine regularly to keep it interesting and motivating.

At one time my favorite form of exercise was swimming, and my Super Swim apparatus was my new best-exercise friend. The Super Swim looked much like a fishing pole, basically a PVC pole with a waist belt, instead of a hook, attached at the end of a 12-foot nylon cord. The pole was grounded at one end of our pool, and I, with the belt securely strapped around my middle, would swim against the pull of the pole. Because I had to maintain an even speed to avoid being pulled back to the pole, I could swim in place rather than trying to swim laps in our small pool. I loved my Super Swim, and my one-and-a-half hours of swim time several times a week were sacred. The physical exertion provided a great sense of calm that was crucial to me and allowed me to be the mom, teacher, and spouse I wanted to be. But for this to work, I required that—barring blood or loss of limb—my family could not under any circumstances disturb me when I was bonding with my Super Swim.

"I don't care who calls, what you think you need help with, or how hungry you are. *Do not disturb me.* Got it?"

I thought I had made myself absolutely clear, but my husband Jack was the first to test my directive and got the full force of my wrath. He interrupted my swim by screaming my name to tell me I had a call from Becky Bailey, someone he knew was important to me.

*No, I'm not taking any calls. No, I don't care who's calling. And no, leave me alone. What part of "NO" did he not understand?* I shut him down like the snap of a steel trap. "Take a message!"

He stepped back as if I had just slapped him on the cheek.

Two days later—same time, same place, same bonding with my Super Swim—I was having the swim of my life, doing a fast-paced crawl and feeling the endorphins and dopamine surge through my body, when I felt myself being pulled backwards. Before I could figure out what was happening, I was yanked to the edge of the pool. I turned to see what the hell had caused the Super Swim to malfunction only to find Bart standing there with the pole in his hand like Mr. Starkist himself, quite proud of his catch. I leaped out of the pool, pushed my face toward his, and turned into a raging bull.

The steam snorted out of my nose as I screamed, "What the fuck are you doing? How many times have I told you to leave me alone when I'm swimming. How dare you?"

Bart, wide-eyed with shock, tried to justify his behavior. "I just wanted to know if you would drive me to Palm City so I can hang out with my friends."

"Are you fucking kidding me? You are so selfish! What did I tell you about my swimming? Who the hell do you think you are?"

"Okay, okay. Sorry, Mom." Bart quickly left the pool deck without retort, escaping into his room. It was highly unusual for him not to engage in an argument, especially when provoked, but my wrath had gotten the better of him.

I paced the pool deck ranting to Mother Nature, the only one brave enough to listen. After several minutes I finally calmed down enough to reflect upon my behavior. That ugly place I had just returned from did not at all feel like me. Someone or something had possessed my body, flushing down the toilet every principle I valued. I lost sight of my higher self—the kindness, compassion, composure, and respect for others that I hold most dear.

The ugly, hurtful me seemed to come out of nowhere. *Wake up, Ginny. He's just being 15.* From a distance, I had watched myself acting stupidly, trying to grab a hold of myself yet always finding myself just out of reach. It was like reaching out to touch a loved one only to find an unseen glass door between you and them. Rather than the familiar warm flesh you were longing for, the hard glass was icy-cold to the touch. When I was in the depths of emotional hell, I could not connect with myself.

A cloud of shame rolled over me. I took several deep breaths and calmed myself. I should have known better. After all, I was not only the adult in this situation, but the one who is considered a professional in managing emotions. *How many times do I have to teach it before it becomes natural to me?*

I realized that "should-ing" myself would not erase what just happened or solve the problem. While sitting with myself, pondering what triggered me to lose my cool, a flashback from my childhood zapped my brain and instantly I understood. I needed to reconnect to my higher self and repair what I could with Bart.

I cautiously tapped on Bart's bedroom door.

"What?"

"Can I come in? I want to apologize."

"Okay."

"I am so sorry that I lost it out there. The way I screamed at you and blamed you was disrespectful and entirely unfair to you."

Bart was silent, lying on his bed distracted by a book he was reading, but I could tell he was listening.

"I'm not sure what happened to me out there, but rest assured I was triggered by something other than you. Once I calmed down, a story from my childhood flashed into my brain. One of the antics my brothers used to pull on me when we were growing up was to taunt me with their spit. They'd pin me down on the floor and hover over me with mouths puckered, allowing threads of saliva to drip down, laughing as it dangled above my face. Just before it hit the target, they would suck it back up into their mouths like a snake retracting its tongue. No matter how much I squirmed, I could not free myself from their clutches. When you pulled on the pole, I went right back to that powerless state, only this time I was able to break free and I attacked you for all the rage I felt for my brothers back then. It was not fair to you, and I hope you can forgive me. God willing, this won't happen again, but I can't promise that I won't be triggered again. I suggest you honor my boundary when I'm swimming so I can be the best of me to listen to you."

"It's okay, Mom. I understand. Now, can you take me to Palm City to see my friends?"

What I learned from this was that I am human and that everyone loses it from time to time. I am not perfect, nor should I expect to be because of my profession. Some unhealed wounds from past experiences stick with us until we have an opportunity to understand them. Sometimes you just have to lose it to become aware that they're even there. This was an opportunity for me to honor the wounds, heal, and be grateful for the connection Bart and I were eventually able to share: Bart in learning to respect my limits and understand that mistakes are opportunities for learning, and myself in learning that some of my deepest emotions are stories waiting to be healed.

## *Chapter 22*

# YOU ARE NOT YOUR LABEL

*The way we talk to children becomes their inner voice.*
—*UNKNOWN*[24]

Labeling children is something most adults unconsciously do to the children in their care. Our intent is determined by how we see or judge a situation. At the core of every label lies a positive or negative intent—a good or bad perception of the child and their behavior. Young children, having limited language proficiency, are more adept at picking up on the energy behind the intent, rather than focusing on the actual label. So even if they can be interpreted as having positive connotations, labels delivered with a negative energy can become imprinted in children's core beliefs about themselves and still be a major part of their inner dialogue later in life.

Two labels attached to me as a child still affect me to this day. The positive label was *cute*. "Isn't she cute?" people would say, as if I weren't in the room hearing their judgment of me. "Cute" was how I was labeled in my junior high school yearbook. "Cute" is what I continue to see when I am not beating myself up with my negative label, "stupid." Negative energy has a way of creeping in and taking over when positive energy is lulled into quiet complacency, especially in early adolescence when we are questioning everything about ourselves and none of it looks good. In no time at all "stupid" became such a major part of my inner dialogue that it still impacts actions in my adult life. It's the president of the itty-bitty-shitty committee in my head, and I will be consciously working to transform this misnomer most likely for the rest of my life.

Bart had been labeled "smart" at a very early age. Even when offered with a positive energy, "smart" can provoke a negative response. Bart had heard the word applied to him so many times that he began to think of himself as unfailingly smart—as smart as any adult. It became difficult for him to accept that he could be wrong. He was relentless in attempting to get me to admit that he was right and I was wrong. His endurance in debating an issue was beyond exhausting. I had to remind him several times that he was not his label.

"Bart, smart is not *who* you are. It doesn't define you. It just happens to be a gift you have that you can use to be helpful to others. Being smart does not mean you have to be right all the time. You will make mistakes; you will be wrong sometimes. Everyone is. You are so much more than smart. You are kind, helpful, tenacious, persistent, and more. Remember that."

Every teacher Bart ever had either loved him or hated him for his precocious and unrelenting behavior. Those who tried to control him, but couldn't, often labeled him defiant.

In an effort to keep him busy, his first-grade teacher would ask him to color in his math worksheets when he finished his work before the rest of the class. Bart hated coloring, especially when he was told to color within the lines. He would declare war, and the power struggle began. The teacher would send the completed, but uncolored, math paper home for him to color as homework. It would go back to school uncolored simply because I was not going to spend my evening taking the teacher's power-struggle baton over the issue of coloring. My time was much better spent choosing ways to connect with my son rather than trying in vain to control him. Every night these papers would come home with increasingly larger print from the teacher: *PLEASE COLOR!* Underlined three times. Now I felt like she was in a power struggle with me. It was time to conference with the teacher.

"Bart is a very bright boy," she began.

*Another label for smart.* "Yes, he is. He is quite precocious and persistent."

"But he doesn't follow directions. Have you seen all the math sheets he hasn't colored?"

"I have, and I also know that Bart hates coloring. I'm a little confused. Is this a coloring activity or a math activity?"

"It's a math activity. But he finishes so quickly. Coloring keeps him busy while the others finish."

"Oh, so you want him to be busy so he doesn't disturb others while they're working?"

"Yes."

"Keeping Bart busy with activities he doesn't like is hard for him. What works for me is to give him a couple of choices of things he can do that interest him. He is so much more compliant when you give him positive choices. This might help you avoid struggles with him."

"He needs to follow my directions."

"That is true, but I have had enough power struggles with him to know that I must choose my battles with him. Otherwise, it's a constant fight. When I choose to fight with Bart, it never ends well. We both end up losing. So, I want you to know I am not willing to struggle with him over coloring, unless you think it will interfere with his academic performance. Honestly, I would rather spend the time reading to him."

I could tell by her silence she wasn't pleased with my response. She may have thought I was an irresponsible parent, but no further math papers came home for coloring.

I knew her struggle with Bart all too well. He was so good at engaging adults in these battles. At times, I felt like a bull with a ring through my nose being pulled into my paddock. Bart tested adults as if intentionally challenging them to look at themselves and consider if it was more important to be right or be connected. Connection was becoming a more valuable strategy for me in achieving compliance than insisting to him that I was right.

Bart was very adept at reading people's intentions. He instantly knew who was supportive in a connected way and who was trying to coerce him into compliance. After all, he honed his technique on me. I was a great model of both styles. He could smell a power struggle a mile away. Controlling adults did not fare well with him because they didn't ask themselves the right question: control or connection?

In middle school Bart started the gifted program as a sixth grader. A call from one of his teachers soon followed.

"Hello, Mrs. Fletcher?"

"This is Bart's mom, Mrs. Luther."

"Yes, well, I am having a problem with Bart and his homework."

"Is he having difficulty completing his assignments?"

"Nothing like that. He is completing all his work and doing well, but I require all the students to check off their completed work on the checklist inside their planner."

I found myself questioning her motives. Was it about taking responsibility for completing his work or teaching him to respect her wishes to confirm who was in charge? It may have been a combination, but my gut told me it was the latter. She was completely unaware that this was fodder for a power struggle she would never win.

"Could you make sure he does this?" she asked.

"Well, I am willing to discuss with him the reasons for doing it and suggest that he do it, but I can't guarantee he'll follow through. I believe it's something that he should work on with you, since it's your request."

'Well, I would hate to see his grade fall because he does not follow my direction."

"I would too, but it's his grade, not mine."

"I really don't want to give him a C for not checking off his assignment. Can't you do something about it?"

"As I said, I am willing to encourage him, but I think that if you think he deserves a C, you should give him a C. He'll learn."

We ended our conversation with nothing resolved, other than I was not going to get in the middle of it. I let him know the teacher called and what her concern was, and then left it in his lap. His performance in school was his responsibility, not mine. I was willing to help him see his choices, but I refused to become the Homework Police. I can't remember if his teacher gave him a C or not, but in general, the middle school years were tough for Bart. He didn't take his academic work seriously. On a scale of one to 10, academics ranked around a four; friends ranked a definite 11.

One interim report in middle school indicated that Bart's grades were dropping precipitously.

"What's going on, Bart? This is not typical for you."

"I hate some of my teachers. They're so boring. It's not a big deal, Mom. It's just a grade, not my life."

"I know friends are important to you now and school is not, but to go to high school you'll have to pass. Is it important to you to be with your friends in high school?"

"Duh! But it's not a big deal, Mom. Really. I'll pull them up."

"Bart, I know you don't want to fail and be left behind your friends, so here's what will happen if the next report shows further decline. You and I will conference with all the teachers of courses you are struggling with, got it?" This was not a request.

Silence.

Lo and behold, the next report showed continued decline in one subject, so I scheduled a conference with his teacher, Mrs. B, whom Bart did not admire.

Before we got there I had a chat with Bart about our upcoming meeting. "I just want you to know that I am there to support you in this conference, but it is going to be your conference with Mrs. B. The point is for you to solve the struggle you are having in her class with her so you can begin to remedy the problem, much like we do in our family meetings at home."

"What if I don't want to say anything?"

"That's up to you, but I hardly think you'll solve anything that way. You can be part of the problem, or you can be part of the solution."

Silence.

When Bart and I arrived at the school, we were instructed to wait for Mrs. B in the media center. People were flowing in and out. When Mrs. B arrived, I introduced myself and told her of my intention of supporting Bart in his discussion with her.

Regardless, she directed her concerns to me, pointing out in a passive-aggressive tone everything inappropriate Bart was doing. "Bart is a very smart young man." She peered over the top of her glasses. "But he is not performing at his aptitude. I don't understand why he doesn't participate at the level he's capable of."

Bart did not challenge her but looked to me for help as he slunk back in his chair. After I redirected the conversation to Bart, both he and Mrs. B were able to talk through some of her points and gain some understanding of each other's point of view.

Just as we were ending, in walked his math teacher.

"Hi, Bart. Is this your mom?"

Bart's eyes widened in alarm. I introduced myself.

"You know, I was meaning to contact you about Bart's progress. Do you have a minute?"

"Isn't it really Bart you want to talk to?"

"Oh, sure."

Round Two of this boxing match began, once again with his teacher showing concern for Bart's effort in his class. "You know you are not working up to your ability, Bart. It's hard to see you underperform when the material is relatively easy for you."

Bart started to slink further down in his seat so that all I could see were his shoulders and a defeated grimace on his face.

Another teacher walked by and acknowledged Bart. "Hey, Bart. This must be your mom. I'd love to talk to you some time, but I have another meeting right now." He scurried past us.

Bart was about to wave a white flag of surrender when Mr. Hager, his band teacher, stopped abruptly as he was passing our table. Bart could take no more. He seemed to be drowning in a sea of worthlessness. His head plunked down on the tabletop in despair.

"Hi, Mrs. Luther. May I sit for a moment?"

Bart could not lift his head to acknowledge his favorite teacher. He was expecting the worst, and that would be the last straw. His self-worth couldn't take much more.

"Mrs. Luther, I just want you to know what an amazing and talented son you have. He is so enthusiastic about music and such a great model to all the other kids in band class in his discipline toward practicing and playing. You should be proud of him. You're doing great, Bart."

Bart's head popped up. At last, a moment of triumph! He had been thrown a life ring, saved by someone who truly believed in him. A smile illuminated his face.

"I was wondering if it would be okay if Bart plays in our local jazz band? It's basically a bunch of older guys that play for free at various community events. Bart, do you want to join us?"

No words were necessary. His face was a beaming, affirming yes.

Labels can be so powerful, especially when offered in a positive light. Bart's relationship with Mr. Hager and their local band was the catalyst for his participation in marching band throughout his high school years.

Marching band became the basis of his social life. Its requirement of self-discipline and a full calendar of events throughout the year gave Bart little desire or opportunity to engage in some of the risky behaviors that many teens engage in, and his transformation from adolescent to adult was a safe and healthy one.

In Bart's first year of high school, he declared that he wanted to attend a military academy in his college years. After his experience in middle school, I was cautiously optimistic about his ability to discipline himself to get the grades he would need to be accepted into one of the academies. When he showed me his first-semester report card, I was ecstatic. It was all A's except for one B+.

"Woo-hoo! Yay for you! You must be thrilled."

"Well, no, actually I'm not. I'm not happy."

I was stunned. His expression was serious disappointment. This report was the best I had ever seen. How could he possibly be disappointed?

"But this is the best report card you've ever had. As long as you did your best, that's all that matters."

"I want to get into West Point, remember?"

"Don't you feel you did your best?"

"No. I didn't study enough. That B+ could have been an A."

I was dumbfounded. And then I realized that I had just ignored my own advice: By judging Bart's grades, good or bad, I had just labeled him. I had interfered with his perception of his own success. The expectation I had set for him was lower than the expectation he had for himself. It wasn't for me to tell Bart how he had done; it was for Bart to tell me how he thought he had done. That was his, and only his, responsibility. My job as a parent was to help him understand what he wanted and to support him in that journey.

"That must feel very disappointing, Bart. Getting to West Point is important to you and earning all A's will help you get there. If there's any way I can support you next semester to achieve your goals, please let me know."

He turned and walked toward his room. Knowing my son, he was probably already planning his path.

## Chapter 23

# BART'S RITE OF PASSAGE

*Alone we can do so little; together we can do so much.*
—*Helen Keller*[25]

By the time Bart was 14, I had been growing increasingly disenchanted with the emphasis on consumerism for the December holidays. Christmas was becoming an event I loved to dread. I loved the family traditions, but dreaded the hustle and bustle of shopping, wrapping, and delivering. When the boys were in their mid-teens, we had a family meeting regarding the upcoming holidays. We decided that we had had enough with the stress of it all. We wanted to spend the time together without all the pressure. Instead of the gift-giving chaos normally associated with the holiday, we would give ourselves a four-day cruise to the Bahamas in the spring.

The trip to the Bahamas was the kids' first cruise, and probably their most memorable. They had their own space to hang out with other teens and met many new people. In fact, the ship was Bart's *Love Boat*. Jack and I watched from a distance as he became increasingly smitten with Renata from Portugal. Their budding romance was so cute to watch, especially because we knew it would end almost as soon as it started. He followed her around the ship like a puppy dog eager to engage in play. He had a perpetual smile that I imagined made his cheeks ache. I have to admit I was a bit apprehensive about where Bart's resourcefulness, at 15, would take him with the opposite sex.

Within 24 hours of returning home, Bart was knocking on my bedroom door. He entered with a look on his face that triggered an *uh-oh* in my brain.

"Hi, sweetie. What's up?"

"I want to ask you something."

"Okay, shoot."

"I want to go to Portugal this summer and see Renata."

"Stop right there. First, we just came home from a cruise, so sending you to Portugal is not in the affordable category right now. Second, even if we could afford it, you are only 15 so I would need to go with you. That's two plane tickets *and* my time, which is already booked through the summer. Doubly not in the cards. You'd also only have two months to come up with the money. Hardly sounds possible."

"I can fly by myself. I do it three times a year to see Dad. And I've figured out a way to pay for it. I can sell my paintball gun."

"That won't cover it, Bart, and besides there is more to it than just the finances and flying by yourself. You would need to get a passport, find a place to stay, and, most importantly, be supervised while you are there. I would need to talk to Renata's parents about whether they are even interested in supervising your visit, and if so, what that would look like.

"Okay, I'll arrange for you to talk to her parents. About the money, I have some other ideas about how to earn some. And I know I can find a place to stay. I can do this. I just need you to support me, like take me to apply for my passport and drive me to the airport."

As far-fetched as this idea sounded, I knew there was no turning back for Bart. Tenacity was oozing from every pore of his body. I could feel myself being sucked into the quicksand. If I didn't do something quickly and calmly, I'd be swallowed alive.

"You are 15. As a minor, you are my responsibility. This is a big undertaking for a 15-year-old. If you go alone, I need to know that you will be safe."

"Please, Mom. Please! I can do this. I will be safe."

The quicksand was up to my chin. It was time to offer conditions I was sure he wouldn't be able to achieve. "It is only under my conditions that this will ever happen. First, you must pay for everything out of your own pocket because Dad and I are not paying a cent. Second, I need proof of itinerary, including where you are staying and who will be supervising you. Third, I need to talk to Renata's parents to get confirmation that they are willing to support this on their end. Fourth, you will make all the arrangements. Now, if you can do all this in the two months you have to accomplish it, then yes, you may go."

"Thank you, Mom. Thank you! Thank you! Thank you!" He picked me up off the floor in a huge bear hug.

As Bart hurried out of my bedroom, I wondered what I had done. I had just unleashed a caged bull who was running headlong toward the matador's cape without a clue as to the swords that lay in store for him there. What responsible parent would ever allow their 15-year-old child to embark on this risky a trip? How would I ever explain this to people without them thinking I'm a delinquent parent?

But intuitively I knew that Bart needed exactly this type of challenge in the journey of his life. Challenge was his middle name; he thrived on it. If I didn't support the positive challenges, like this, he could delve into the dangers of the negative ones. Making his way to Portugal and back was better than racing his car down some back road after drinking a six-pack of beer just for the rush. If he felt this trip was an adventure, maybe we could avoid a catastrophe. Deep down, though, I was certain it would never happen. It was too tall of a task for him to accomplish based on the limits I set.

Like clockwork, he sold the paintball gun he had never used for 500 dollars, made an appointment for me to take him to get his picture taken, and then applied for his passport. That he was willing to give up this "gun" to spend time with a girl—in my mind, a much better choice—indicated the depth of his passion to make this trip a reality. He made his arrangements to stay at a youth hostel two kilometers from Renata's home. Her parents were not willing to have him stay with them. I'm sure they too were considering the raging hormones in both kids at that age. He arranged for me to talk to Renata's mother who assured me that Bart would not be allowed in the house without supervision. She also offered to feed him, so he wouldn't need money for meals. Bart had some money in his savings account, and he worked tirelessly at extra chores around the house to earn money for the remainder of the trip. His plans were truly coming together. The day his passport arrived was the defining moment of Bart's rite of passage. He had accomplished what had seemed impossible. It was going to happen.

As I left him at the airport gate and headed back to my car, I reconsidered my decision. He's only 15. What if something seriously bad happened to him? I could not be there to support him in any way. Could I trust Renata's family to handle it if it all went wrong? Then there was my work to consider and my credibility as a parent consultant! My ambivalence with it all overwhelmed me in the decision to let him go.

This was one of those moments in life, for both Bart and me, when we stood on a precipice contemplating the risk that lay ahead. Would failure be our outcome? Would I lose all that I had worked for? Would he lose his relationship with Renata after sacrificing so much? I was sure Bart had no qualms about risking the security of his current life for an unknown adventure. He was challenged by it but had the confidence that no matter the outcome, he would handle it. I rode it out with angst every moment he was gone. It just seemed so much bigger than anything I had risked in parenting before.

No sooner had Bart returned from Portugal than he was asking to go back. Interestingly, it was not to be with Renata. His love for Portugal was greater than his love for her. He wanted to immerse himself for an entire year in Portuguese culture as a foreign exchange student through American Field Service. He had evidently spent a significant amount of time researching it because he was able to answer all my questions.

"Mom, I want to spend my junior year there. I want to learn Portuguese fluently. It'll be great on my application to West Point when I get back. I'll live with a Portuguese family for a year. I've already contacted the AFS representative here. She wants to meet with us."

This was the drive I had been dealing with his *whole life*. "Slow down. You just got back! You need to think this through. If you do this, you'll be a senior when you return. You'll have to make up your junior year when you get back to be able to graduate on time because in Florida you won't receive any academic credit for attending school in Portugal. And if you want to go to West Point, you'll need to pass all your junior and senior classes with flying colors—all in one year. There is no way, Bart. Think this through. It's too much!"

He stopped in his tracks and looked at me for several moments. His eye contact was intense and probing. He said slowly and calmly, "Something you need to realize is that *your* agenda for my life is not *my* agenda for my life. I'm going to do this, with or without your support. You can fight me, or you can support me. It's up to you."

I was speechless. There were no words that could refute this wisdom. I reminded myself, *What we overprotect, we make weak!* I admired his courage immensely.

Bart's sophomore year required a lot of planning to make his exchange-student dream happen. He needed to earn much more money than he had for a two-week stay in a youth hostel. There were applications, interviews, and searches for families who would host Bart. He was also required to meet his obligations at home, like earning his spending money for the next school year. Although he did extra chores around the house to earn money, he realized it was not going to be enough. He asked me if he could request sponsorship from the clientele of my parenting classes. Bart had helped teach some of these classes with me, and he was fully aware that all my clients knew him from the "Bart stories" I had shared with them over the years.

To my surprise, the checks came pouring in; Bart's heartfelt email request yielded much more than he expected. My village had come through to support him, which spoke volumes for their regard for him. It was the catalyst that enabled his dream to come true, and I am forever grateful to them. After their generosity, he only needed a small bit more to reach his goal. He contacted AFS, told them how close he was to his goal, and asked for assistance. They awarded him a scholarship that sealed the deal.

Bart's departure for Portugal was no small event. He had a barrage of friends to see him off as they were sure to miss him. Before getting on the plane, he gave each one a letter to make sure their connection would not be broken during his yearlong absence. Social media was not yet a part of our lives and Bart had no email address to give to them, so he had taken the time to handwrite each of them letter.

Just before he turned to walk down the jetway, he handed me a letter. "I love you, Mom," he whispered after giving me his goodbye hug.

"Love you too, son," I squeaked as tears rolled down my cheeks.

I stuffed the letter into my purse to read later, knowing I would not be able to hold it together for the two-hour drive home if I read it there, watching him disappear into the tunnel of the jetway.

> Dear Mom,
>
> Hey Mom, I know that you are probably crying right now, and it is hard for you to read this, but if you are I am on the plane right now heading for DC into unknown territory that is sure to make for an interesting year. I just wanted to let you know that I never could have done this without your dedication for me to succeed. I wanted you to know that I did realize it and how much I appreciate it even when it seems sometimes like I don't. I also wanted to tell you that I love you and that I am gonna miss you a lot. Trust me, no mom in Portugal could ever replace you and you know it.
>
> I want you to take care of my girlfriends for me while I am gone. I have to have someone to do it for me and they all need someone to go to for advice and most of my advice comes from you

anyway. So, do me a favor and invite them over once in a while to talk and look at pictures or something, will ya?

God, this is so hard for me to do, it is so bittersweet for me I don't know whether I like it or hate it, but I am strong and I know that I can get through it. So you don't have to worry about me, ok?

It has been 16 long years with me, and I am finally starting to live away from home. This is probably very scary for you, and you probably feel like you're useless now. Well, that's not true, I still need you, just in sort of a different way. And, besides, it's not like I am not coming back.

I can't get through this letter without crying. This is sooo hard for me, but I will be fine, just visualize a great time for me and it will happen.

Well, I have said about all I need to say except for "good-bye."

Love you Mom.

Your son,

Bart

I think I read his letter 50 times before I could read it without crying. I cried for the depth of the love we shared and for Bart's openness and consideration in expressing his thanks to me. I cried because of the double sting of the empty nest all at one time. Both Nic and Bart had reached new milestones; Nic was off to his first year of college and Bart to Portugal. My "Mommy" role had abruptly ended. They would never need me in the way they had done all their lives up to this point, and the loss of that role was the death of someone near and dear to me. With John off on his own as well, it was going to be a lonely year.

I put on the saddest music I could find and cried for three days. When I couldn't shed one more tear, I got up, turn off the music, and snapped back to my life with gratitude for all that I had shared with my children as their mommy. From now on in I would be just Mom. Soon they would create their own family tribes, and my involvement would come from the periphery. Advice would be given by me, when asked for, and heeded by them if desired. And maybe one day I would be an oma, encouraging my grandbabies as they grew and supporting them as they followed their dreams.

*Chapter 24*

# WHERE THERE'S A WILL, THERE'S A WAY

*Dreams should never die. Nothing can stop them except for self-uncertainty.*
—*Bart Fletcher*

The following was Bart's essay in his application to West Point:

When you see someone in a nice car, wearing nice clothes, or a person that is just happy where they are in life, did you ever wonder how they could be so successful in their pursuit of success? After all, personal success, for most people, is difficult, if not nearly impossible, to achieve. To most people, success exists in some secret society, where only the people experiencing it know the secret and won't share it with the rest of us. Most everyone has received, in one form or another, some "personal action plan" or "steps to success" self-help but have never understood the real key to reaching their personal goals.

The truth about success is that there is no one single way to achieve it, and it looks different for every person. I have discovered in myself that I can never achieve success in anything unless I truly want it. When I have found something that sparks passion inside me, I follow that passion with a "no holds barred" kind of determination that will carry me to my goal. Thinking about my goals, I am reminded of a foreign exchange program in which I participated that sparked this same, very passionate, desire and gave me the determination to take success by the reins.

A few years back, I took a vacation to visit some friends in Portugal. When that vacation ended, I came away from it a changed person. I had gotten a taste of a new culture, people, and life that were different from my own, and I truly desired to experience more. When I finally decided that a foreign exchange program was what I wanted to do in order to have the experience I needed to quench my desire—my thirst for a life outside of the norm—I used that passion to find the determination to reach my final destination. As a 15-year-old kid with no job, no car, and no money, it was going to take a lot of determination to get the $6,500 the foreign exchange program required for a one-year stay. "What can I possibly do to get all this money? There is no way!" I thought to myself, but my passion wouldn't let go. This was what I wanted; it was my dream, and I would have it no matter what it took.

I started my quest by searching for a job, but try as I might, there was no job to be found for a kid my age. So, I did what any other person does who can't find a job and feels total desperation without lack of fortitude: I wrote to people; family, friends, friends of friends, and to anyone who might have been willing to support me. I implored, I begged, I inspired these people to help me raise money for my personal culture crusade. "Someone has to see my dream as worthy of giving," I thought. So, they did. As the weeks went by, the money kept rolling into the bank. However, after all the beseeching, the money of my benevolent benefactors was still not sufficient. "I've made it so far," I said, "I can't give up now!" Though I was discouraged, I held steadfast to my goal. I wrote to the exchange program to petition for a grant to decrease my deficit. They were so impressed by this resolve that they promptly responded with a $1,000 scholarship to ease my struggle. Their grant was just enough for me to enter the program. After all that work, I had finally done it; and all of it took just a little determination to persevere.

So, it remains said that "where there is a will, there is a way." I cannot think of a greater law that governs my life so necessarily. I know that what I put into my goals and dreams is exactly what I get out of them in return, and without the passion of dreams, no one can find the determination to achieve success. Stay determined not to let fear get in the way of your passions and let them lead you to your dreams. This is the one key to success, and it is no secret, it is a universal law.

Bart Fletcher, February 2002

# Chapter 25
# A MAN RETURNS FROM PORTUGAL

*There is a world of difference between insisting on someone's doing something and establishing an atmosphere in which that person can grow into wanting to do it.*
—*Fred Rogers*[26]

In the first few months after Bart's return from Portugal, he slowly adjusted to the culture shift. He was quiet and reserved in his demeanor, sticking to home for a while until he was ready to re-enter the social circle he'd had before his year abroad. It was during this time that he met Katie, and they officially began to date. One evening while I was reading in my bedroom, I got that signature "something's-up" knock on my door.

"Mom. I've got something I want to talk to you about," he said in a reluctant voice.

"What's up, sweetie?" I put my book down.

"You know, since I've come back from Portugal, I've realized that I learned a lot while I was over there. There is so much you don't know about what went on there, but trust me there were some pretty rough times. My Portuguese mom and dad weren't around much. I had to rely on myself a lot and learned that I am totally responsible for my choices. I feel like I grew up to be a man while I was there."

"That's great, Bart. I am so glad you had that experience. Learning can be so big when life is tough." I waited. I was clueless as to where he was headed with this epiphany.

"Well, now that I am a man, I've got a question for you."

I slipped my reading glasses down my nose and peered at him cautiously. I could feel a big disclosure coming on. "Go ahead."

"Well, you know I've been dating Katie since I got home. I just want to be respectful and ask if it's okay that she and I have sex…you know, here in the house?" His eyes were focused on his feet as his toe scuffed the tile floor.

I can't imagine what my face looked like at that moment, but it felt like the blood had drained from my face and landed in the pit of my stomach.

"Excuse me?"

He assumed the stance of a lawyer about to give his closing statement. "I want to be able to sleep with Katie here. You know we are going to do it anyway, so why not in the safety of our home?"

I tried to pull myself together to maintain the calm I wanted him to see, but inside I was fighting a scream of *Over my dead body!* I paused for a second. *Breathe, Ginny. You got this.* I forced the air into my lungs and then out again.

"Mom?"

"I so appreciate you asking me, Bart. That was respectful, and the answer is 'no.' Not because I want to control you having sex with Katie. If the two of you want to have sex, there is nothing that will stop you except your conscience. My decision is not about you. It's about me. Personally, I do not want to have to wonder what I am going to walk into when I am home, any more than you would want to walk in on me and Dad. I want to walk into my house knowing I don't have to worry about a potentially awkward moment. So, no, you may not sleep together here. I know this is disappointing for you, but I know you will handle it." I wanted to be as respectful as possible since he had trusted our relationship enough to have the courage to ask. I didn't want to discourage him from this kind of trust in the future.

The determined Bart began to emerge. "But, Mom, it's not fair! You have no idea what I did over in Portugal and what I handled. I was robbed a few times. Did you know that? My Portuguese mom and dad were never around, and I mean *never*. My sister was the one who was there for me, so most of the time I was left on my own. I could do whatever I wanted," he emphasized none too subtly.

"I'm not sure that what happened in Portugal has anything to do with you and Katie having sex in this house. This is about respecting our personal boundaries, Bart. End of conversation."

"But this is my house too. It's not fair."

"Yes, it is your house and, as you know, our family commitment is that everyone has a right to feel physically and emotionally safe here. This crosses my emotional boundaries."

He stormed out of the room, huffing, and puffing. I heard his bedroom door slam.

Two weeks later I returned home from a weekend retreat to find Katie, Bart, and Nic hanging out in the living room. Jack was in the kitchen, and as soon as we made eye contact, he signaled me silently, summoning me to the bedroom.

"Correct me if I'm wrong, but didn't you have an agreement with Bart that there was no sleeping with Katie here?"

"Crap! What happened?"

"Well, this afternoon I took a nap, and when I woke up I saw Bart's door was closed. I knocked and opened the door, and there were Bart and Katie lying naked in bed together. I didn't want to say anything until you got home. I just wanted to make sure I understood what you had told me."

If I had not just returned home from an *Understanding Yourself and Others* self-growth retreat, I would have stormed out of the bedroom and raged at both kids. I was furious at Bart's defiance, but I knew I had to calm myself before I could talk this out. Bart was not one to surrender to someone's threatening posture. My calm would be the key to him hearing me. When I regained my composure, I walked back out to the living room. Katie was in the recliner seemingly preoccupied with texting on her flip-phone. I assumed she was attempting to avoid the anticipated confrontation while still supporting Bart with her physical presence. Clearly, she did not want to be included in the conversation. Neither did Nic, who abruptly left the room.

"Bart, I want to talk to you. Now. Exactly what part of our conversation about sleeping with Katie in this house did you not understand? I believe my answer was a very clear 'No!'"

"I'm a grown man, and I should be able to decide what I do in my room. I live here too, you know."

"If you are so grown up, then be my guest and move out to live as you wish to in your own house where you pay for rent, utilities, food, and everything else that an adult is responsible for. But as long as we are financially and legally responsible for you, we expect you to respect our boundaries. Dad and I provide for you in the way we do because we are in the process of preparing you to be able to do just that, to live independently. If you are not willing to respect this boundary that I requested of you, then I will ask you to leave. Then you can behave exactly as you please because you will have all the say you want in a home paid for by you. If you choose to leave, I will understand. I'll even help you move if you'd like. But I must tell you, I would truly miss you."

He ranted and raved for a few minutes and then fell silent. Would he honor our request? The choice was his. But this time he knew that if he chose not to comply, he would have to leave. His future actions would indicate his answer.

Before leaving the room, I turned to him. "Let me know how I can support you."

He nodded reluctantly.

Bart did not move out and, to our knowledge, complied with my boundary until the day he left for military service five years later. Of course, parents never know everything that happens when their teens are home alone, and I had no desire to know. This was not about controlling Bart and Katie's sex life, or any other part of his life for that matter. This was about connecting through respect for a personal boundary.

## Chapter 26

# ENOUGH IS ENOUGH!

*Stop shrinking yourself to fit into places you've outgrown.*
—*UNKNOWN*[27]

What never ceased to amaze me was Bart's uncanny ability to teach me so clearly about myself. His intense defiance and our frequent conflicts always prompted me to look in the mirror and reflect on my part in it, my acceptance of it, and my commitment to a personal transformation.

By the time Bart was 17, I was well into my journey toward becoming more mindful of disciplining myself first before teaching him to discipline himself. I was becoming aware of the unconscious beliefs that were getting in the way of my authentic self and triggering me into reactive responses that were controlling rather than connecting.

One area of struggle for me was my inability to be truly assertive with others in my life. People-pleasing was, and still is at times, my modus operandi for sustaining my false belief that people will leave me if I set a boundary they don't like. I also felt responsible for other people's upset, especially anger. Anger in others scared me, and I tended to capitulate to avoid conflict.

At this time in Bart's life, I was teaching parents and adults working with children that to be authentically assertive you must be able to set a boundary without worrying about how others feel about it. That's easier said than done because if you carry any guilt about how someone feels about a boundary you're setting, then you set them up to walk all over you and your ability to be heard is greatly diminished. Guilt is the catalyst for giving in and giving up.

In theory this made sense to me, but in practice I was constantly challenged by the guilt that lay beneath my boundaries. I had discovered that with children and teens I was able to be completely assertive—without being permissive or aggressive—90 percent of the time. I was able to set a boundary with a tone of confidence, knowing that if that child was upset, I could follow through without trying to happy them up or shut them down.

With adults, however, this was more difficult. With women, I was beginning to know my boundaries and feel confident in setting them. With men, on the other hand, I submitted frequently to my perceived assessment of their displeasure. I'm sure this was related to the responsibility I took on in childhood of making my dad happy. I was constantly taking the pulse of his mood, sensing that he was deeply unhappy even when he tried to be cheerful and fun. His anger would trigger me. If he argued with my brothers over who would help him rake the yard, I would offer to do it just to make peace in the family. Most of the time it worked, and his resulting happiness helped me feel safe. The belief that became embedded in my 11-year-old brain was that I was responsible for his happiness. The pressure of that responsibility caused me extreme anxiety, but it was a price I was willing to pay. I thought that if I could just be good enough, conflict would be avoidable. The big blow came when he took his life. I had failed. I was supposed to make him happy, and I couldn't do it. It was *my* fault. What a burden for a 15-year-old girl. As a result, I made an unconscious decision not to piss off men, or anyone else who displayed extreme anger, or they too, I believed, would leave me.

When I felt strong and confident, I was able to be assertive with Bart. But there were days when I failed miserably. One evening Bart asked me for a ride to work the next morning; he had a job waiting tables and it started at 10:00.

"Sure, but I have an exercise class in the morning that starts at 10:00. I want to be on time for my class, so you need to be ready and heading to the car by 9:30. Are you willing to be in the car no later than that?"

"Yeah, but I don't have to be there until 10. That means I'll have to wait around till Red Lobster opens."

"You'll have to get a ride from Katie then. I'm not willing to be late for my class."

"Okay. I'll be ready."

Fast forward to the next morning: I was ready to go at 9:15, and I discovered Bart had barely wrestled his way out of bed. Trigger. Alarm bells went off inside me; anxiety signaled that a struggle was imminent.

I knocked on Bart's bedroom door, which was ajar. "Bart, you up?"

"Yeah," he said in the middle of a yawn.

"I'm reminding you of the agreement we made last night about taking you to work. It's 9:15 now, and I'm planning on leaving at 9:30 so I can get to my class on time."

"I know. You don't have to remind me."

"That means you have to be dressed and ready to go in 15 minutes." I tried to keep my voice light and breezy.

"I *know*, Mom. Just let me get dressed."

"If you are not in the car by 9:30, I will be leaving to go to my class and you will have to find another way to get to work." I was beginning to nag. I could hear it, yet I couldn't help myself. My anxiety was taking charge.

If he couldn't get Katie or another friend to drive him, he would need to take a taxi, which would be costly for him. I didn't want him to lose his job or have to deal with his blame and anger as a result of it. Now guilt and anxiety began to mix with my anger—a toxic brew. I immediately busied myself with cleaning counters and doing mundane tasks that I had intended to do later. This was my ineffective method of trying to distract my anger. I could not sit still and wait for what was to come. The adrenaline was racing through my veins. I was about to get sucked into a power struggle when I had so clearly articulated my limit to Bart the night before. And now the guilt I was feeling over him potentially losing his job, coupled with the tapes of my childhood telling me I was not good enough, was causing me to question whether I could follow through. I groaned. Power struggles always ended in abuse, either to myself or to him. I wondered who the victim would be this time.

At 9:25 out strolled Bart in his tighty-whities, scratching his jewels while yawning as he opened the refrigerator door. I could feel myself losing it.

"Bart, what did I tell you? You have five minutes to get yourself together so I can take you to work. I'm not kidding when I tell you that I will leave without you if you are not ready by 9:30."

"I *know,* Mom! If you tell me that one more time…!"

"You can't possibly think you will be ready in time. I'm serious. I *will* leave you here."

"Chill, Mom! I'm getting ready. Quit barking at me!"

By 9:30 Bart had managed to get into his uniform and was heading to the bathroom to brush his teeth.

I was seething. "Okay, I'm leaving." I slammed the front door as I left, got into my car, and searched for my keys, desperately hoping that this small delay would give him time to get out the door and into the car. I pretended to search for the keys to distract myself from the reality of having to follow through with a boundary I had been afraid to set. My guilt was pounding on the door of my heart, screaming at me to rescue Bart. After a minute of stalling, I relented and grabbed the keys. I paused, knowing I was about to compromise my assertiveness, the only thing that would make my voice matter. I slammed on the horn. No Bart. Now there was no turning back.

In full watching-myself-act-stupid mode, I got out of the car and opened the front door of the house to find Bart in the recliner, bending over while tying his shoes.

I went into full rant.

"I *told* you that I was going to leave at 9:30 if you were not in the car. What part did you not hear? Just so you know, I'm *really* going this time. I'm leaving *now*!"

It's debatable who I was really trying to convince, him or myself. I must have looked like an idiot to him. Bart knew this dance. He knew he had me over a barrel and I would not follow through. For the second time, I slammed the front door closed and headed for the car. By now I was 10 minutes late.

This time I got in the car, started it, and with tremendous fury and resentment backed out of the driveway and headed out of the neighborhood with my itty-bitty-shitty committee tapes playing in my head at full volume. *Why does he always do this to me? Dammit, Ginny, what's the matter with you? Why can't you set—and keep—a boundary with him? You travel all over the nation teaching people how to do this, and you can't even do it yourself? What are you afraid of? Just do it, you idiot.* All this was going on in my head as I turned into the next driveway, backed out, and reversed my direction back toward home. As I turned into the driveway, there was Bart, shaking his head as if to say, *If you had just waited for me without this tantrum, you wouldn't be so late.*

What followed was a response that was anything but normal. Normally, I would have transported Bart in a seething silence of guilt and shame that I would have energetically projected onto him. I would have blamed him for my actions and told him I would never bail him out again. I would have imposed my guilt on him. The verbal vomit from my past would have exposed the victim in me and would have sounded something like this: "This is your fault. It is *so* disrespectful. I don't know why I am doing any of this for you. It must be because I'm a such a kind mother. I hope you are happy now that I will miss my class. You owe me one."

But somehow this time I was mindful enough to know this was *my* issue, not his. He was just the catalyst for me to observe it, learn from it, and hopefully grow from it. So, this is what happened instead: Bart got into the car and I got up into his face and proceeded to rant. "I JUST WANT YOU TO KNOW I AM NOT MAD AT YOU! I AM MAD AT ME. I AM FURIOUS AT MYSELF FOR NOT FOLLOWING THROUGH WITH WHAT I SAID I WOULD DO. I ONCE AGAIN HAVE DENIED YOU THE OPPORTUNITY OF LEARNING HOW TO SET BOUNDARIES FOR YOURSELF. SHAME ON ME! I AM SORRY, BUT I CAN PROMISE YOU FROM THIS DAY FORWARD I WILL NOT GIVE IN AGAIN!"

Through all this, Bart was wide-eyed. For the second time in a conflict with me, he was speechless. Nothing in his teenage brain could tell him how to respond. Defiance, argument, guilt thrown at me, manipulation of the situation—none of that would work here. I was taking full ownership—not so gracefully, but certainly there was no need for him to go on the defensive. I continued ranting for a few minutes, at and about myself. As we approached Red Lobster, I was calm enough to remind him of his accountability to me in letting me know how and when he would return home.

He quickly opened the door and scooted out. "Okay, Mom. I love you."

I missed my class at the gym, but I spent two hours on an elliptical machine sweating anger and toxins out of every pore in my body. I internally ranted, confirming the shame I felt at the inadequacies of how I handled this incident. I reflected on the voice I struggled to find with my mother when I was 16 and set my first boundary with her. I didn't have the ability to understand it as deeply then as I could now. Guilt had so overwhelmed me then and threatened to overwhelm me now as well. But this time I had awareness, and with awareness comes change.

Once I was done beating myself up, I was able to see that this struggle was another level of growth. This needed to happen for me to get it. *Enough is enough!* I was furious because I was victimizing myself and Bart in the process with my own guilt. Guilt. It felt like a cancer to me, eating away at my self-worth as it lay silently, a blanket over my anger. I was tired of allowing it to take charge of me. I was determined to take back my power. I wanted to seal the deal with myself, finally, about how important my voice was in helping others find theirs. I felt fortunate to have been able to witness myself acting stupidly so I would never forget. I would always have that image to confirm my resolve in making a transformation.

From that day forward, my ability to be assertive grew significantly in all of my relationships. Bart and his siblings never again doubted my "no." When I said it, they knew I meant it. My voice had a knowing—an internal understanding—a tone that said *Just do it,* and a clarity as to what I was and was not willing to do to follow through. I felt powerful and I gained integrity with Bart—but most especially with myself. There was a new respect in our relationship. We reached a new level of trust for the better part of our journey. Oh, the gratitude—the bittersweet gratitude—for these struggles.

Chapter 27

# THE SECRET THAT SAVED ME

*The face is the mirror of the mind, and eyes without speaking confess the secrets of the heart.*

—ST. JEROME[28]

People keep secrets for many reasons. Some are kept to create the happy element of surprise, like a party for a landmark birthday or an unexpected visit home for the holidays. Others, however, may hide a shameful truth.

Keeping a joyful secret is easy; imagining the delight of the one who will benefit from it is enough to secure silence. Keeping a shameful secret, on the other hand, must be more carefully considered. At first the tendency is to keep the secret closely guarded rather than revealing to anyone, even a close friend, a shameful moment of your life. The shame of it might leave you feeling vulnerable, ostracized, unworthy of inclusion in the human race. But eventually the shame begins to weigh on you, becoming too much for you to bear alone, and you consider revealing it to someone carefully chosen and completely trusted. The sharing of that secret can then forge a unique bond between the two of you forever, simply because you are the only two people on the planet who know it.

One of the deepest connections that Bart and I shared was a secret that was revealed when he was 17 years old. It was a secret that we each kept without knowing the other also kept it. It was a secret charged with shame, for both of us, because to reveal it would have been shocking. No one would have believed us. They would have thought it preposterous, outrageous, unthinkable. They would have shaken their heads and suggested we were irrational. But eventually this secret became too heavy to carry alone and once revealed, it became a sacred bond between us.

One night I returned home from a parenting class to find Bart sitting on the couch by the front door, waiting for me to return. He was staring off into space as if trying to solve the most challenging problem of his life. His pensive demeanor concerned me.

"Hey, you okay?"

"Can we talk?"

I rushed to put my stuff down. In these moments I knew that when Bart asked to talk about something, it would not be superficial or trivial. I sat down on the edge of the couch across from where he sat studying his fidgeting fingers. I worried about what he was about to reveal to me. Was Katie pregnant? Maybe he was failing school and wanted to quit and join the army? I waited in trepidation.

"Mom, I know this might be hard for you to hear, but I think I am not going to live a long life."

I immediately froze. Trying to keep eye contact with him was impossible. A flood of anxiety surged through my veins upon hearing Bart's words. Viscerally it felt like that adrenaline rush you get when a car driving next to you suddenly cuts you off, and in a nanosecond that sensation of almost-death races from your gut to the tips of every extremity.

My anxiety was not for the reasons most would think. I was not worried about my son's preoccupation with thoughts about dying young. No, my anxiety was because I had known this too. I became aware of it the moment he was born. Shamefully I had tucked this nagging secret down into the depths of my soul, not sharing it with anyone because I was afraid to think it. It was easier for me to defer thinking about it by focusing on the mundane daily worries my role as a mother held. It carried an energy of truth, truth that felt like a knowing—not a thought derived from logic but one created of undeniable knowledge. I had never revealed it to anyone for the simple reason that it had an edge of insanity to it. What kind of mother would think that thought and ascribe a truth to it? Was I crazy? For the sake of my son, I should have just shoved it out of the way and denied it. What would people think if they knew that I had harbored this secret for years, protecting it from the light of day?

A flood of worry, confusion, and shame rushed through me in anticipation of what would happen next. Should I tell Bart I *too* knew his journey with me would be short? It was not one of the normal worries that nags most moms. That mother-bear fear in every mother's DNA has two intentions, to protect and nurture. This was different. It wasn't an instinct; it was a knowing. My whole being told me I had to reveal it, but should I? I was too afraid of the impact it might have on him. What would he say once he knew that I knew? Would he be devastated? I didn't want to make eye contact with him for fear he would see my secret. But Bart was astute at reading people's intentions, and he would know I was lying if I faked ignorance. My head was going in circles trying to figure out my path, Bart's path. I was the parenting expert and should know what to say or do in these tough situations, yet I was stifled.

"Mom?" he said, imploring me to respond with some guidance, some words of wisdom.

I locked eyes with him, speechless until our souls met. It was an awkward moment. The secret was the elephant in the room, and I did not want to acknowledge it. All I wanted was to deny this moment. Our eyes probed each other's until he found the truth, my acknowledgement, my shame. It bonded us immediately, an unspoken truth requiring no words.

"I know," I finally said with remorse, knowing it could be the biggest mistake I ever made as a parent.

What I witnessed in Bart was far from what I expected. I saw the most subtle change in his expression, an ever-so-slight relaxing of his jaw, a downshift of his shoulders, a release of the waves of anxiety on his forehead. It was as if hearing my confirmation allowed the shame of it to be freed from his soul. He heard the truth in my response. I saw it in his eyes. He understood.

Both of us had been struggling with this shame, and the unveiling of it allowed us to confirm the connection we had with it. I am not sure when his truth came, but I had known it from the time our eyes first met on the day of his birth—a silent spiritual contract that had been established lifetimes ago. The secret we both carried alone for so long now became a sacred connection, one that drove us to be on this journey together with such intensity. The connection had been revealed, the shame lifted, and there was nothing else to say and no other person to tell. It was just a matter of waiting for the when of it. And the irony of it was, this would be the secret that would save me.

## Chapter 28

# WEST POINT DECISION

*Feel the fear and do it anyway.*
—SUSAN JEFFERS[29]

Bart's senior year in high school was one of the most challenging of his academic life. In addition to taking all the junior and senior classes required for graduation in one year—to make up for the academics he missed out on the previous year while he was in Portugal—he was applying to college. He had decided in middle school he was going to attend the United States Military Academy, West Point. The application was a much bigger endeavor than the typical college application. Among a mountain of other requirements was the need to secure a congressional recommendation, which is not an easy task.

Bart took it all in stride and paced himself well for a procrastinator. He had had a habit of waiting until the last minute to complete his school projects, but this year there would be no room for delay tactics. There was too much to do within a limited timeframe. At the end of March, he submitted his application, a bit late because he was missing some teacher recommendations. Ironically, it was the teachers who struggled to get the recommendations done on time, not Bart.

Bart graduated, and at the end of June a letter addressed to Robert Bartlett Fletcher arrived in the mail from West Point. Bart opened the letter and was somber during the read. When done, he carefully placed it on the table and slid it in my direction. He then turned and walked to his bedroom.

I was expecting the worst. He had worked so hard for this moment. And he had no backup plan. I picked up the letter and said a quick prayer before my eyes hit the page. *Oh, please, dear God.*

The first words registered. *We are pleased to inform you…* He was accepted, but with a caveat. His math scores were weak, and they wanted him to attend a preparatory class which would delay his start date until the January semester. At the bottom of the letter were explicit instructions to not let his decision to attend be influenced by his parents in any way.

"Yes!" I sang out in celebration while dancing about the kitchen. So what if he's delayed for a semester? He was going to be able attend the school of his dreams.

"You got in! You got in!" I howled with delight as I skipped into his room.

"I'm not going."

"Wait a minute. What?"

"I'm not going. I don't want to spend an extra semester and be behind all my friends graduating. Like the letter says, don't try to change my mind."

It took me a few minutes to process his decision. I backed off with an intention to respect his boundaries, yet the parent in me was chomping at the bit to lecture him about his decision. I wanted him to think it through before deciding in such a rash manner, but I couldn't help myself. I had to, at the very least, let him know my stance regardless of his decision.

"Okay, Bart, I know I am not supposed to influence you. The choice is up to you. I will accept it and love you no matter your decision. But I have to tell you what I think only because I do not want you coming back to me 10 years from now blaming me for not pushing you to go. I think you are making a big mistake here. An extra semester is nothing in the scope of your life. This is a huge decision, so take some time before you decide."

Ultimately, he chose not to go. I found out several weeks later that secretly he did not want to leave Katie.

What he did choose to do was to attend one of the top 10 community colleges in the country which happened to be located in our area. Bart did not settle in his decision, however. While maintaining a heavy academic load—completing the required courses that most freshman and sophomores would complete at university—he became president of the student council and was selected to be on the Florida State Academic Team. His plan was to attend University of Florida with a full scholarship starting in his junior year.

"Why don't you want to go to UF now?" I asked. "You can be with your friends there."

"The first couple of years at university are all party, Mom. I know that's what my friends will probably do. Been there and done that in Portugal. I have a chance to earn some serious scholarships for ROTC and the Academic Team there. And if I get a 4.0 here, a transfer to UF in two years will be much easier than trying to get in freshman year. *And* I get to be with Katie here." And that is exactly what Bart did.

He made his path clear and there was no turning back. His summers were taken up with ROTC boot camps, and after two years he received enough scholarship money to pay for himself at UF with some left over to support Katie's room and board there as well.

In the spring of 2006 Bart graduated from University of Florida as a top ROTC cadet with a 4.0 grade point average. He would be commissioned as an officer and serve his country for the next several years. There was nothing more exciting to him.

But nothing ever goes off without a hitch. Two months before he was to be commissioned, Bart had a serious episode of supraventricular tachycardia (SVT), an abnormal racing of the heart that at times would rise to such dangerous rates that he would lose consciousness. In these episodes, his heart was clocked at over 200 beats per minute. Apparently, Bart had struggled with a racing heart for the past year and no one but Katie knew. He didn't want it to interfere with his military endeavors. After passing out a couple of times, he realized the situation was serious and needed attention. He was diagnosed with Wolff-Parkinson-White Syndrome, a congenital cardiac condition that does not emerge until the heart grows to its adult size.[30] Bad timing.

The army gave him two options. He could go on beta blockers for the rest of his life and revoke his commission or get ablation surgery to calm the SVT and the army would re-evaluate his commission in a year. Either option was tough, but in Bart's mind there was only one choice. He scheduled surgery at Shands Hospital in Gainesville one month after graduation.

The surgery lasted six hours because it was a cauterization process essentially to snuff out the over-firing of electrical impulses. In recovery, Bart developed a hemorrhage in his leg. The recovery nurse and I had to put pressure on it for three hours. His hospital stay was extended because of this complication, but he never lost his hope for a completely successful outcome.

Three months into his recovery, Bart's relentless spirit kicked in, and he began to pursue the arduous red tape of getting an earlier commission date from the army than they had originally planned. He managed to convince his major from ROTC training to agree, clearing him to be commissioned six months earlier than was intended. What no one knew is that Bart was experiencing more episodes of tachycardia, although not as intensely as prior to surgery. This was a secret he did not reveal to anyone in the military. If they had discovered this, Bart would have been medically discharged. He did not want to risk missing out on his dream of deployment. He was eager for the fierce challenges that abound on the front lines of war. He proceeded with eight months of training to prepare him for deployment as a tank commander.

Bart was never one to allow any obstacle to get in the way of his mission. In his mind, failure was not an option. He was willing to feel the fear and overcome it to reach his goals.

## Chapter 29

# THE BLUE STAR

*Have faith in life. Faith comes from knowing that there is a bigger picture, and all is well.*

—*UNKNOWN*[31]

The secret we shared resurfaced in the third week of October 2007 when Bart called.

"Hi, honey, what's up?'

"It's that time, Mom. We're being deployed to Iraq in a couple of weeks." I froze for a moment. Neither one of us talked about it, but I knew we were both wondering the same thing. Would this be the time our secret would come to fruition?

"Why don't you come home next week so we can spend some time together before you leave. Dad and I will pay for your flight."

In my mind, I had to see him one last time. During the time he was home, however, I didn't want to face the secret. It was the elephant in the room, stomping between us, around us, and in our faces. Yet neither of us would bring it up. If Bart was not going to live a long life, it seemed so logical that his deployment would be the time, but neither of us was willing to discuss it for fear we couldn't handle it. I didn't want to say my last words to him. I hadn't even thought about my last words. What mother thinks about that? I didn't want to face the potential of losing him forever. I wanted our last visit together to be positive. I wanted to set him up for success, not failure.

On Bart's last day with us, I racked my brain trying to think of what I could say to him. I saw a blue glass star lying on a shelf. I had a plethora of them to give to participants in my parenting classes and national conference trainings as reminders to breathe. They say that often a soldier's last word on the battlefield before he dies is "Mom." This would be the perfect way for me to be there with Bart.

Bart was playing on the computer in my office. I approached him and gently put my hand on his shoulder as he engaged in his game. When he turned to face me, I asked for his hand. Delicately I cradled it, placing the blue star in his palm. Our eyes locked in the very same way they did when the secret was revealed.

"You know what this star means in my business, right?"

"Yeah, Mom. It's that breathing thing you teach: **S**top, **T**ake a breath, **A**nd **R**elax."

"You are a warrior, Bart, and you have trained well for this deployment. You'll be off soon to enter unknown territory; that is sure to bring some fear. No matter the training you've had, there will be times your soldiers are scared, and there will be times *you* will feel scared in helping to keep them safe. I want you to keep this star to remind you to breathe so you can stay composed and help them stay focused. Keep the star with you and know that when you forget to breathe, I've got your back. I will be breathing for you, always."

Tears began to well up in my eyes while I desperately tried to restrain myself from uncontrollable weeping.

Bart stared at the star in his hand for a moment. He glanced at me nonchalantly. "Thanks, Mom," he said, and abruptly returned to his computer game.

*Well, that went over well,* I thought. *I won't be surprised if it's in the garbage the moment I step out of this office.*

There was some satisfaction, however, in knowing I had done it. I had addressed the secret without really talking about it. My feeling of dread was comforted and quieted just a bit—until I had to say goodbye.

Bart had to leave at 6:00 the next morning to catch a plane for his return to Fort Hood. From the moment I awoke to prepare for saying goodbye, I tried to ignore the lump in my throat by keeping myself busy with mundane tasks. I made some coffee and Danishes for breakfast. Jack and I had decided that it would be best if Jack drove him to the airport. I honestly could not do it with any sense of serenity or safety. All I could do in the moments before he left was try to smile for what could be the last photo of us together.

When it was time to head for the car, my heart was pounding out of my chest while sweat oozed from my pores. The lump in my throat became a deep pulsing ache and I struggled to hold back tears. Yet the mother in me was desperate to be upbeat and encouraging for this honorable venture of service he chose. I did not want to lose him. Seeing me as a pathetic emotional pile of poo who could not handle his leaving would not help. The internal struggle stopped me from taking more than one step beyond the front door.

Bart was wearing his army regalia, including a beret atop his head, looking so proud and utterly happy.

"Love you, son…to the moon and back. You got this." I hugged him.

"Love you too, Mom." He gave me one last peck on the cheek before stepping out the door.

Oddly, the weather became the metaphor for the situation as it began raining in the midst of sunshine. While watching Bart walk down the front walkway to the car, time downshifted like a movie slipping into slow motion. He turned and locked eyes with me as if to say, “I'll be fine, Mom. I love you.” When they drove away and I turned to go inside, there, radiating across the sky, was the brightest double-rainbow I had ever seen, a celestial suggestion that all would be well no matter what. It can't be easy for any mother sending a child off to war, but in our case the moment was even more bittersweet because of the secret that lay beneath.

A week later, on a Saturday morning, I was attending a spiritual awakening workshop when my cell phone flashed. I recognized Bart's phone number and quickly exited the meeting room to answer. On the other end, Bart was sobbing and trying to catch his breath. “Mom, I'm leaving now. I'm going. I'm about to get on the plane. I just want you to know I love you. This may be, ya know, the time,” he said, referring to the secret for only the second time, “and I want you to know how glad I am that you're my mom. How much I appreciate everything you have done for me.”

Suddenly I was desperate for more time. I just wanted to hug him, hold him one more time. I wanted to kiss away the boo-boos and wipe away the tears. I wanted to be his mommy, just one last time.

There was no doubt in my mind that I needed to leave nothing unsaid. With tears streaming down my face and an unrelenting ache in my throat, the words just poured out. “Oh, Bart, my sweet baby boy. I love you more than words can say. We are two souls that have been together before our time on this planet. We have known each other for eons. If this is the time, know that we live in love, forever connected. Nothing will break that. I love you forever, sweetheart. For always. Be safe. Remember your star. I am with you, no matter what.”

“I love you, Mom,” he said, choking to get air.

“I love you too, sweet Bart. To the moon and back.”

Both of us, satisfied that the secret had been acknowledged, disconnected with a click of our phones. I paused, feeling the intensity of what had just happened. There was sadness, but it was shifting to a sense of relief, for now. I would have no regrets. If this was Bart's time—the time the secret would become a reality—I had said all that I ever wanted to say as my last words to this precious son of mine.

*moments before leaving for deployment*

# Chapter 30
# DEAR FAMILY AND FRIENDS

11-20-07

Dear Family and Friends,

I am writing this email now because I don't know that I will have the time later to write one. I am very busy. I work long hours, about 30–40 hours without a break. I have dreaded telling you all this, but yesterday I was confirmed that my platoon has been picked for a somewhat dangerous mission. All the other platoons have been tied up guarding Patrol Bases and we need to explore an area that hasn't been touched by American or Iraqi forces for some time. It is very difficult for me because I don't really have that much time to get to know the platoon, but I still have the duty and responsibility to lead. Enough bitching though. I am writing this letter to tell you all what I am thankful for on this Thanksgiving Day.

First, and foremost, I am thankful that I have such a wonderful person to share my life with. Without her, nothing else would matter much to me. She is my perfect match, and I thank God every day that I was lucky enough to find her.

Secondly, I am thankful for my family. I have never known a family to love so much and be there for each other in the way that we are. It is the best family, the best.

Third, I am thankful for all my loyal friends that I have come to know over the years. They have become my extended family, my family away from home. They were there for me when my family could not be, and for that I am in a debt I can never repay to you all. Thank you.

Finally, I am thankful for my country. I love the fact that I live in a place where I get to choose. It is not my privilege, but my God-given right to choose who I want to be and what I want to do. Our nation's sons and daughters fight for this every day, and work so hard you will never know.

I am so thankful that my country has entrusted in me the responsibility to protect their most precious resource and am amazed at how hard these young men work for our unit, our country, and our way of life. I am so proud that I get to lead them.

As I trudge on in this journey, it becomes increasingly clear the importance for me to bring each and every one of these brave soldiers back to their families because everyone is thankful for them. They are thankful for their own families, and they so desperately need to be with them again, no matter what the cost to me. God bless us all, in everything we do, but take time to be thankful for what you already have. You never know when it's the last time you'll see it. I hope that bringing these soldiers home earns me the right to see my country again and be with all of you, for which I am so truly thankful.

The price of freedom so seldom comes for free. —*Stephen E. Ambrose*

Very sincerely yours,

2LT Robert B. Fletcher, AR

United States Army

## Chapter 31

# HELLO FROM TAJI, IRAQ

12-25-07

Hello from Taji, Iraq,

I just wanted to have the opportunity to wish everyone a merry Christmas. I want to thank all of my friends and family, and their friends and family, who have supported me so much in the past months.

The soldiers here have endured so much over the past year or so; some of these young guys are barely out of high school, but they have grown into men. I am so proud and honored to have led these battle-hardened warriors in combat, and I take great pride in my duty to make sure they all come home safe to their families.

The best gift we could have given to these guys was the gift of connection with their families for the holidays. So many of you have supplied the phone cards to make that possible, and I want you all to know that all of Demon Company got to call home because of your love and support. So, great job and mission accomplished. Thank you.

As I begin to undertake my last mission here (Operation Homecoming), I will tell you that you all can feel proud that our country has produced such a high caliber of people. These men have spilt their blood to protect their family and their country and ensure the lasting peace in a war-torn and broken nation. I cannot think of greater people to spend this Christmas and New Year's with if I could not be with my family. I hope that you all have the chance to meet great men such as these one day, and I am humbled just to share my name with this unit.

I want to wish you all a happy holiday season and hope that all of you make this new year the best new year. You only can live in the present, so take advantage of the time you have with your family, friends, and loved ones, enjoy their company and take a second to remember all that is good in your lives. I know that I am truly blessed to be in the presence of such an honored group and will soon take advantage of the little time I get to spend with my own family.

From everyone in the Demon Family, 2-8 CAV, and the 1st CAV Division have a Merry Christmas and a wonderful new year.

Yours truly,

2LT Robert B. Fletcher, AR

United States Army

# Chapter 32
# GO BIG OR GO HOME

*The truth is of course that there is no journey. We are arriving and departing all at the same time.*
—DAVID BOWIE[32]

Bart had been deployed to Iraq to replace the fallen leader of his new platoon, Lieutenant Dan Reardon, at the end of Demon Company's scheduled tour. Bart served a tough, but short, three months before returning to Fort Hood, Texas. At the beginning of his tour, his oma,—his grandmother—was diagnosed with stage-four lung cancer. I was sharing the responsibility of her terminal care with my older brother Gordon while maintaining a very busy work schedule. I was unable to attend Bart's homecoming at Fort Hood, which was deeply disappointing to me, but my mom's care was much more critical at the time. The only thing that really mattered was that the secret Bart and I shared had not become a reality. We did not have to see each other to celebrate that. I wanted to hug him, hold him, and see the light in his eyes, but it would have to wait. Waiting was a piece of cake, a blessing, compared to having to face the reality of the secret, if it had come to pass. *He made it home alive! He made it home alive!* I celebrated.

The first time I saw Bart after his deployment was a month after his return. I was coming home from a week of work in Arizona when Bart phoned me to say he was coming home for a brief visit. He was scheduled to arrive on a redeye flight the morning after my return.

"Hey, Mom. I know it's last minute, but Katie and I are coming home for a wedding this weekend. Just wanted to let you know. It's okay if we stay with you, right?"

"Of course! Oh, my God, I finally get to see you. But I want you to know Oma has been really sick, and I'll be caring for her to relieve Uncle Gordon who has been tending to her for the past week while I was away. I'll be pretty consumed with that, but we still can be together. There's a pool at Oma's condo you can use. Oma has been asking us to look at her furniture or anything else we might want to inherit once she passes."

"Mom, how can you say that? She's not gone yet."

"I know, sweetheart, but her time is coming, and as long as you are here it'll be a good time at least to look."

"I can't think about that right now."

Bart clearly was unaware that my mom was in her last stage of life. She had just received her third round of intense chemotherapy treatments within a two-month period. In her exhaustion, she was showing signs of anger over things she had never been angry about. She accused the home-health nurse of stealing bread from her freezer, among other things. To calm her, I bought seven loaves of the bread she loved hoping she would feel like she had enough—a fear that probably stemmed from her experiences in the Netherlands during World War II, but that I had never seen before. She called me every day while I was working in Arizona, pleading for me to come home, which was unusual. I didn't know it at the time, but these were signs that she was declining rapidly.

Jack picked me up at the airport at 11:30 that night; we were to return to the airport to pick up Bart and Katie at 6:00 the next morning. Jack had been caring for my mother and was exhausted.

"Man, I'm glad you're home. I just spent the last 24 hours with your mother, and I can officially say I'm done."

"Uh-oh! Something happened."

"Uh, *yeah*!" as if it was a no-brainer.

My mom and Jack had struggled for the first 17 years of their relationship. She did not like his mannerisms, his humor, and, most importantly, the fact that he did not have a college degree. From the get-go, Jack was excluded from my family's events and celebrations. Needless to say, it created a fracture in the family. Rarely did my mother attend the Luther family get-togethers. There had to be a reason, and an important one at that, like Christmas or a birthday. When she did make an appearance, she often left as quickly as possible after the meal. More often she chose to spend the holidays with Gordon and his wife. I was stuck in the middle, sometimes appeasing my mother and other times siding with Jack. Someone was always hurt, and I constantly felt guilty over never being able to please everyone.

It was only in the last year that my mother and Jack finally repaired their relationship. Jack and I had recently made a trip to the Netherlands where we connected with my mother's family. Her siblings relayed to us my mother's heroic acts as a young adult during World War II, bicycling about the countryside and stealing food from the backs of trucks or from whatever markets were open on the streets to keep her siblings fed. They revered my mom as a hero, and Jack was impressed to his very core. From that moment on he saw my mother in a new light.

After we returned, my mother came to our house for a Mother's Day brunch. Jack was eager to talk to her about how we connected with her sisters and her experiences in the war. For the first time, I felt enthusiastic about a family gathering that included Jack and Mom in the same room.

"Mom, do you realize how much your sisters appreciate what you did for them?" I asked her.

"That took so much courage," Jack added.

"Naw," she refuted, waving away the acknowledgement with her hand. "Really, you just do what you have to do when you are faced with that situation."

Jack stood up and walked over to her with his hand in his pocket. He knelt in front of her. All in attendance stopped in their tracks; none of us had any idea what was about to happen. Jack pulled a small box out of his pocket. "Cora, this is a medal I received for my service in the army. It really doesn't mean that much in terms of the duty I served. I want to give it to you because I think you are the true hero, and you deserve this more than I." Jack offered her the one and only military medal that he had received for his distinguished service in the army during the Vietnam War.

In that moment there was not a dry eye in the room. She reluctantly accepted it, wanting to honor his kind gesture, yet she struggled with accepting this moment of celebration of herself. "Oh, no, I'm not a hero. Really, I'm not," she continued to deny. "I had to do what I had to do. That's all. Really, Jack, I shouldn't take this from you." He insisted she keep it.

She held it for a moment and turned to Jack, reaching to embrace him and this honorable moment in which she recognized in Jack his integrity and respect. This was the first genuine hug I had seen between them in the 17 years of our marriage.

"Do you want to know about the day I had with your mother?" Jack asked.

"Sure."

"Just so you know, your brother gave up his Mom Duty yesterday and, well, the only person left to take over was me. She had a little bell that she must have rung 75 times to order me to do something. I had to make her meals, change her clothes, help her shower, and help her with the toilet. Let's just say we were closer than either of us wanted to be. When I asked her what she wanted to eat tonight, well, you won't believe it. She said she wanted me to mix broccoli with some special cheese and some ice in her bullet blender. I had to clarify her request twice because I couldn't believe what she was asking. A broccoli and cheese smoothie?" He looked at me incredulously.

"Oh, my God! How did you keep a straight face?"

"I didn't want to cause a rift, so I went along with it. I told her the kind of cheese she wanted was not in the fridge. All that was there was macaroni and cheese. She insisted the cheese was there. I took everything out of the fridge and freezer and dumped it on her bed to prove to her the cheese she wanted wasn't there. But that didn't sway her. I felt so helpless I started banging my forehead on the refrigerator door, pleading with the Lord to help me in this moment as she's ringing her damn bell. We battled for a while, but she finally gave in because she could not get out of bed. So, I asked her again if she wanted me to put the macaroni and cheese in the drink instead. She said yes and told me not to forget the ice. I could barely hold my cookies while making it. It was disgusting! Who would drink that?

"When I brought the drink to her, I told her, 'If you can drink this Cora, you're a better man than I am.'

"She took one sip and made a noise of disgust. 'This is awful. I can't drink this!' When I offered to go to Boston Market to get her something else, you know what she said?"

"Nope. Tell me." I was trying to be sympathetic, but it was all I could do not to laugh.

"She said, 'Oh, *now* you tell me!' There was nothing, and I mean nothing, that I could do right. That's for sure. Tag, you're it. I hope you got some rest on the plane because I'm dropping you off there. I'm going home to get some sleep."

That meant I was not going to get much sleep, and we had to be back at the airport in fewer than six hours to pick up Bart and Katie.

When I got to my mother's condo, she was calm and relieved to see me. We talked a bit, and then I slipped under the sheets in the guest bedroom for what I hoped would be a restful, if short, night.

My eyes snapped opened just before the light of day. I was happy to have had some decent rest, but fearful my mother might be dead in her hospital bed. I was hoping I hadn't slept so deeply that I missed her call. I hopped out of bed and checked on her. She was sleeping soundly, *thank God.*

I called my brother Gordon to ask him to take over the breakfast shift with Mom so Jack and I could pick up Bart and Katie. He was not anxious to return to Mom's so soon but complied because he knew I hadn't seen Bart since his deployment, and he knew I should be the one to pick him up.

On our way to the airport Gordon called, concerned about Mom. "She's all of a sudden in a lot of pain. You need to call the doctor."

I would have told my brother to call the doctor himself, except that mom's doctor was not willing to talk with my brother anymore. Apparently, Gordon had overstepped the doctor's boundaries during an office visit, so I became the designated liaison. I called the doctor, told him what was going on, and asked for guidance on how to proceed.

"It sounds like it's time to make a decision, Ginny. You can have her come here to the hospital, and we will do everything we can to keep her alive, or you can sign me off and have hospice come into her home. If you choose hospice, you need to know I have to be officially signed off from being her medical caretaker."

One thing I knew is that my mom did *not* want to die in the hospital. She had made this clear to me years before. This seemed like a decision that needed more time. But there was no time.

"Hospice. I know that's what she would want," I told him, not really sure I was making the best decision because there really wasn't a good option. Both would result in her death in the end, and it sounded like the end was not very far away.

"Great. I'll make arrangements for hospice to get involved ASAP." We ended the conversation 10 minutes before Jack and I arrived at the airport.

Picking up Bart was a mix of extreme emotions. I was elated and grateful to finally see him, yet I couldn't ignore the sad reality of where his oma was in her illness. It all seemed surreal. The only thing certain was uncertainty.

Bart's eyes were bloodshot from the flight. He had been unable to succumb to sleep. Once in the car, we informed the two of them about what had transpired with my mom since talking to him two nights earlier. Both Katie and Bart were somber and exhausted. I suggested they go home and take a nap before going to Oma's to see her.

"Hopefully we can make a nice dinner tonight," I said in an attempt to change the topic to something more positive. "What do you want for dinner?"

Jack chimed in. "Oh, I forgot to tell you, we don't have a stove."

"What? When were you planning on telling me that? It's going to be a tinge difficult to cook this weekend," I added.

"It broke the day before you got home. I managed to get it out and put it on the curb, but I haven't had time to get a new one. I was too busy taking care of Oma."

When it rains, it pours. Life seemed to be careening out of control, like a game of Whac-A-Mole. There was no time to reflect on how to respond, only enough time to react.

"No worries, Mom. We're going to be at a wedding for part of the weekend. We'll figure out the rest," Bart said in an attempt to lighten the load.

Beginning to sense the urgency of the situation, Bart and Katie decided they wanted to go to Oma's now.

When we walked in there was utter chaos. She was in excruciating pain. When I went into her room, Gordon was all too eager to get out. It was too distressing for him to see her like this.

"Has the hospice person come yet?" I asked.

"No. We had a nice breakfast, and then she just started moaning in pain. Pain in her legs, she says." Gordon seemed desperate, hoping I'd know what to do with that information.

I shooed him out to relieve him of the stress of it all. "You go. I'll take care of her."

After we visited Oma briefly, I told Katie and Bart to go home and rest. "Come back later. This is not a good time." I needed as little distraction as possible to deal with the situation at hand.

I sat by Mom's bed and held her hands. Her viselike grip cut off my circulation until eventually my hands went numb.

"Please, Ginny, help me. Make the pain go away. Please. It hurts so much."

"Breathe with me, Mom. Breathe. You can do this." I wasn't sure *I* could do this. I felt so helpless. All I could do was help keep her calm in her pain. "Breathe with me, Mom. You can do this," I repeatedly whispered in between the breaths we were taking together.

"We're getting you medicine right now. We're waiting for the pharmacy to fill the prescription." Hospice had assured us the medicine would come soon.

"I can't wait. Please. Ginny, help me." She was in agony.

This went on for five hours while we anxiously waited for the hospice nurse to arrive with meds in hand. It was a Friday, during the height of tourist season in Florida. The pharmacy was running far behind with filling prescriptions, and hospice was abnormally busy. It was one of the most trying times of my life to watch my mother in so much pain for so long, pleading for help I was not able to give her.

When the hospice nurse finally came, she could see the situation needed immediate remedy. She pulled me into the kitchen. "Here is the morphine. Give her one capsule at a time. Break it open and put it under her tongue. Wait a half hour. If she's still in pain give her another one. Keep doing this until you see she is not suffering."

"Wait. You want *me* to administer this to her? Why not you?"

"It's hospice standards for in home treatment. We are not allowed to administer the medicine."

"What if I give her too much?" What I was really thinking was, *What if I kill her?*

"That's not going to happen. Not the way I have instructed you to do this. Trust me. You can handle this."

I'm glad she was sure about that. I certainly was not. But desperate times call for desperate measures. My brother wasn't there. He had exited, stage left. Jack, Katie, and Bart would return soon to support me, but there was no time to wait. It was up to me.

After four doses, I finally watched my mother fade into a drug-induced state that freed her from the pain. She was not conscious enough to have a conversation. She was in la-la land. I questioned my proficiency in administering the drugs, yet I felt enormous solace for not having to watch Mom in such agonizing pain.

When I could relax from this high-level stress, I realized a slew of family members had congregated in the living room and were chatting and laughing together.

"When did you all get here? I didn't notice you come in." I briefly greeted everyone with hugs and informed them of Oma's status.

In the middle of explaining it all, the hospice nurse returned to check in for the night. "I'd like to speak with the immediate family, if possible," she said, after checking on Mom, "to answer any questions you may have."

Jack, my stepson, John, Bart, and I went into the guest room, and the nurse proceeded to update us on my mom's prognosis.

"I want you to know that your mom, your grandma, is in the last stage of life. She could live anywhere from two days to two weeks. There are lots of signs that will indicate when the time is near. I'm giving you this brochure to read. It will be very helpful in understanding the transition. When you talk to her, she can hear you but she probably won't be able to answer." She handed the brochure to me.

After the nurse left, I went back into the bedroom while the others sauntered back to the living room. They began to talk about retreating home for the night. I was feeling insecure about being alone with Mom. It had been a very long week for me, and some company would help me relax. They were all tired, but so was I.

I went to the living room. "I know it's been a long day for all of us. I'm sure Oma appreciates all of you being here. Not all of us can go home. I am going to stay here, and although I am not expecting anyone to stay with me, I really could use the support. Anyone interested?" I tried not to sound as if I were pleading, but I was.

Silence. No one peeped, not even Jack who is usually the first to come to my rescue. I stood there for what seemed like hours, ruminating in my mind about the drudgery of what lay ahead and having to endure this alone for possibly two weeks.

"I'll stay with you," Bart offered. "Katie and I will stay."

"Oh, Bart, you are so tired. You've only had a few hours' sleep in almost three days." I provided him an opening to back out, but the soldier in him continued the mission.

"It's okay. I want to be here."

Suddenly I could see him as the lieutenant he was to all the soldiers he cared about so much. I could see him sacrificing his safety for the sake of others. It was the soldier in his heart, the motto he always professed: *Go big, or go home.*

Jack had told Bart about how blessed he'd felt to be with his stepfather just before he died and encouraged Bart to take the opportunity to be with loved ones in their last moments if he ever got the chance.

After the others left, Katie, Bart, and I had a glass of wine together with some cheese and crackers. I finally had a chance to read a few sentences of the brochure before my heart was calling me back to my mom. Bart and Katie settled in on the couch, relaxing and mindlessly watching TV. As much as I wanted to be with them, I didn't want to leave my mom for another moment. She had told me this past year that when she died, she wanted me to lie next to her, holding her.

At midnight Bart retired to the guest room, and Katie sacked out on the couch in the living room. Finally, I was alone with Mom. She looked so peaceful, but her breathing was labored and rattling. At least she was not in pain. I would find out later that this breath was referred to as the "death rattle" by the medical world.

Life can change so abruptly, like a flash of lightning. Mom was supposed to get a pedicure that morning. You think you have it all planned out, and then in an instant you feel like you're living in another world. It all seemed like a bad dream.

Sleep was impossible for me. All I could do was be there with her, holding her hand. "I love you, Mom. You are so courageous. We have had a great journey together. Even with all of our ups and downs, I know you love me too. Just know that we will all be fine, whenever you decide to go. Don't be afraid." I recited the Lord's prayer. I wanted to climb in bed with her, but I was afraid I might hurt her. Maybe tomorrow would be a better time. She had had a long day.

A few minutes later her breathing seemed to get better. *It's a miracle! She's getting better.* Her breathing was peaceful, devoid of the rattle. But in the next few minutes her breathing was becoming more and more shallow. She was not getting better; she was dying.

"Shit! She's dying. They said two days to two weeks. *Shit*!"

I ran into the living room, shaking Katie awake.

"She's dying. Go get Bart."

I ran back into the bedroom and turned on a dim light. Mom had stopped breathing. I had read enough on death to know it takes about an hour for her brain to die, perhaps for her soul or spirit to leave as well, so this was our last chance to say goodbye. Bart and Katie, stunned in their sleepy states, joined me.

Mom's eyes were at half-mast. They looked like Jack's eyes when he sleeps. I could see the pupils, but they didn't connect with the outside world. I tried to close them, but they snapped back to half-mast. She didn't seem to be breathing, and I couldn't feel a pulse, yet I wasn't sure she was gone yet so I asked Bart and Katie to join hands so we could sing a song to say goodbye. Bart knew this song from an early childhood book by Robert Munsch I used to read to him and Nic called *Love You Forever*. I started singing with tears streaming down my cheeks.

I'll love you forever,

I'll like you for always,

As long as I'm living

My mommy [grandma] you'll be.[33]

We repeated the song over and over until we could feel she was gone. The room was filled with love and peace. The oppressive weight of death had disappeared; the sadness had subsided. Experiencing my mother's transition out of this world was an ethereal moment. Love prevailed, similar to the moment a baby is born into this world.

Bart turned and hugged me oh-so-tightly. "There was something so beautiful about that, Mom. I am so glad I stayed tonight."

While Bart and I were reflecting on this magical and surreal moment, Katie began calling family and friends to let them know of Mom's passing.

"Hey, Jack. I hope I didn't bother you, but I wanted to let you know…"

"I know," he said.

"What? How did you know?"

"I woke up about 20 minutes ago when something came over me, like a spiritual wave or something. I said to myself, 'Cora just passed.' I think it was her letting me know. The best part was I felt like I was there with you all in her last moments. I said a prayer, and then you called. That's how I know."

Katie sighed. She didn't for one minute doubt his words.

## Chapter 33

# YOU DON'T WANT TO KNOW

*The soldier above all others prays for peace, for it is the soldier who must suffer and bear the deepest wounds and scars of war.*
—DOUGLAS MACARTHUR[34]

In all the chaos of Bart's short visit home for his friends' wedding and Oma's unexpected death, there was no time for me to talk with him about his tour of duty in Iraq. I was ecstatic that he had come home alive and was able to be with Oma for her passing. Those moments were so surreal, yet rich in truth and love; their intensity, however, did not allow for any real down time for Bart and me to connect. I had hoped that his spontaneous visit would be an opportunity to resolve some of the residual guilt I felt for not being able to receive Bart at his grand return from war at Fort Hood. After all, I wasn't there to welcome him into the loving arms every soldier dreams of when anticipating their return from serving their country. Instead, my life was completely engrossed in helping my own mother pass this life while balancing a busy load at work.

A few weeks after Oma's passing, Bart and Katie were engaged. This was exciting news. Bart had been planning this moment for a couple of years.

They wanted to get married after Bart's return from his next deployment the following year, which meant another weekend visit home to make plans. This would allow them to have a last-minute engagement party and start the search for a venue for the wedding. They wanted me to be there to support them in their planning.

My work involved a lot of travel, often delivering keynote speeches at conferences followed by multiple-day training sessions for up to 500 people. I had to commit to a schedule as much as a year in advance. Canceling was impossible, making it hard to attend any personal celebration or event that wasn't planned before my commitment. Guilt for missing some of these important life events was the blood that flowed through my veins. These conflicts between my professional and personal lives were the part of my job I hated. It was always my personal life that took the back seat because backing out of a professional agreement could cost me my job if my reason wasn't a major emergency.

Luckily the weekend Katie and Bart planned to come home was right after an out-of-town event. In fact, I was flying home the day of the engagement party. I had just enough time to race home from the airport, arriving in the middle of the party at Katie's parents' house. It gave me a few hours with them at best. I missed being a part of the preparation, but at least I was able to attend. The next day, we had a relaxing day together visiting potential venues for the wedding.

That evening we finally had downtime on the patio. We shared funny stories about Oma and what had transpired over the last six months. As the evening wound down, Bart and I seized a moment to be alone. I was curious about what he would reveal about his time in Iraq.

"I'm so relieved you made it home alive, son! So, how did it go? What was it like? Was it everything you dreamed it would be?"

Bart looked at me with an intensity difficult to explain. I could sense a burning, secret shame lurking in his soul. He was trying so hard to conceal it, but was unable to deny or ignore it. He pleaded with his eyes, as if to say, "Please don't ask, Mom."

I couldn't help myself. I wanted so badly to support him, take away his pain, alleviate his guilt. "Tell me, Bart. I can handle it."

"Mom, trust me. You don't want to know," he said with a reverent determination.

I could see the horror, either of what he had seen or done while serving in Iraq—or both. His face told me all I needed to know. The energy of it felt raw and ugly. These horrors could become his demons for the rest of his life, and he wanted, at all costs, to protect me from them. Once again, the soldier in him was sacrificing his safety for mine. I could not insist that he tell me, and now I was too scared to know, frightened because he didn't want me to know. This was a secret he had no intention of sharing with me, or anyone.

Truth be told, I was grateful he was alive. I didn't want to know his truth that could potentially haunt me forever. I didn't need to share his demons. It was all I could handle in the midst of grieving for my mother just to face his second deployment. But one struggle at a time. For now, I would just enjoy being present with my son and focus on his upcoming marriage to Katie. There was plenty of time to worry later.

## Chapter 34

# THE UNFORESEEN GOODBYE

*Here comes the sun,*
*Here comes the sun, and I say*
*It's all right.*
—THE BEATLES[35]

It seemed that lately I was always seeing Bart when the energy of life was intense. I just wanted the mundane part of normal to return, something predictable that I could look forward to without stress. From funerals to engagement parties, the guilt and frustration of never having time to spend with him were the demons that kept me seeking any opportunity to connect until we finally got it right. As luck would have it, I had a training scheduled for mid-August that allowed me to arrange a weekend with Bart and Katie in Texas on the back end of work.

"Finally, I can come see you guys. I have a gig in Dallas, and then I can drive down to see you, if that's okay?" I was hoping there would not be a glitch on either end to kibosh this opportunity. Nothing had seemed to be going right for me this year.

"Okay, Mom, but you need to know I'm really busy filling in for some people in my company who haven't had a vacation since before our last deployment. I was only in Iraq for three months, but they were there for 15. They deserve time off more than I do. And now we're getting ready for the next deployment, so I'll have to work but would love to have you come anyway." His enthusiasm overrode the stress of having to squeeze me into his busy life. I was thrilled. Nothing was going to stop this mother bear from getting some much-needed connection time with them.

After working a few days in Dallas, I drove to Killeen to stay the weekend in their off-base apartment. Bart arrived home late as his hours were long, but we were able to go out to a local restaurant for a nice dinner.

Bart seemed to convey a more serene demeanor than I had seen in the past. It was unusual, to say the least. Should I be concerned? Could this be PTSD? Maybe I was overreacting, but the normal Bart would engage in conversations that were emotionally intense, sanctimonious, or doggedly seeking positive change for a better world. Now he was more accepting and present, listening more to other people's ideas rather than always working toward his own agenda. Maybe he was humbled by his experience in Iraq as a tank commander and had matured to a new level. I wasn't sure if I should be scared for him or proud.

The next morning Bart surprised both Katie and me by announcing he was going to follow through with the Christmas present he had bought for each of us while on tour in Iraq—gift certificates for massages at a local spa.

"Don't you have to go to work?" I asked.

"No, I was able to take the morning off. I don't go in till this afternoon." He had found some way to rearrange his schedule for the day so he could fulfill this mission with Katie and me first.

I remembered the Christmas present and had wondered at the time when I would ever get to Killeen to use it. And now that I was in Killeen, I didn't have the gift certificate with me. But Bart figured it all out and went out of his way to make it happen. I think he got more pleasure out of the giving of this gift than we got out of the getting of it. He had a perpetual grin on his face as he confidently transported us to a lovely spa after breakfast.

I had never seen Bart drive the speed limit before. If it was 25 miles per hour, he actually drove 25 miles per hour.

"Bart, why are you going so slow?" I asked.

"Better safe than sorry. We've got all kinds of time." I could see he was truly appreciating the simple things in life. The drive alone was enough to bring him peace and joy.

"Wow! They taught you something over there in Iraq. Or maybe this is the way you're used to driving those army tanks."

He rolled his eyes at me in jest.

Once in the spa, I could see that Bart was looking forward to relaxing in the waiting room for more than an hour while we were having our massages. He was enjoying every precious moment with us, as if they were his last. When we were done, he greeted us with a satisfaction I have never seen in him before. Either he had been brainwashed in Iraq or he was just at peace with himself, I decided. The latter was an easier choice for me.

Bart had to report to duty later that afternoon. He had been designated the HHC executive officer, which meant he was temporarily in charge of his company while his commanding officer was on vacation. He encouraged me to come with him so he could show me around the base and I could meet some of his company.

Although visiting a military base was not in my comfort zone, I was eager to accompany him because of the pride I saw in every part of his being while on base. He wanted to show me every aspect of his working life. He took me to his office and introduced me to some of his fellow officers. As soldiers passed, they saluted him. You could see he was not used to being saluted—he was often surprised and delayed in returning the respectful acknowledgement.

"I keep forgetting," he said almost sheepishly. "I'm substituting in this position and not used to all these people saluting me." Nonetheless, you could see his pride—not for himself, but for the entire base and for those with whom he served. He was living his dream.

When he took me to where the tanks were stationed until the next deployment, he seemed most excited. "Wait till you see these amazing machines, Mom. I wish I could show you what they do. They are so awesome."

By the time we got there, it was approaching dusk. He described every detail of the tanks with the utmost enthusiasm and admiration. At one point he hopped on top of one. He squatted down, looking at me eye-to-eye with an enormous smile on his face. Suddenly, the movie of Bart's life slowed in motion, like it had the day he left home just before his deployment. I wanted this moment to last forever. He was the happiest I had ever seen him, crouched down, his army Stetson on his head, beaming from ear to ear, and silhouetted against a beautiful, emerging sunset. I yearned for a photo to capture this moment.

"Oh, Bart, this is a perfect picture, but I don't have my camera," I moaned in frustration.

This was before cameras on phones were ubiquitous.

As a family we had always dealt with the absence of a camera by going through the motions of taking a picture, making sound effects that confirmed the action would solidify the moment in our memory banks forever.

"Okay, so I'm going to take a picture."

Bart stood perfectly still in the sunset with that beautiful smile while I took out my invisible camera and framed the image in my imaginary viewfinder.

"Smile!" I told him. He posed, as if it were a photo shoot, while I pushed the imaginary button.

"Zzzzt...zzzzt! There. It's a keeper. I just filed it in my memory bank."

Somehow taking pictures this way actually does make a more memorable imprint on my brain, perhaps because the printed version would never be a reality. I could carry with me forever the image I wanted to see—just as I hungered to see it—and view it as often as I liked.

After the tour, Katie and I went back to the apartment and puttered, planning and making dinner to share with Bart when he returned home from work. As it turned out, Bart had to work extended hours that evening. He never did make it home for dinner. I stayed up, waiting for his return, as I didn't want to miss him before going to bed. I didn't want to miss saying goodbye before leaving the next morning. I was disappointed not to get to spend the evening with him, but not surprised at his 200 percent commitment to his job. I admired him for it.

He walked in too tired to eat or talk. A kiss goodnight was all he could manage before retiring to his bedroom. He yawned a humongous yawn as I kissed him on the cheek in the same way I did when he was my towheaded boy.

I had scheduled an early morning flight home because Bart, once again, had a full day of work, and Katie needed time to study for the MCAT. She would be applying to med school for the following fall. In order not to wake Katie and me, Bart had snuck out of the apartment to report to work at dawn. I was grateful for the goodnight kiss the night before. Little did I know it would be my last.

Katie dropped me off at the airport that morning. When I got home, I was exhausted but filled with gratitude for the 36 hours I had with them. Later in the day I called to let them know I had arrived home safely—another family ritual that was established when the boys were in their teens.

At one of our family meetings we were trying to find a solution to accountability issues that were disruptive to our family dinner routine. We came to an agreement that the boys would check in with us by phone by a designated time or leave a note telling us where they were. If they broke the agreement, they would not be allowed to leave the house for the following week to see their friends, although friends were welcome to come to our house to visit instead.

"Yeah, but what if you and Dad don't check in?" Nic asked. "What's *your* consequence?"

"What do you mean? We are accountable," I countered.

Nic persisted. "That's not true. Lots of times you and Dad just leave when you want to go to the grocery store and such. You don't always tell us or leave a note to tell us where you are going."

"You know what? You are right, Nic," I confessed. "I never realized it bothered you. So, what do you think our consequence should be if Dad or I forget to check in with you?" Jack and I were curious. Was he going to offer something punitive or teachable, and if so what would it be?

"How about you owe us a pizza and a video if you forget?" There was instant consensus. It was a brilliant idea. And, yes, there were several times Jack and I had to eat crow and provide pizza with a video from Blockbuster because we forgot to check in. Accountability was a big deal in our family.

It was early evening in Texas when Katie answered my call.

"Hey. I'm just calling to tell you I don't owe you a pizza. I'm home, exhausted but safe and sound."

"Okay."

I immediately sensed stress on the other end of the line. "What's wrong, Katie?"

"Nothing. I'm just really worried about my MCAT tomorrow. I've studied, but I'm studied out and I'm not sure I'm going to do very well."

"Would you like a suggestion?"

"Okay." She hesitated.

I offered Katie some strategies for breathing that might help shut off her stress response. "You've got to keep breathing while you're taking the test, Katie. It will help you stay present and focused. I talked with Bart about this before he was deployed to Iraq. I gave him a blue glass star to carry with him to remind him to breathe when he felt overwhelmed. Why don't you take his blue star and put it on the desk tomorrow while taking the test, to remind you?" Although I offered this to help Katie, I also had a hidden agenda. I was never sure that Bart had kept that star. Now I would find out for sure.

"What blue star? I've never seen it,"

*That little shit*, I thought with a grin. As I originally suspected, Bart had thrown it away five minutes after I gave it to him.

"Ask him when he gets home," I said.

At that very moment Bart entered their apartment, returning from work.

"He just walked in the door!" She seemed astonished at the coincidence.

"Go ask him. See if he'll lend it to you."

As she put the phone down to inquire, all I could think was, *At least I'll finally know if it really meant anything to him.*

Katie juggled the phone. "He has it. He keeps it in his shirt pocket, but only when he's in uniform." She seemed surprised at having learned something new about Bart.

I was touched that it did mean something to him after all. "Will he lend it to you?"

"Yes, he said I could have it for tomorrow." The star seemed to have more importance to Katie, knowing that Bart carried it with him.

"Just remember to breathe whenever you look at it. And good luck tomorrow."

It was at this moment that I realized, at a deeper level than ever before, the power of connection as a parent. You never know if your children really hear you. You never know what their perceptions of you are or the impact you will have on their lives. You never know if what you offer them will be considered valuable. That's not yours to determine. I just knew that while my baby boy was in peril, I would be with him. I didn't need to be there to say goodbye. I would be there, always, close to his heart.

# Chapter 35

# THE TRUE MURDER

*Three things cannot be long hidden: the sun, the moon, and the truth.*
—*Unkown*[36]

CITY OF KILLEEN, TX
911 POLICE DISPATCH
08 SEPTEMBER 2008
08:30 CDT[37]

| | |
|---|---|
| Dispatcher: | This is 911. What is your emergency? |
| Bart: | Yeah, I got an emergency. This is Lt. Robert Fletcher from HHC, 1st Cav. I'm on 1702 Second Street. |
| Dispatcher: | 1702 Second Street. Okay. What city? |
| Bart: | I got a soldier and he's armed. |
| Dispatcher: | What city? |
| Bart: | Uh, Killeen. |
| Dispatcher: | The apartment number, sir? |

Bart: The apartment number is 9.

Dispatcher: He's currently armed?

Bart: Yeah.

Dispatcher: Okay. And what's going on with him?

Bart: He's, uh, he's.... He's suspected of stealing some goods, so we came down to confront him about it. He's armed now, and he's making threats, so we're calling police.

Dispatcher: So, he's suspected of stealing some army stuff?

Bart: Yeah.

Dispatcher: Okay. Now what's going on?

Bart: We had the manager open the door, and he came out of his room armed with a nine-millimeter.

Dispatcher: Okay. Hold on one moment.

Jones: (Staff sergeant in background giving Bart information.)

Bart: I got the address wrong. It's 1807 Second.

Dispatcher: Okay, so it's 1807, not 1702, right? Okay. That's no problem. We can change that. So, it's apartment 9? And so you guys are at the apartment, right?

Bart: Say again?

Dispatcher: Okay, so after he came out with the nine-millimeter, you left the apartment?

Bart: Yeah. He came out for a second with the nine-millimeter, and now he's gone back inside. We just went to the window to talk to him, and he was making threats.

Dispatcher: What kind? What's he saying?

Bart: "This is my house. Get out of my house." And he's got the weapon, you know, so we're...we're just staying back. We wanted to call the police to make sure everything is safe.

Dispatcher: You were talking to him through a window? I'd like you to move from that location so that he doesn't shoot that way, okay?

Bart: Yes, we're staying away from it.

Dispatcher: Okay. Did he point the weapon at you, or was it at himself?

Bart: Uh, he was just trying.... He was brandishing it to kind of.... He didn't really aim it at anybody, but he was definitely being in a threatening manner, so....

Dispatcher: Okay.

Bart: He's got alcohol in the apartment and says he's not feeling so good, so....

Dispatcher: Says he's not feeling good? What's his name?

Bart: Uh, his last name is Wirawan. (Speaking to his staff sergeant) What's his first name?

Dispatcher: Can you spell it for me?

Bart: Uh, W-I-R-W-A-N.

Dispatcher: First name?

Bart: First name is Jody. (Speaking to his staff sergeant) J-O-D-Y?

Dispatcher: J-O-D-Y?

Bart: Yes, J-O-D-Y.

Jody: (In the background) Who are you fucking talking to?

Bart: You hear him?

Dispatcher: Huh? So what's his first name? J-O-D-Y?

Bart: (Speaking to Jody) Just calm down. (Then to dispatcher) "Yes, J-O-D-Y.

Dispatcher: What do you mean, "Just calm down." What happened?

Bart: He's out here. He put the gun down. As far as I know.

Dispatcher: As far as you know? Do you see the weapon?

Bart: No.

Dispatcher: Okay. Okay. He's outside the apartment now?

Bart: Yes, he's outside the apartment.

Dispatcher: Can you see him?

Bart: Yes. He's standing here.

Dispatcher: Do you see a weapon?

Bart: No.

Dispatcher: Do you see both of his hands?

Bart: Yes.

Jody: (Talking in the background)

Dispatcher: Okay. Stay on the phone with me, okay?

Bart: Yes. He's back inside now.

Dispatcher: He went back inside?

Bart: Yeah.

Dispatcher: Please back up, away from the house.

Bart: Yes, I've backed away from the house.

Dispatcher: What did he say when he came out there?

Bart: He's got something in his pocket. I don't know what it is.

Dispatcher: He has something in his pocket?

| | |
|---|---|
| Bart: | Now he's coming back out. |
| Dispatcher: | Can you see both of his hands? |
| Bart: | Yes. He's jumpy though. |
| Dispatcher: | He's what? |
| Bart: | He's pretty jumpy, so I'm just gonna have to stay away. |
| Dispatcher: | Okay. I'm really concerned about your safety. I just really want you to back away from him and…. Is he saying anything right now? |
| Bart: | Nope. |
| Dispatcher: | Does he look like he's intoxicated…possibly high on anything or…? |
| Bart: | Oh, no. He…. I…. Uh, no. I'm not really sure. |
| Jody: | (Talking incoherently in background) |
| Dispatcher: | Okay, you back away from him, all right? |
| Bart: | Yeah. |
| Dispatcher: | Yes, you did? I want to make sure you're safe, sir. |
| Bart: | Hmm, yeah. He just broke his window. |
| Dispatcher: | He what? |
| Bart: | He just broke his window. |
| Dispatcher: | What window? |
| Bart: | His own window. |
| Dispatcher: | To his car or house? |
| Bart: | It's, uh, no. It's to the apartment. |
| Dispatcher: | He just broke his own window to his apartment? |
| Bart: | Yeah. |

Dispatcher: How did he do that?

Bart: He dropped the glass. Hey.... Hey....

Dispatcher: What do you mean, "He dropped the glass."?

Bart: Hey, man.... Hey....

*(Muffled sounds on the phone)*

Dispatcher: I need you to back away from him.

*(Seven popping sounds in the background)*

Dispatcher: Is that gunfire? Hello? Sir? Sir? Hello? Sir?

*(Two more popping sounds)*

Dispatcher: Oh, no. Sir? Sir? Hello: Sir?

*(Shouting voices in the background)*

Diepatcher: Hello? Sir? I need you to say something to me. Sir?

*(Voices of police in the background)*

Dispatcher: Hello? Hello? Sir, are you okay?

*(Voices of police in the background)*

Dispatcher: Oh, you just, God, okay. Sir, I'm gonna go now. (*crying*)

Five rounds hit Bart directly in the skull at close range. He collapsed instantly, and his blood flooded the balcony, dripping into the parking lot below.

As the police arrived, they heard the gunfire and immediately pulled their guns to prepare for engagement. As they reached the front of the building, they saw the blood flowing off the balcony and immediately called for Jody to put down his gun. Jody refused, and the police fired. Jody turned his gun on himself and collapsed on top of Bart.

We did not learn this factual account from the army. We had to obtain a copy of a report from the local police department to find out what really happened that day. Bart had been shot—not in the chest, as the army had told me (but maybe that's what Mike Doyle was led to believe), but in the head; and not once, but five times—at close range with a semi-automatic handgun. This is why we didn't recognize him at his own funeral. When I discovered this violence that had been done to my son, it nearly made me vomit. My only consolation? He died instantly. He didn't suffer.

Needless to say, the military community was in shock. The news spread rapidly from Fort Hood to military bases all over the world, and then to the public. The prevalent question: How could this happen? How is it that Bart was safer serving in Iraq than in the United States of America? Everyone who has a loved one, a friend, or a relative serving in a war zone knows the stress of deployment. One rarely ever considers the terrorism that occurs in their own backyard.

# PART III

# CALM IN MY HEART

Chapter 36

# THE SCENE OF THE CRIME

*The true courage is in facing danger when you are afraid,*
*and that kind of courage you have in plenty.*
—*L. Frank Baum, The Wonderful Wizard of Oz*[38]

Four months after Bart's death, Jack and I were invited to Fort Hood for a memorial dedication to Bart by the 1st Cavalry. We gratefully accepted and attended the thoughtful ceremony. Afterward, Captain Mike asked if we wanted to attend the roll call for holiday leave for his company. Bart had led this roll call several times as acting commander, but we had never witnessed it. Essentially, before any kind of leave, including weekends, the soldiers go through a farewell ritual in which they are reminded of the rules for "good soldier behavior" while off duty. There are four main rules that every soldier should abide by while on leave:

1. You may drink, but no drinking and driving.
2. No drugs.
3. Do not beat your wife or girlfriend.

4. If you got a woman pregnant, take responsibility

In the days that followed, I couldn't stop thinking about these four rules. I remembered Bart had said to me several times, "Mom, don't worry about me in Iraq. The chance of injury here at home is greater because of the poor choices that soldiers make when they don't have the battlefield to keep them focused. There are a lot of alpha males with poor self-control."

I assumed that these four rules needed to be constantly reinforced because of issues the military had with soldiers who had experienced the trauma of war: living in a constant state of vigilance, the never-ending evaluation of potential threat, fear of death around every corner, and the horrors experienced on the front lines. Bart experienced these things in his three months in Iraq, and they changed him forever. Jody, his killer, experienced them for an interminable 15 months. Would Bart's tragedy have had a different outcome if Jody had gotten the support he needed, if he had been taught the skills required to manage the trauma of ground war? I believe it would have.

Since we were in Killeen, Jack and I decided to go to the scene of the crime to gain closure in Bart's death. It was time, but it would be hard. Maybe being at the scene would allow me to feel for a moment what Bart went through—what he was thinking and feeling. Did he have a way out in those final moments of his life? I had to see it for myself. It was another way to connect—to say goodbye to him.

The apartment building was a motel shade of light pink, facing Second Street with a parking lot between it and the street. Access to the second-floor rentals, where Jody's apartment had been located, was provided by a stairway situated in the center of the building. The apartment was on the far-right end of the building; the only access to and exit from it was that stairway. With my heart pounding and hands trembling, I began to climb the stairs. Once again, I was having to face the reality of my son's violent death. But it felt so much more vivid knowing I was following in Bart's footsteps.

At the top of the stairs was a balcony that ran the length of the front of the building. I walked along it, gliding my hand over the top of its railing to #9, Jody's apartment. There were no signs that a murder had occurred here, but my brain played out the event as depicted in the police report as if I had seen it on TV. I imagined the fear Bart must have felt the moment he turned to flee. There was no way out. He was trapped in the corner at the far end of the balcony, blocked by Jody from passing the apartment and getting to the stairs. Was there a moment he knew this was the end, or did it all happen too quickly for it to register? I envisioned the quantity of blood spilled here, both Bart's and Jody's, dripping over the edge of the balcony onto the parking lot below. I visualized his staff sergeant wailing below, helpless to save an army brother from imminent death.

As I played the scene in my head I was overcome by nausea. No sooner had I reached the apartment than I realized, *I'm done.* I needed to get off the balcony. Jack took the cue from my hasty retreat and followed me to the stairway. As we descended the last steps to ground level, a woman who lived on the first floor, below Jody's apartment, was leaving her apartment. Jack and I stopped her to ask if she had witnessed the event.

"Yeah, I was here," she answered. "It was awful. I stayed in my house. When I heard the shots, I knew what was going on. I thought somethin' like this would happen."

"How did you know?"

"I saw that boy in passing just the day before it happened. He was gettin' out of his car. When you looked into his eyes, you could see somethin' wasn't right. There was somethin' dark going on there."

It suddenly became clear to me what Captain Mike was talking about when he picked me up at the airport the day after Bart's death. He told me that Jody wasn't in the military for "the right reasons." Something was off with Jody. Was it a mental health issue he had brought with him into the army, or was it because of what he had had to deal with while serving? We would never know, but his mother had made reference to the army knowing better than to "tread in his personal territory." Did the army know about Jody's dark side, or was this something his mother thought they should have picked up on? It was anybody's guess, at best, but if the army knew that Jody was a loose cannon and that he could be stealing equipment from the armory, why would they have risked sending Bart to Jody's apartment without military or civilian police backup?

## Chapter 37

# NO NEED TO FORGIVE

*You don't need strength to let go of something. What you really need is understanding.*
—GUY FINLEY[39]

A couple of months into the grieving process, which felt more like a numbing process, I finally had a quiet moment with Jack. I say "quiet" because Jack had had knee replacement surgery three weeks after Bart died, and his recuperation had been anything but quiet. For some reason, the medication he was given was ineffective in relieving the excruciating pain he experienced post-surgery. Personally, I think his physical pain was at least partially attributable to the emotional pain of losing Bart. Jack had not cried yet. In his efforts to support me in this tragedy, he forgot about his own emotional needs. The pain in his knee was the manifestation of the pain in his heart. My grief had to be put temporarily on hold while I tended to my wounded man, and I felt powerless to help him.

In addition to my caregiver duties, I was working full time, traveling about the country. Bills still had to be paid, and with Jack in retirement the onus of providing financially had fallen to me. In the midst of all this, thoughts of my mother were returning to remind me of the impact of that loss. She had died six months earlier and, with all the chaos that had occurred in the interim, I hadn't had a chance to think about how much I really missed her.

In my overwhelmed condition I was fortunate to have neighbors and friends who checked on Jack while I was gone. As much as I hated to leave his care to others, work travel became my refuge. It was a relief to be able to focus on something other than suffering for a while. But now, Jack's pain was finally beginning to subside, and we were able to have a conversation that didn't involve knees, pain, or doctors.

"Who are you angry with?" Jack asked, out of the blue.

"What do you mean?" I had been so immersed in just staying functional; it did not occur to me to reflect on anger—or any other emotion. It was easier to be numb and busy. I just focused on getting through one day, and then the next day, and then the next.

"Who are you mad at with this whole thing about Bart's death?"

As I began to reflect, I proceeded to spew out a long list. "*So* many. Let's see. I'm mad at the army. I'm mad at the 911 dispatcher. I'm mad at the police. I'm mad at Bart for trying to be the hero and take care of everyone but himself. I'm mad at myself for supporting Bart down this path of life." As I caught my breath, I made eye contact with Jack who sat, mouth agape, staring at me in disbelief.

"What?" I asked, challenging Jack to question any of what I had just said.

"You never mentioned Jody. Aren't you mad at the one who killed Bart?"

I stopped, shocked at my own unconscious exclusion of Jody from the mix of people and situations. I was speechless. I had no answer to justify my omission.

Over the next several days I kept returning to this question, asking myself over and over, *Why didn't I mention Jody?*

A week later I had an epiphany. On that balcony in Killeen, where both

Bart and Jody died. Bart had met his counterpart. Bart had struggled throughout his young life to have a voice and connect with others who would hear and support him rather than try to subdue him and his will. Was Jody any different? What kind of upbringing did Jody have? I didn't know, but something told me that he didn't have an adult in his life who chose to help him find his potential and become the person he envisioned he wanted to be.

Poking around on the internet, Jack and I found a website about Jody that his sister had created.[40] We learned that Jody experienced significant strife as a child. When he was an infant, his family was smuggled into America from Indonesia. He lived a short time with his grandmother, with whom he developed a close relationship, possibly the only stable relationship in his young life.

During his parents' turbulent marriage, Jody spent much of his life in and out of homeless shelters and foster care. As a teen he spent many months in a home for adolescents because of a dysfunctional relationship with his mother. Prior to the military, according to his sister, "he'd witnessed several incidents of gun violence and vowed to buy a firearm to protect himself as soon as he was old enough. When he turned 18, Jody purchased his first firearm, a Saiga-12, a Russian semiautomatic shotgun. He became increasingly interested in firearms and learned as much as he could about them." Clearly, Jody had not experienced the security and safety that every child needs to develop trust and build resilience. In fact, much of his life was viewed through the lens of survival.

For a split second on that balcony, there was Bart, face-to-face with the very person I once feared he would become. Jody was the person I had envisioned the day Bart challenged being spanked with a wooden spoon. I could visualize little Jody having the same passion for life as Bart, but never receiving the guidance he needed to discipline himself and allow his light to shine. How could I be mad at the deprived boy who shot my son? All I felt was empathy. Jody was wrong in what he did, but the truth was that he had reacted from a place of threat and fear. He chose to fight because he lacked the skills to manage the situation peacefully. Jody had spent at least one 15-month tour in Iraq on the front lines, which was enough to solidify, or possibly enhance, his illusion that the world was one continuous threat. Experience had taught this young man that his only viable choice was to kill or be killed.

Whom do I blame for Bart's death? Is it a parent or teacher in Jody's younger years who didn't hear his call for help or connection? Perhaps the laws that allow the general public to so easily purchase guns? The army for not providing police support to investigate the possible theft of government munitions? Maybe the police whose sirens triggered Jody to panic and snap? Worse yet, maybe it was Bart's fault for not running to safety when he had the chance? Most difficult to accept was the blame I imposed on myself. Should I have helped Bart to pay closer attention to his internal guidance to get out of harm's way? Who exactly *was* at fault here?

As I began to emerge from the cloud of numbness into the clarity of reflection, I concluded that there was no one entity to blame. We, as a culture, are at fault for these kinds of terrorist acts in our own United States. We must all take responsibility for not meeting the emotional needs of our children and giving them the coping skills required to get along in this world. Blaming the fall guy will not help any of us heal.

Blame is the ploy we use to appease our anger when we are not willing to accept our mistakes as opportunities for growth. Anger—the silent, pervasive seething I directed mostly at myself for using the threat of punishment as the last straw to try to make Bart listen to me. I metaphorically carried that wooden spoon in my back pocket—my secret weapon that gave me the confidence to regain control. Punishment may seem to work in the short term, with some children who surrender rather than resist, but in the end, it only teaches conflict resolution through violence and revenge.

Collectively, punishment is the culmination of a society believing that fear is more powerful than love. That we rely on the proverbial "last straw" of war to create peace in the world is, to me, an oxymoron. I feel angry when our society glorifies war, making it the ultimate sacrifice, while government disguises the ugly reality of it and its collateral damage with politics. I feel angry that we mourn deeply the thousands of lives lost and honor the sacrifice with triumph, yet never allow the sacrifice to teach us to do anything differently. It may be in our DNA to be territorial, but is it in our DNA to kill our own species in order to feel safe?

Days, weeks, and even months after Bart's death, the media would call or visit, asking to interview us. They especially loved the military holidays—Memorial Day, Veterans Day—or any time a similar tragedy occurred on a military installation. They wanted to keep fresh in the minds of the public the sacrifice our soldiers are continually making in the face of threat and to keep alive the story that without them we are in imminent danger of losing our freedom.

One reporter, Tim Malloy, was fascinated by our story and kept asking me the same question: "How will you forgive the soldier who killed your son?"

"I don't need to forgive him, Tim. I never judged him in the first place."

"What do you mean, you never judged him? I don't understand. You have to judge him. He killed your son!"

I did feel angry about what happened, but I wasn't angry at Jody. I only saw a lost soul who didn't receive the soothing and security he sought or the help he needed as a child. In a world without soothing and security, a child will interpret most things as threats, something he needs to defend himself against. He saw Bart as a threat when there was no threat. This murder was not something Jody planned. He was planning to go on vacation with his mom after he was discharged. This was an impulsive reaction that was tragic for both of them. Forgiveness is not necessary when there is no judgment. I am choosing empathy over anger.

# Chapter 38
# FREE TO FORGIVE

*As I walked out the door toward the gate that would lead to my freedom, I knew if I didn't leave my bitterness and hatred behind, I'd still be in prison.*
—NELSON MANDELA[41]

Several years after Bart died, I was watching a *60 Minutes* segment that focused on victims of crime forgiving their perpetrators, sometimes after years of harboring intense anger, hatred, and desire for revenge. I watched in fascination as the victims who were interviewed spoke of the liberation they felt at being able to forgive, divulging how important it was in their recovery. Forgiveness had given them the power to heal their pain and move forward in their lives. While watching, I contemplated the role of forgiveness in my life.

Most people who know my "Bart stories" would think the hardest person for me to forgive would be my son's killer, but in fact it was my mother. I blamed her for my dysfunctional adolescence and everything that ever happened in my life that was wrong. Why, Mom? After all, it was my father who ignited our family's dysfunction with his years of secret gambling, bankrupting the family finances, and eventual suicide. I couldn't blame him at the time because I believed his happiness depended on me. I was his little girl, the one who made him happy. If he died in misery, then I had failed him.

My guilt and shame over my father's death paralyzed me. Unlike other emotions, shame doesn't pass through you and move on. You can stamp and scream out anger. Sadness will pass after you seek comfort and cry it out. Fear evaporates when you find safety. Even remorse will release its clutches after a good dose of self-acceptance. But shame? It doesn't like to be revealed in any way. It loves secrecy. It is a muddy bog. When you try to take leave of it, the muck oozes around your ankles and sucks you in deeper. It strangles the core emotions you are born with that are designed to provide internal guidance.

We are not born with shame. It's derived from the perception of others, from a person's projected judgment that can suck you under until your self-worth is left gasping for air. I spent most of my life hiding in fear that someone might discover who I truly am, an unworthy, stupid piece of shit. I had plenty of evidence to justify this belief. In my mind, all the mistakes I had made in my life obliterated any value I offered. The responsibility for my dad's death was too much for me to bear at the raw age of 15, so unconsciously I chose my mother as the victim of my blame. I could deflect my shame by projecting it onto her. I became an angry teen. I missed my beloved father terribly and took it out on the entire adult world, but especially on my mother.

Everything she said to me was perceived as criticism—from comments about what I was wearing and my posture to the people I chose to hang out with. I could never satisfy her. If she ever had something complimentary or encouraging to say, I didn't hear her. Yet my friends' parents would say to me, "Your mom is so proud of the things you are doing." I would look at them in shock and disbelief. They couldn't be talking about *my* mother! If it was true, I didn't want to know about it because then I would have to take responsibility for my unhealed emotional wounds. Blaming my mother was so much easier. My blame was fierce, loaded with judgment about her self-centered behavior and her unwillingness to place her children's well-being above that of her own self-indulgent drinking.

Revenge was my modus operandi. As a teen, my revenge was to run away from home for 18 months. I imagined her alone in that house with no one to pour her helpless heart out to. As a young adult, revenge was keeping an impenetrable wall between us, a barrier to any love, acceptance, or forgiveness she might care to toss my way. In my early years of mothering, revenge was keeping me so impossibly busy that I didn't have a moment to spare for her—and always had a ready excuse for having to get off the phone. I unconsciously wanted her to suffer, to feel the abandonment I had felt as a child. I felt she hadn't been there for me for most of my life, so why should I let her in now?

For the first couple of years after my dad died, I had to endure her nightly rituals of alcohol-induced pity parties and pretend I cared, which of course I did at some level. But mostly what I felt was guilt, guilt for not being able to save my dad. I felt her pain, but I wanted her to feel mine too. I wanted her to hold me, hug me, and tell me everything was going to be all right. I wanted her to be my *mother*. But it seemed the roles were reversed. I was angry, but the anger was only a disguise for the guilt and shame. As long as I stayed angry at my mother, I didn't have to acknowledge the self-blame that lay beneath it.

It took me more than 30 years to realize the only person who was suffering from this anger and blame was me. My feelings weren't teaching my mom anything about loving me, and I was growing weary of my anger and resentment. Misery flowed through me like a seething river of lava, slowly but deliberately destroying everything in its path. I was becoming a miserable person.

One day it finally occurred to me that it was my responsibility to shift how I was seeing my relationship with my mom. My life stories and experiences were, after all, only my perceptions, narrated by my internal feelings. I would ruminate for hours, creating stories of what I thought others should be to me and what they thought of me. The reality was that I did not know what they were thinking. How does anyone *know* what someone else is thinking? The stories I was projecting onto my mother were really *my* stories being reflected right back at me. I could just as easily shift my perceptions toward seeing our relationship in a more positive light by changing my interpretation of the story and seeing her actions with positive intent. Rather than searching out criticism, I consciously began to listen for love and concern.

I began by listening to every comment or criticism my mother made and choosing to interpret it with the intent that she was trying to be helpful. Every time she would "should" me about something I did, I consciously sought to see it as her way of trying to prevent me from the disappointment of my own "mistakes." She did not want me to experience disappointment because she loved me and wanted the best for me. I needed to learn to erase the tapes of my childhood that told me that my parents' threats, bribes, and criticisms were meant to make me feel like a failure and unworthy of their love. Instead, I needed to interpret them as a sign of their *love* and hopes that I would have a happy life.

A year before Bart's death, my mom said to me, "I think that you should never have let Bart go into the army."

At first, I felt the familiar trigger as my usual blaming thoughts emerged. *She always has something negative to say! As if I have any control over what Bart chooses! Why can't she…?* Blah, blah, blah. But I caught myself and paused, took a deep breath, and consciously shifted my intention. I actually listened without judging her and thought, *What is she really trying to communicate to me?* When I allowed myself to be present with honesty, I was able to see—really see—that she was trying to be helpful. Instead of defending myself, I reflected to her, "You don't want me, or you, to worry about Bart while he's on the front lines, do you? You see how stressful his deployment will be for me, and you wish I didn't have that stress in my life."

In one of those rare moments in my life, my mother looked into my eyes with love. It seemed that by my looking for the good in my mother, and verbalizing it, she was able to see it in herself in a way she never had before. As Bart had taught me over the years, I had to dig down deep into my heart to find the best in her. I knew it was there; I just had to have the patience and empathy to find it. In that moment, I felt forgiveness begin to melt all the ill will that had accumulated between us from the moment I was born.

Forgiveness would take lots of conscious practice on my part. Being aware of the positive intent behind my mother's comments and criticisms meant I had to be present without focusing on my own story of why I thought she saw me as unworthy. Even with my intention to shift from a place of fear to a place of love, my brain was patterned to trigger negative, defensive thoughts. The brain loves pattern, whether helpful or not, and fear compels you to maintain the status quo: go for what you know, whether it feels good or bad.

The biggest trigger was my mother's "should" language. Every time she said, "You should have done this instead," or "This is what you should do," the hair on the back of my neck bristled with anger. My first attempt at shifting the status quo was to ignore her, but I found that without honesty my responses became passive aggressive. "Well, I gotta go, Mom. I'm busy. Got lots to do." I could not get off the phone or out of her space fast enough.

It occurred to me this was only putting a Band-Aid on a deep wound. To be able to approach it differently, I needed to first see it differently and remind myself that this was her way of preventing me from feeling disappointment or regret if I made a mistake.

It didn't take me long to get to practice the technique again. In the very next conversation on the phone, her familiar words started to flow like a bird gliding on the wind, "Oh, Ginny, why did you do it that way. You should have...."

I let her finish, and then I said, "Mom, I know that you are trying to help me and prevent me from making a mistake. And I know you want me to succeed. But when you tell me I *should* have done it another way, I feel frustrated because I am helpless to change what has already happened. I feel like a failure, and then I want to get off the phone with you. It's that 'should' word. I know you are trying to be helpful, but it just doesn't feel helpful."

Silence. "Okay," she said with guarded anticipation.

I continued. "What would be most helpful to me when I am sharing my struggle with you is if you could find some encouraging words like, 'You will get through this,' or 'That must have been hard.' I know it will be difficult to change your habit, so when you slip into the 'should' mode I am going to signal you by telling you, 'You shouldn't "should" on me, Mom.' Okay?"

To my surprise she laughed. She *laughed*. She got it. She understood. She heard me, and she wanted to honor me. This was a major breakthrough. I had cracked through her shell and found love underneath. Our new way of communicating was our little secret. I had to signal her several times in the following months, but it didn't take long for her to make the shift. One time she even confided in me that she didn't want to talk about negative things with me anymore because I was such a positive person. She wanted to be more positive with me.

Mulling over this breakthrough, I realized I had spent 47 years expecting her to know what I was feeling. She was my mother. She should *know* what I think and need. We were mirrors of each other—mother and daughter, right? But she didn't know, and I shouldn't have expected her to know. I knew she wanted what was best for me, that she loved me at her very core. I even believed she lived vicariously through me and wanted me to accomplish all the things she was never able to achieve for herself. But the shift had to come from me. I needed to speak up and *be* the love that would help our relationship shift toward an alignment of peace and joy.

One day, early in this transformational process, we went to lunch at a local restaurant. We had a nice connection over lunch, and when we left we stood chatting in the parking lot for a moment. *Now's the time, Ginny. Choose love. Hug her, and don't let go. Just hug her with all the love you have to give.* So I did. I'm sure that hug lasted no more than 30 seconds, but it seemed a lot longer to Mom. It clearly was uncomfortable for her as she made several attempts to pull away from my embrace. I kept chiming in, "Not yet, Mom. I'm not done. I just want to hug you to let you know how much I love you."

When I released her, she had a loved that/hated-that smirk on her face. The hug had felt so foreign to her, yet I could see it felt good.

"You're so silly with your hugs." With an inconspicuous smile on her face, she got into her car and went about her day.

For the first time, I felt love from my mom just by choosing to offer it to her without expectation of getting anything back; but the love she gave me in return changed my life.

Forgiveness requires empathy. Empathy was easy when I could see her perspective without trying to resist it, fix it, or change it. I began to reexamine all the stories of blame and anger about my mom, and others, that I continually replayed on the tapes in my head. I worked hard to transform my previous perceptions, opening my heart to love rather than finding reasons to be angry. But how would I shift my perception of my adolescence? This was, after all, where the blame-shame game began.

With a lot, and I meant *a lot,* of practice—and lots of oops-ing—I was able to see that during my chaotic adolescent years, my mom had it rougher than I originally thought at the time. She had lost the man she so dearly loved in a most violent and unexpected way. She learned for the first time that he had been gambling away the family fortune for years, and she was left holding a shitload of debt from his gambling binges. She was broke and unemployed—not because she had chosen to be unemployed, but because my father thought his wife working outside the home was socially unacceptable in the affluent lifestyle he tried so hard to portray. My mother had given up the intellectual stimulation and personal satisfaction of a career to make her husband happy and, as a result, had no experience or prospects when she found herself in need of a job. She was suddenly the single parent of four grieving teenagers.

The more empathy I projected, the more compassion poured into my heart, and the judgment was replaced with forgiveness. Once I began to forgive my mother, we began to develop the loving connection we both had always desired. In my infancy and early childhood years, she was too preoccupied tending to four children, all born within three years of each other, to focus on me. During my teen years, she was too devastated by the loss of her husband and the mess he left behind. In my young adult years, she was too disconnected from her own self in her alcoholism for her to know how to connect with me. But the truth is that my blame-and-shame stories were what got in the way of allowing *me* to connect with *her*.

I had to learn to love myself first before I could see and be that to Mom and to my children. I had the power to choose love in any moment. Love was not something that I had to earn or that I had to rely on others to give me for me to feel and be it. No, love, I discovered, was right there in my core and had been all along. By offering it to others, I only strengthened it in myself. Loving unconditionally is a lifelong journey, and I am grateful to have found empathy and positive intent for my mother before she passed. It was because of this journey with her that forgiveness of Jody was not necessary. I was able to choose love.

## Chapter 39

# OH, SHIFT!

*Everything you seek is inside you.*
—JOEY KLEIN[42]

Forgiving my mother and the man who killed my son seems easy to me in retrospect, but the road to that destination was long and winding. It began with the threat of a wooden spoon, when I discovered that controlling through fear not only didn't deter Bart's disrespectful behavior, it actually provoked it. I realized then that there had to be a better way to be the best mom I could be to both Nic and Bart, but it took me years to figure out how.

The road began in the mid-eighties, after my divorce. We needed a change. I decided to move from upstate New York to a small town on the coast of southern Florida where my mom and brother Gordon lived, and where I would have some support starting anew. It would take me a couple of years to save enough money and find a job before I could move, but I was determined to provide a better life both for myself and my children.

Amid my plans to move, I met Jack. With all my might, I resisted falling for this man. I refused to stay in New York to start a life with him—or anyone—but as our relationship began to grow, I found him too compelling to let go. It was hard to resist his humor, his enthusiasm for honest communication, and his open heart. A year in, things were looking serious.

"I just want you to know that I love you, but I am not staying in New York," I told him. "If you want to be with me then you'll have to come with me. If you choose to stay, then we'll just call this a short-but-wonderful romance I will never forget." Deep down I hoped he would join me. There was no turning back on my plans, but I didn't want to let him go.

A year later we married, blending families. Jack and I headed south with John, age 10, Nic, eight, and Bart, six. Kristy, 15, chose to remain in New York with her mom; she didn't want to leave her friends.

Our first year together was not easy. We had three major simultaneous stressors: new family, new jobs, and custody issues with the boys. Most difficult was Bart's strong will. Everything seemed to be a battle with him, and it was getting in the way of his relationships with his new stepdad and siblings. There were times both Jack and I wanted to throw in the towel and go back to New York, but we decided returning would be much harder than trying to work out our struggles to be a happy, connected family in Florida.

I had landed a temporary job as a speech pathologist in a school for children with varying exceptionalities. A condition of my hiring was that I become certified to teach in the state of Florida. I was given temporary teaching certification based on my master's degree but was required to pass the Florida state exams by the end of my first year of employment. Part of the exams involved algebra, which I hadn't touched since my early college days, so I enrolled in an adult algebra class to prepare for the exam. This was where I met Sue, another teacher seeking to pass the exams. Sue was not granted temporary certification, so until she passed the exams she was self-employed and planning to teach parenting classes. She asked if I would be willing to be a guinea pig in her *Redirecting Children's Behavior* (RCB) class. She wanted to hone her skills before starting her business. I was all in. Anything that could help me to be a better parent would be a blessing. I needed all the help I could get given the struggles over the years and now the dynamics of our newly blended family.

RCB opened my eyes—wide. Through this parenting course, I realized that my need to control Bart was getting in the way of my connection with him. My relationship with him up to then had relied on a false, fundamental belief that he was responsible for my upset, and he needed to change his behavior for me to be happy and connected with him. I constantly lamented, "If he would just follow my rules and stop these crazy antics, this disruption in the family would stop."

My change in behavior after taking the course confirmed that the real problem was not him, it *was* me as I first suspected when I threatened him with that wooden spoon. For so many years, my emotional outbursts of frustration had been operating from a place of fear. My intention was to shift this fear to love in the discipline of my kids. I wanted to relate to Bart—and, quite frankly, to everyone around me—in a more connected way.

At that time, my normal emotional state was stress. There was never enough time in my day. I was a hamster running on a wheel to nowhere, obsessively checking off items on an interminable list of tasks that I thought needed to be completed before I could relax. But there was always more to be done, and I never allowed myself any time to recharge. Friends and family who greeted me with "How are you?" got a consistent, maniacal response: "Busy, busy busy!" I blamed everyone and everything except me for my stress. *If only Jack and the kids would do this or that, then I would have more time for me.* I even blamed my dirty house for my unhappiness. But really, the only person to blame was myself. I had set an unachievable goal that only confirmed I was not enough and never would be.

RCB taught me that to create the relationships and peace I desired in parenting, I had to stop blaming others and change myself. And so, the mindful journey began bringing awareness about the patterned behaviors that were ingrained in me from early childhood. They were keeping me stuck and preventing me from being the person I wanted to be. The course had a dramatic impact on both me and my family and inspired me to become an instructor. I created a side business, *Peaceful Parenting*, and started teaching classes at night along with my full-time teaching job by day.

Part of my RCB certification required that I attend a very intensive, self-growth weekend course called *Understanding Yourself and Others* (UYO). The name of the course speaks for itself. I was reluctant to tell Jack about the course because of the expense. I had never spent $500 on myself at one time; it felt selfish.

As expected, he tried to talk me out of it. "That's too much money! It feels like a rip-off…" Blah, blah, blah.

Guilt crept through my veins, once again, telling me I wasn't worthy. If I attended, would he leave me? I couldn't stand the agony. "Are you going to divorce me if I do this?" I blurted out.

Jack looked at me, startled. "No, of course not. You're going to do what you want to do. I can't stop you. But I am not leaving you."

This risk I had just taken to make my voice matter with an adult male was a pivotal step toward asserting myself and becoming the me I wanted to be. I loved Jack, and I wanted him to be happy with our relationship. I didn't want to lose him like I had lost my father, but it was important that he heard my voice, that we were equals.

That weekend in my UYO course, I learned all the ways I was blaming myself and others for things that had happened in my life. I was victimizing myself and, in the process, rendering myself powerless. After discovering this pattern of behavior, I committed from that time forward to take my personal power back.

When I got home, I was exhausted but enlightened. My family noticed a change the moment I walked through the door. Rather than the half-crazed, task-obsessed control freak, they saw the authentic, loving me. I was lighter, calmer, and more at peace with myself and them. They were so impressed that they not only insisted on attending my course graduation the next day, but wanted to take the course themselves on the next available weekend. It seemed the course was worth every penny. I became an assistant UYO instructor, attending up to 10 classes a year for the next several years and eventually supervising the courses. My family attended at various times over the years as well.

As I became more empowered, so did people around me. Our family began to function with respect and dignity for the most part. We replaced arguing and yelling with family meetings and negotiation. But most importantly, UYO eventually gave me the opportunity to repair my relationship with my mother.

Peaceful Parenting was growing in popularity, requiring me to work both my day job and many nights as well. My family was beginning to suffer from my absence. I was overwhelmed trying to balance it all. I saw myself return to the edge of the old Ginny, trying to control my outside world because of the stress on the inside. It became obvious to me I had to choose one job or the other.

Giving up my teaching position meant giving up a secure salary and retirement benefits. If I chose Peaceful Parenting full time, there was no guarantee of success. Yet my heart told me to devote myself to my business so I could follow my dream of making a bigger difference in the world. Without being restricted to a classroom, I could make a considerable impact on children and families.

Jack was concerned about the financial implications, but being the wonderful man he is, he encouraged me to follow my heart. We saved enough money so I could let go of my teaching position at the end of the following school year without financial distress. To bolster my business, I continued my education by getting certified to instruct a variety of relationship-based courses related to children, adolescents, and educators.

In my last year of teaching, I attended a workshop called *Brain Smart Discipline* taught by Dr. Becky Bailey, the chair of the Department of Early Childhood Education at the University of Central Florida. After reading her book, *There's Got to Be a Better Way,* which was in complete alignment with my approach, I applied her strategies to teaching adults how to effectively discipline themselves and their children. Learning the newest brain research related to the development of self-control would be helpful for future parenting classes.

It was at this workshop that I made a personal connection with Becky. During a break, we discussed how fascinating and helpful the material was and how I would include it in the business I planned to start full time at the end of the school year.

"Yeah," she said, "I'm quitting UCF at the end of next year. They wouldn't give me a parking space."

We laughed.

"Actually, it's true. They gave me a parking space, but someone always takes it. But seriously, I took a sabbatical this year to write a book called *Conscious Discipline*. Hopefully the book will be published by next August because I'm going to lead a week-long Conscious Discipline Summer Institute. Want to come?"

"Where do I sign up?" I called her office as soon as I got home. There was no way I was going to miss this opportunity to pursue a better way. I was the first registrant.

I became hooked on *Conscious Discipline* because it is a transformational approach that focuses on changing yourself first before disciplining children. As Becky asserts, "Discipline isn't something we do to children; it is something we help to develop within them." You can't teach children to discipline themselves if you can't discipline yourself. There are seven powers that help adults take their personal power back by shifting their resistance of children's challenging behavior to acceptance, and seven skills that are used to motivate and teach both adults and children to take full responsibility for managing their feelings and choices.

Immediately following the summer institute, Becky asked me if I would become the first certified instructor for her company, which would require my traveling nationally to present Conscious Discipline's transformational approach to educators and adults working with children. Conscious Discipline was paving my path of self-actualization. By teaching others, I was teaching myself. It allowed me to work on changing the false beliefs that were getting in the way of some of my relationships—particularly those with my mother and Bart—which seemed like perpetual struggles. I dove into a deeper level of experience by strengthening my personal power with awareness.

The essence of change for me happened when I discovered the power of acceptance and the power of love, both of which lie at the heart of Conscious Discipline. The power of acceptance—seeing this moment as it is—allowed me to stay present in the moment without judgment. Suspending judgment enabled me to stay positively connected and offer empathy to the person I was conflicted with. The power of love—seeing the best in others—challenged me to shift from offering a negative intention, manifested by judgment, to offering the highest intention to others, love. No matter how hurtful a person's behavior is, choosing to see the best in them allows them to see the best in themselves. On the contrary, if I choose to see the worst in someone, then the worst in them always comes back to me.

As we discussed in chapter 22, you are not your label; it is important for parents to be very careful about the intention they offer to their children. Intention creates labels, or beliefs, for our children that they can carry with them for the rest of their lives. In my mind, the powers of acceptance and love are the core of the journey toward being the change we want to see in others. They are interdependent; you can't practice one without the other.

There seemed to be endless opportunities to practice these beliefs and skills in my relationship with Bart. At first, I viewed his behavior with a negative intention. When I saw Bart as an out-of-control, disrespectful child who needed to be put in his place, that intention had a direct impact on how he saw himself in that moment and, accordingly, he responded to me negatively. This was evident by his response to the threat of the wooden spoon and to the teachers who saw him as defiant throughout his academic life. It is possible that continual negative intention could have led Bart down the same path that Jody went down. He could have become the incorrigible label I offered to him if *I* had not changed. Instead, I chose to see Bart's defiance as a call for help. He lacked the skills to manage his struggle with a world that wasn't going his way. Providing a positive intention, empathy, and choice, within the limits I was setting to keep him safe and accountable, allowed Bart to flourish and live the life he was meant to live.

By the time Bart was killed, it was not difficult to offer the same love and acceptance to Jody, his killer. In fact, I did it without even realizing it. With endless practice I came to a deeper understanding of unconditional love for others and myself.

Conscious Discipline also taught me to let go of taking on other people's upset by blaming myself for it, although this continues to challenge me. It is simply hard to own my perception as nothing more than *my* reality, not the truth. Every thought I "knew" to be true was really based on a belief that was neither true nor false. All my beliefs are based on my perceptions or stories of my past experiences, usually established in early childhood. The power of perception says that my upset is created by me, not by other people. No one *makes* me upset. Only *I* can make myself upset. My pattern of thought had typically been, *That makes me...*, or *They make me....* These thoughts consumed me and would create an inner state of upset, the antithesis of peace.

Changing that thought pattern meant that when I perceived that someone was blaming me or getting upset with me, I had to focus on the knowledge that it was their perception—their upset—not mine. This helped me to not take Bart's and others' behaviors and antics personally. When I was stressed, I tended to fall back into old patterns of blame. Over time, I learned to re-pattern myself to pause and take deep breaths until I could address the situation with composure rather than internal emotional chaos.

Hardest for me was to learn how to shift from being passive-aggressive to being assertive. To this day I continue to struggle with finding my worthy voice. At times, guilt will still wriggle its way in and I give in, surrendering my boundaries like I did when my kids used to whine to stay up longer. "*Please?* We never get to see you." Often, I'd let them stay up because I felt guilty about not spending enough time with them like a "good mother" should. My kids were astute at knowing all my guilt buttons and when to push them.

But as my guilt began to wane, my voice of knowing began to emerge. I was able to be clearer in voicing my expectations without preoccupying myself with how others felt about the boundaries I set. I began to feel my integrity. It required me to constantly shift my focus from the outcome I didn't want to the outcome I did want, enabling me to express to others how I want to be treated. I perpetually practice setting boundaries by verbalizing "I am not willing to do that, but I am willing to do this."

One of the most powerful transformations for me was shifting from blaming others to owning my choices. I shifted from a world of "shoulds" to accepting what my choices were in the moment. Choices freed me from a feeling of resistance to one of acceptance and focusing on what I wanted. If I was having a glass of wine with a friend and thinking, *I should be home working on a presentation for work*, guilt would slither in and I would immediately resist myself and everything in that moment. Instead, the power of free will allowed me to see choice in the moment by telling myself, *I could be working on my presentation, but I am choosing to spend time with my friend. Do I want to go home and work right now, or continue to be with my friend?* What I choose isn't important. What is important is to accept whatever I choose. When I take responsibility for every choice I make, I am empowered to change direction when *I* choose.

At the core of my growth was shifting my perception about connection. I was so disconnected from myself that I couldn't establish the closeness I yearned for in my struggling relationships because I was too preoccupied with satisfying certain mistaken conditions. My belief was that love must be earned, that if I could somehow achieve the goal of being special, then being enough to others and belonging would magically happen. That need for others to love me in order for me to feel lovable cornered me into relationships with a ball and chain around my ankle. In my first marriage I desperately tried to "get" Jerry to love me the way I thought he should. *If only he would stop this or do that, then I will be happy and feel loved.* Unfortunately, the cost of my need to control was connection. It was a false premise that if I could "get" others to love me, I could love myself. Relinquishing those chains allowed me to unconditionally love myself first.

Conversely, I believed that the people in my life who were what I thought they should be to me deserved my love. If not, then they weren't worthy. I would denigrate myself mercilessly because I couldn't be enough for them to make me a priority in their lives and, ultimately, I disconnected from my own self.

I've come to learn that transformation of self is a journey, not a destination. You can't hurry it up; it's a lifelong process. Growth comes from accepting that struggle is the catalyst for transformation. Feelings such as disappointment, angst, anger, love, and happiness guide us, awakening us to see and challenging us to see and be the love that we are.

Prior to the onset of my transformational journey, my belief about being unworthy led me to feel guilty about my sheer existence. When I began to see my self-worth with open eyes and an open heart, I could begin healing the many internal wounds that festered in me in that jail cell of shame.

## Chapter 40

# GOLD STAR MOM

*Imagine there's no countries.*
*It isn't hard to do.*
*Nothing to kill or die for,*
*and no religion too.*
*Imagine all the people*
*Living life in peace.*
*You may say I'm a dreamer,*
*But I'm not the only one.*
—JOHN LENNON[43]

I officially became a military designated Gold Star Mom the day Bart died, but I didn't know it until a Veterans Day celebration two months later when a petite woman decked out in red, white, and blue approached me before the ceremony and introduced herself. "Hi, I'm Joanne. I'm the president of the local chapter of Gold Star Moms. Are you aware that you are officially a member?"

I had no clue what it even was. "Uh, no. Tell me more."

"Well, the American Gold Star Mothers—or Gold Star Moms, as it's more informally known—is an organization for mothers of fallen soldiers. We are a special group of people." She winked at me.

*No kidding. That can't be a club that any mother wants to be a member of.*

She must have read my mind. "Yeah, it's not a group we chose to be in, but here we are!" She flashed me a bright smile with a tinge of sadness tugging down at the corners, something I guessed she'd worked hard to hide over the years. She went on to explain how her son had died in a motorcycle accident while serving on active duty, and how the Gold Star Moms had helped her to feel honor for her son's sacrifice. She described some of the military activities they participated in, such as commemorative ceremonies and parades.

I tried to picture myself in a military parade in my patriotic Gold Star Mom outfit, waving to all the people on the sidelines as they dabbed at their noses with hankies and fluttered their little American flags with patriotic pity. I wasn't sure I had it in me.

I didn't know how to respond to her. A mix of emotions flooded my gut at the thought of being a part of this group, none of which I could clearly decipher. Questions began to pop into my mind. *Why should I be honored? I felt neither proud nor privileged. It was not my sacrifice; it was Bart's. He was the one who had defined his dream, set his path, and accomplished it all—only to lose it all.*

There was something wrong with this picture, but I couldn't put my finger on it. I felt pressure to be grateful for their attempts to honor me as a mom of a fallen soldier, but I sensed that there was a hidden agenda in it all. I questioned if this was the military's misguided attempt to apologize for the unintended consequences of war. Or was it to pacify women who had lost a child they had borne, raised, and deeply loved, making them feel special and honored so they show up at all the military spectacles in their patriotic mom uniforms, smiling for the crowds and displaying their pride at having made the supreme sacrifice for their country? *No hard feelings! It was an honor for me and my family! We'd do it all again if we could!* To me, acknowledging the title would feel like condoning the military's hypocrisy, and this didn't work for me.

Certainly, the moms weren't to blame. Their intent to make me feel virtuous and proud was well-meaning. They had lived the pain and the struggle to get through it. They only wanted to support me in my struggle, but I was sure this was not my path to healing. The only virtuous thing I had done in this journey was to accept Bart's chosen path and encourage him to live his dream. I was just collateral damage in the tragedy of his death.

I didn't know how the other Gold Star Moms felt about this. I was afraid to ask. Grief is a very personal thing. Everyone goes through it in their own way. Asking how these women felt about the military's role in this could reopen some recently healed wounds, and I didn't want to go there. But am I the only one who is angry that the loss of my child is labeled as a sacrifice when there was so much more to it than that? Am I the only one who feels shame that I was not able to prevent this from happening? Maybe I could have been more persistent in convincing Bart to go about his dream another way. When did patriotism become the rug for the military to sweep their mistakes under? Am I the only one who feels guilty about wanting to speak out because it could be perceived as unpatriotic or dishonorable to my son? My voice was a silent scream, the kind you experience in a nightmare when you try your hardest to make your voice heard, but no matter the effort all that comes out is a pathetic whisper of an exhale.

With all due respect to the Gold Star Moms: don't honor me; honor my son. He received no medal for his sacrifice, and it won't be long before his sacrifice is forgotten. If we continue to use violence as the means to bring peace to the world, there will be other fallen soldiers who will replace Bart in the headlines.

Did the army even know the Bart I knew? Did they know of his commitment or witness his dedication to the mission he chose to serve? Did they know that he was planning this journey from the time he was a little boy, that first he dreamed of being a Navy SEAL, then a Green Beret, and then of getting into West Point? Did they know the lengths he went to to overcome his fears so he could serve with courage and dignity? Did they know his passion for history so he could serve as intelligently and bravely as great military officers have through the ages—a leader to his men? Did they know his ultimate goal was to be a diplomat, to support international relations in achieving world peace in a way much more humane than the way he died?

No. I suspect even his immediate superiors didn't know this about Bart, and this is what was truly sacrificed. For this I feel incredibly proud, not for some vacant patriotic implications of duty, honor, and country. Lieutenant Bart Fletcher was a soldier of the highest military integrity, and he is the one who deserves the honor, not me. I was just his mother. I was the one who resisted his dream for many years because of the fear I would wind up exactly where I am now, mourning the loss of my son for a cause I don't believe in.

We need to stop forcing our chosen way of life on countries we share this planet with, and to stop using our economy and politics as the drivers of our hidden agenda. Force is not the answer. Force instills fear and begets defiance; whatever you are aiming to achieve by trying to control the outcome will not endure. When I tried to coerce Bart as a child into following my rules, I was met with defiance. What human being does not want to have choice or free will in their life? Choice strengthens and empowers them to take full responsibility for their life. Why can't we listen more to what people want and empower them to get it without hurting others? It is only through empathy and compassion that we can create cooperation. Love is more powerful than fear.

One day when I was walking my miniature schnauzer, Lily, we came upon the neighborhood cat: a solid black, domesticated stray belonging to no one particular family but adopted by the neighborhood at large. Nobody knew where she came from, but everyone cared for her because she had such a sweet and loving nature. As soon as protective Lily saw her, she began to bark with her sharp, threatening alpha bark. Rather than take a defensive posture, the cat's response to Lily was to offer more love! She did not exhibit an ounce of fear, but continued to approach Lily, trying to rub and nuzzle against her. To my surprise, the cat calmed Lily with her affection, enough so that Lily gave up the aggressive bark and started to quietly sniff the cat. Before my eyes was the power of love at work. This cat was remarkable! When encountering aggression, her focus was on love and the threat began to dissipate. If this wasn't detente, I don't know what is.

What if we discontinued our attempts at coercion and worked toward compassion? Can you imagine a world with no violence? Violence defies the Golden Rule, which virtually every culture and religion based in love on this planet espouses in one form or another. Violence destroys human lives, individual free will and well-being, and personal property. Human beings killing other human beings is unnatural. If you don't believe me, look at the history of post-traumatic stress disorder brought on by what soldiers have witnessed on battlefields over the centuries. We have a Mount Everest to climb here, but it can be done—one step at a time. Bless the generations that follow, for they hold the seeds of change.

Despite my conviction that war was not the answer, I chose to support Bart in his journey because there was no denying that he was a warrior at heart and thrilled by the challenge of bringing positive change to the world. Knowing that I could never control his choice, the only option for me was to love and support him unconditionally. But I also knew deep down that Bart did not believe war was the answer either. He had a higher goal—diplomacy—but he wanted the military experience first to understand the issue from the other side.

All I am left with are the tears of loss and the joyous memories of having had the privilege to be his mom. There is no Band-Aid—no military extravaganzas or Gold Star Moms club that will bring honor to my loss, no matter how red, white, and blue. They will never bring my son back to me, or heal my wound, or alleviate the pain our family will live with for the rest of our lives. The pain will always be there, and the best I can hope for is peace. I don't ask that the noise, trouble, and hard work that has become my life will disappear because I know they won't. All I can hope for is that in the midst of all those things, I can find calm in my heart through love and compassion.

## Chapter 41

# AN UNKNOWN SOLDIER

*As we express our gratitude, we must never forget that the highest appreciation is not to utter words, but to live by them.*
—JOHN F. KENNEDY[44]

My year of firsts was almost complete. For most who experience the tragic loss of a loved one, it is a huge relief to accomplish the one-year milestone of grief. To experience every birthday, holiday, and traditional ritual in that first year with the conspicuous absence of one who was always there and never will be again is deeply painful. The events continue without them but will never be the same. The joy they used to bring to the occasion is now a gaping hole that can only be partially filled with a tender memory.

For me, the loss of Bart was more than missing his presence at family events. I missed the spontaneous, drop-in visits from his friends I had "adopted" over the years. I was second mom to some, and I could never play that role again. Nor could I be a part of the military friendships, rituals, and events that Bart had celebrated in previous years. The recognition of his service and sacrifice had been reduced to Veterans and Memorial Day parades.

I was internally conflicted by the remembrance holidays that honor the military. There seemed a delusion of patriotism to it all. So many souls lost, some dead and some still living. The ones who live suffer on the inside, grappling with what they lived through for the sake of freedom, some with regret and some deeply scarred by their experiences on the front lines.

For many years I celebrated Memorial Day as the holiday that kicks off summer, enjoying three luxurious days at home with my family, laughing and splashing in the pool, and enjoying grilled hot dogs and hamburgers on the patio until the warm evening faded into starry night. Somewhere in there, we would hang the American flag in front of our house and take a few moments to remember and honor the soldiers who had made the ultimate sacrifice. I used to acknowledge the holiday by wishing people a "Happy Memorial Day." But since my son died while serving his country, the holiday takes on a totally different meaning, none of it happy. Now holidays and rituals that include Bart focus on his sacrifice as the supreme act of patriotism.

It was for this reason we decided that the first of several holidays after his death, including Memorial Day, we'd go on vacation. Despite being asked by several event coordinators to attend various Memorial Day observances that first year, it was just too painful to stay and participate. Instead, we rented a cottage on Seneca Lake in upstate New York where we could privately observe the holiday with campfires and s'mores.

The second year after Bart died was different. On Memorial Day 2010 our family was asked to attend the annual Memorial Day event in a neighboring town as special guests. They wanted to honor Lieutenant Bart Fletcher, I surmised, because he was one of the more recently fallen heroes in our community. We were given front-row seats at the event where State Congressman Tom Rooney, among other local patriots, would address the crowd.

It was a hot and humid day, and the forecast called for rain late in the morning. I approached the event subdued on the outside but battling a flood of emotions on the inside. Vacillating between angst and pride, pride became the stronger contender. This event hardly felt like a celebration.

Was it anxiety? No, it was fear. No, anger. No, sadness. I was not sure which one was the prominent emotion, but I was a hot mess internally. In my mind, the logical thing to do was run—just get in the car and drive to the beach, watch the waves tumble to shore until I felt calm again, and try to have a happy day. But I had made the commitment to be at the ceremony, and so I'd stay. I was positive it would have meant a lot to Bart, as it did to Jack, so I put on my pseudo-celebratory face and pulled up my proverbial bootstraps.

Surely some people would recognize me and express their gratitude, but the pity within them would seep out like blood from a fresh scrape on the knee. I had been victimized but I never saw myself as a victim, and I didn't want others to either. When they expressed their gratitude, I wondered if it was gratitude for Bart's service or gratitude for not having endured the kind of sacrifice our family had experienced. Were they secretly grateful it was not them?

To avoid the well-meaning condolences, we got there early. We picked seats that were barely shaded by the awning covering chairs that had been set out for guests. As Jack and I sat for a moment, we both noticed a mock cemetery to the right of the awning that was filled with hundreds of white crosses, like Arlington National Cemetery on a much smaller scale. Each cross had a dog tag that hung from its center.

Curious, we strolled over. Standing in front of the display was a cadet from the local military academy. Jack approached him.

"Hey there, young man. This looks awesome. What are these crosses about?"

"Yes sir, well, all the students attending the academy have been making these crosses for months now. They represent all of the fallen soldiers dating back to World War 1 who lived in our local area."

Jack explained our situation with Bart.

"I'm sorry for your loss, sir. I'm sure he's somewhere in here. The dog tag will have his name on it, and if you look up his name in this book there should be a reference to where his cross is placed. Again sir, I'm sorry for your loss."

Jack and I were impressed by the order and the way this military school had chosen to honor all those who had lost their lives serving their country. This felt much more honorable than listening to a bunch of predictable speeches about patriotism. It felt real—a tangible way to connect with Bart in his dedication of serving.

The book was sitting on a pedestal, and we approached it with excitement. For the first time, I began to feel authentic pride. The service men and women were listed in various categories, but I couldn't find Bart's name. I was nervous and confused, so I asked Jack to help. He went through the book several times before giving up.

"How could this be?" I asked Jack, frustrated. "They asked us to come to this event that honors hundreds of fallen soldiers with crosses, but forgot Bart's?" The disappointment began to overwhelm me. I could feel my throat tighten and seething anger grip the muscles in my jaw.

"I don't know, Ginny, but I'm going to find out." Jack went into rescue mode and started asking the servicemen in charge why Bart's name was not in the book. At first, they were very apologetic and embarrassed. They seemed confused too. It must be an oversight. They asked us a series of questions related to the details of his death. For the life of me, I could not figure out why all this information was so necessary. All I could think was that they were stalling, trying to hide their incompetence. Then there was a pause, the type of uncomfortable pause that precedes an uncomfortable truth.

"What?" I insisted.

"There is a reason, Ms. Fletcher, why Lieutenant Fletcher is not represented here," said one of the colonels attending the service.

Another pause.

"Okay. Would you care to tell me?"

"Well, Lieutenant Fletcher is not considered a 'fallen soldier.' Only soldiers who receive Purple Hearts—that is, those who die in the line of duty on foreign soil—are designated as 'fallen soldiers.' If you die in the line of duty in the United States, you are not a fallen soldier." The colonel stared at us, not knowing what else to say.

My throat started to close as it contracted into knots of anger. It was all I could do to hold back tears and words of resentment. No cross for a fallen soldier who experienced the bad luck of falling on the wrong soil. What the hell difference did it make that he fell on American soil? He died in service to his country. I lived with that thought a moment, then—ah-ha—it dawned on me. I knew why it mattered. American soldiers are not supposed to die in America. It's not the natural order of things. When soldiers fall, it's supposed to be on foreign soil, defending democracy from foreign enemies. That's what the military is for. Not for defending themselves from their own soldiers. But my soldier had died on American soil at the hands of one of their own. The army had failed to protect him in the line of duty, and now they wouldn't recognize his sacrifice because recognizing it might be perceived as an admission of culpability, an admission that something had gone terribly wrong.

I thought back to my first visit to Fort Hood the day after Bart died, how the army had told me he had been shot once, in the chest, when he so obviously had been shot five times in the head as we later learned. But not from them. They had never acknowledged what really happened that day on that balcony in Killeen, Texas. And now, for the second time, I was a victim to the military's contrived stories and hidden agenda. How dare they? How dare they use Bart, us, *my* family, as the embodiment of sacrifice in the name of freedom when underneath it all they don't even recognize his sacrifice. They were just glorifying our loss with these stupid ceremonies to cover up their shame and incompetency. The message came across loud and clear: they would keep up their facade until we, the family left picking up the pieces, started to believe it and forgot how the tragedy could have been prevented in the first place.

The mama-bear in me attacked. "If not a fallen hero, then what is Bart? A fallen what?" I did not wait for a response. I knew it was going to get a lot uglier if I did not redirect my attention to something else. Wanting to save some grace for the ceremony that was about to begin, I turned and walked [illegible], [illegible] by a wave of resentment invisible to others but eating me up inside like an aggressive cancer. *Here I am again, sacrificing my feelings to please everyone else.* I could have choked on my anger.

As I marched over to my seat, Jack could see how upset I was and followed. I was stifled by my anger. Streams of tears were flowing down my cheeks behind my sunglasses. Jack attempted to console me, but I couldn't respond. I was afraid that if I spoke, I wouldn't be able to hold back my rage and would make an ass of myself, my family, and Bart.

I sat, totally shut down and unresponsive. As the national anthem played to initiate the ceremony, I barely heard it or paid attention to the muffled words of the hypocritical speeches that followed. Raindrops dripping from the edge of the awning peppered my legs and feet as I sat ruminating and fuming. Each raindrop took on a life of its own, each one falling in slow motion and exploding with a loud splash as it hit my flesh. The sound, not audible to others, was deafening to me, drowning out all ambient noise except for that of my own voice reverberating in the auditorium of my mind. My own speech drowned out the one on the dais in front of me as my inner voice bellowed, *What the hell is the matter with you people? Do you mean to tell me that the sacrifice my son made, dying in the line of duty, is not worthy of being honored? His heroic sacrifice to save his captain, his sergeant, the manager, and residents of that apartment building—even the soldier who killed him—was not enough to deserve recognition in the eyes of the military? If you had handled the whole thing differently….*

The weight of what felt like gallons of water that had been collecting in the awning above me, like the fury in my soul, was more than the awning could bear. A deluge dropped into my lap, snapping me back to the present.

I was soaked from the waist down, but oddly the shock of it had pacified me. The anger and frustration that had been building inside me since the moment I had arrived at this fiasco had been released, like the floodwaters breaking through a dam. My torrent of mixed feelings about war, the purpose of the military, its incompetency, duplicity, and its pretense of patriotism and altruism were mollified for the time being. A temporary truce.

"Oh, no! Ginny…." Jack said, under his breath.

"Well," I said, smiling at him wryly, "when it rains, it pours!"

# Chapter 42
# DEAR CONGRESSMAN ROONEY

Jack and I learned several days after the Memorial Day celebration that Colonel Weierman, the commanding officer of the Southeastern Military Academy (who was not the colonel we spoke with at the event), was the person overseeing the construction of the little cemetery on display that day. The students from the academy had painstakingly created and placed each of the crosses in the cemetery. I do not doubt the dedication and pride they all took in honoring the brave soldiers with such a heartfelt exhibit.

The colonel called us when he learned that Bart had been excluded. He was obviously distraught; he had not considered the impact of excluding soldiers who died in the line of duty, but not on foreign soil. For a nanosecond I could acknowledge his pain, but that did not quash the disappointment, anger, and dejection I felt because of the military's illusion of honoring my son that day.

I felt compelled to be the voice for all those unrecognized soldiers and their families, so I wrote the following letter to Florida State Congressman Tom Rooney who had spoken at the event and served in the same division Bart served in, the 1st Cavalry Division, during Operation Desert Storm.

5-31-2010

Hello Congressman Rooney,

As a Gold Star Mother sitting in the front row watching your passionate, heartfelt speech, I knew there were few who could put aside their pity and truly see the depth of struggle that has been the gift of what motivates you to be where you are today. Your uncle gave you, at a very young age, the gift of knowing that truth and sacrifice is what it truly means to serve a cause that makes a big difference in the lives of others. Something bigger than oneself. Selfless and heroic.

I too know that feeling as a mother who reflects on the struggle of raising a leader who never got to achieve the leadership he envisioned because his life was taken in the duty of serving his country. As I am experiencing the first Memorial Day event after my son Lt. Bart Fletcher's, death (here in the States), I have been struck with surprise, awe, and deep sadness that his sacrifice is not acknowledged as honorable enough to be included with those who are honored as "killed in action." He does not get a Purple Heart. He does not get included on CNN's *Home and Away* listing of soldiers who sacrificed their life for freedom, and, perhaps most disturbingly, I did not find him on the list nor on a cross with a dog tag for soldiers worthy of memorializing at the Stuart Memorial Day ceremony, which I was asked to attend.

I can tell you I was too angry to talk with you today. I was overwhelmed with grief. How can anyone say that my son's death was any less than that of those who died on the battlefield? He had served in Iraq! He, an executive officer, was ordered by his captain to pursue a potential criminal act by one of the soldiers in his company at Fort Hood and ended up being the victim of a murder by one of his own. Tell me how that is not considered an act of combat worthy of a cross that bears his dog tag? Tell me; explain this to me so that it makes sense because it does not make sense to me. I feel outraged and demoralized.

My son, by the way, was accepted into West Point, although he chose not to attend. He was a powerful leader whom many admired and, if nothing else, gave courage to others who doubted that they were capable of pursuing their dreams. To quote Bart in his freshman year of high school, "Dreams should never die. Nothing can kill them except uncertainty." Bart's dream was for all humans on this planet to experience freedom of choice. And he knew the cost of freedom. He served for the same reason all those soldiers were killed in action on foreign lands. Why in God's name can't he be included with them?

I know you said you are working on a bill to include the soldiers in the 2009 Fort Hood incident in receiving the "proper honor" that KIA soldiers get. I can only hope that my son—along with all soldiers that are caught in this trap—is included in this bill and acknowledged with the same reverence. It is time that we all stop closing our eyes to the fact that military casualties of "combat" happen in our own backyard. Why should the fallen soldiers caught in this "home-front combat" have to be the scapegoats for the military's shame?

I give you my permission to share this letter with anyone you choose to, or to consult with me on this matter, as I believe this letter represents the voice of many families who have lost beloved sons and daughters in ways similar to our family's loss.

Thank you for taking the time to consider this letter.

Wishing you and yours well,

Ginny Luther

Lt. Robert Bartlett Fletcher's mother

## Chapter 43
# BLUE STAR MEDAL OF VALOR

*The highest of distinctions is service to others.*
—*King George VI*[45]

Several months after the Memorial Day ceremony, I had not yet received a response from Congressman Rooney but I received a phone call from a reporter for the Stuart News, the primary newspaper for our county. After introducing herself she said, "I want to get your comment on the award your son just received."

"What award?" I asked confused.

"The Blue Star Medal of Valor." She laughed, thinking I was joking.

"I'm not sure what you're talking about. Could you give me more detail?"

"Your son is Lieutenant Robert Fletcher, correct?" Now *she* sounded confused.

"Yes."

"Well, the City of Stuart, Congressman Rooney, and Colonel Weierman from the Southeastern Military Academy are honoring your son as the first recipient of this medal for the sacrifice and service he gave to our country. Could you tell us the story of how this medal came about?"

"Could you hold on a minute?" I had no clue what she was talking about. Excited and bewildered, I put the phone down and went in search of Jack. In order not to sound like an idiot to the reporter, I needed clarification from Jack in case he knew about this and forgot to tell me, which was highly unlikely.

"Uh, Jack, the Stuart News is on the phone asking about some medal Bart was awarded. Do you know what they're talking about?"

"What medal?"

I shrugged and nodded toward the phone.

Jack picked up the other line while I listened in. "Hi, this is Jack Luther. Can I help you?" He went through the same conversation with the reporter that I'd had, and then asked her some questions.

She revealed that the Florida legislature had just approved a Blue Star Medal of Valor to honor Florida residents who have died in the line of duty—on American soil—and Bart was going to be the first recipient.

Jack and I looked at each other and beamed.

Although she hadn't discovered yet how the bill had come about, she was looking into it.

Jack told the reporter about his conversations with Colonel Weierman. "The colonel called me after he found out our son was not represented in the little cemetery the academy made for the Memorial Day ceremony in Stuart." Then he proceeded to share the story about Bart's blue star in great detail. Jack never tired of opportunities to tell Bart's story.

"The funny thing is that we were not aware that there is an organization called the Blue Star Mothers of America. We didn't learn of it until we became a Gold Star Family. A Gold Star Family is the immediate family of a fallen service member who dies while serving in a time of conflict," Jack explained. "Come to find out, Blue Star Mothers of America is a nonprofit that supports mothers of soldiers who are serving in active duty in the US Armed Forces. When Ginny gave the blue star to Bart just prior to his deployment, she had no idea of the full significance of it."

"These are amazing stories," the reporter told us. "We're looking forward to seeing you at the Blue Star Medal of Valor Ceremony at Stuart City Hall and would like to get a photo of you both for the story."

"We would be honored to attend. Thank you very much." We hung up the phones. Jack was grinning from ear to ear with pride. Finally, there was some official recognition of the service and sacrifice Bart had made for his country.

As we later discovered, Colonel Weierman did indeed spearhead the creation of the Blue Star Medal of Valor because of their negligence in recognizing Bart at the Memorial Day event. He had contacted Congressman Rooney who sponsored the bill in the Florida legislature to make the medal official in the state of Florida. Weierman had suggested naming the medal after Bart's blue star because he had been so moved by the story Jack had shared with him. Rooney had also been responsible for getting approval to fly the American flag at half-staff at the state capitol for a day to honor all soldiers who had died in the line of duty while serving on American soil. He too had felt our pain, deeply.

I was overwhelmed with joy at the ceremony in Stuart. The hole in my heart was filled with pride in receiving the medal for Bart. I felt him standing next to me in spirit. The medal honored his purpose, his lifelong dedication to serve his mission for freedom, and I was the hand that received it for him. That was enough for me. My resentment against all those honorary ceremonies that had neglected Bart's contributions began to wane. Bart, and all the other forgotten casualties, were no longer unknown soldiers.

As an added gift, the Sandburgs, a Florida family standing next to us at the ceremony, were the second family to receive the Blue Star Medal of Valor in honor of their son, Brandon, a Navy corpsman, who died in a helicopter crash during a training exercise in 2007. The medal was a symbol of honor to him and his sacrifice in service as well. The tears of joy the Sandburgs cried for their son whose contribution had finally been recognized, bringing [illegible] [illegible] of closure, gratified me beyond words.

*Chapter 44*

# THE STRUGGLE IS THE GROWTH

*We either get bitter or better. It's that simple. You either take what has been dealt to you and allow it to make you a better person, or you allow it to tear you down. The choice does not belong to fate, it belongs to you.*
—JOSH SHIPP[46]

How does struggle become growth? It seems impossible since most of us resist any kind of struggle. Struggle means that the messy emotions we don't like to feel come forth, and all we want to do is numb them away or distract ourselves, so we don't have to deal with them. Somehow exposing them defines us as weak and unstable. We fear disconnection from others for being vulnerable with our feelings. Yet the very thing that keeps us stuck, unable to reclaim our personal power and grow, is not the struggle with feeling the feelings but the resistance of accepting the struggle.

In my life I have had to face two tragedies most would consider overwhelming: the loss of a parent to suicide and the loss of a child to violence.

When faced with my father's death I had no awareness of a grief process to healing. My only recourse was to react to grief rather than to respond to it. From bulimia to excessive use of drugs and alcohol, self-abuse was my only source of healing and a temporary one at that—a Band-Aid over a deep wound.

When faced with Bart's murder, grief loomed like Mount Everest before me. I was afraid I would fall into a crevasse of grief, unable to move or call for help as I experienced with my dad. But this time I was more mature in my awareness and understanding of emotional regulation from all the mindfulness work I had done between the two losses.

Grief. Grief was the game I had to play to get through the struggle. I knew I was going to have to climb that mountain, and I wasn't sure I was completely prepared. There is no prescribed length of time nor precise process for how one gets through grief, only the guarantee that it starts in a very dark and daunting place.

In the first year after Bart's death, I was numbed out of reality, numbed out of joy, and numbed out of feeling present—or feeling anything. I pinched myself daily, not so much to wake myself from my nightmare but to confirm that I actually still existed.

My work mentor, Becky, would call me daily and guide me through a three-step process which I clung to. "Take a deep breath, Ginny. You can do this! You are going to get through this!" She waited a moment while I complied and then said, "Now take a step forward and breathe again."

This was something I taught regularly in my profession to those experiencing emotional distress. Although I did not believe it would work for me in that moment, I thought, *Ginny, you'd better practice what you preach.*

And finally Becky would say, "Have you eaten today? Go to the kitchen and find something, no matter how small, and put it in your mouth." She knew all too well that when stressed I could not eat.

And so, I followed her lead. A couple of weeks into this practice, I realized that I might be okay. Deep down I had a glimmer of hope that this time, with awareness, healing was possible.

For the most part, I functioned primarily from a state of survival. Distraction, busy-ness, and my secret with Bart were the saving graces that helped me to at least function—although somewhat dissociated. It was just a matter of getting through one day at a time. Distraction and busyness allowed me to bypass the grief, hoping to fast-forward 10 years so I could skip over the pain. My fear was that if I allowed grief to rear its ugly head, I would tumble into a devastating emotional pit of hell that I would never be able to climb out of. *What if I can't stop crying for a whole year, like when I was 15?* I thought. *No one would stick by me for that long.* I refused to be the whimpering victim in all this. I needed my support system, my friends. So I plowed forward in numbness. Resistance was working just fine for me.

I worked out a lot and drank more wine than was healthy to temporarily relieve my stress. If people asked how I was, my answer was always "Okay… really busy." "Okay" meant that I didn't have to feel what was really going on. Everyone knew I wasn't "fine," but "okay" was perhaps believable. I used it to bypass the grief that was trapped inside me. And "busy" gave me permission to talk about anything but how I was really feeling.

The funny part was that nobody really seemed to understand the difference between "fine" or "okay." To them, the words were equivalent. But to me, there was a world of difference. I began to become aware of my own mental state using "okay" as a kind of a checking-in tactic. *How are you today, Ginny? Are you okay?* I'd ask myself. It helped me not only to identify what I was really feeling but also allowed me to accept that "okay" was enough. I didn't have to be "fine" to be enough.

It took a tremendous effort to convince myself that I was okay. For a long time it seemed I would never move beyond that state. I was frightened, pondering whether I'd ever feel happy again. Fine, happy—they were foreign to me. There wasn't enough happiness in the entire world that could possibly fill the massive hole in my heart. I just wanted to die. I refused to feel happy because somehow feeling it would diminish the memory of my son and the love I had for him. Feeling joy was something I thought I did not deserve because "good mothers" should be devastated forever.

And then there was the other saving grace: our shared secret. I never anticipated how essential it would be in reminding me I would be able to handle my grief. It saved me from diving head first into devastation. When Bart, at 17, shared with me that he would be leaving this planet early in life, I acknowledged its truth as well. Nothing more was said about it, or needed to be said. I didn't have to question why. There seemed some divine, universal reason for it. It was just a matter of waiting for the when of it and enjoying the remaining time we had together. It wasn't something that I thought about all the time. I was shocked by his death, when it came, and devastated by his absence, especially because it had happened so soon after his safe return from Iraq. And now, in the back of my mind, the voice of our secret whispered, *Remember? You both knew.*

I took comfort from the fact that we had been able to share this connection. My confirmation had comforted Bart. The release of his tension and fear was palpable. He could finally share this terrible burden he had been keeping to himself and was also grateful that I understood, not needing to explain or defend it. My knowing brought him peace, and his peace brought me comfort.

I had not physically been there with my son when he died, but I had been there spiritually just as I had been when I looked into his eyes on the day he was born. Our secret did not change the depth of sorrow or grief or the time it would take me to heal, but the sheer comfort of it helped me to begin to open the doors to accept its truth.

Grief was knocking on the door of my heart, but I would not allow it in until I was willing to feel and be with the pain without it consuming me. I needed to let go of resistance and grab onto a thread of acceptance. It took an immense amount of courage to accept the hell I was about to go through. I wanted to be present with the pain, without fighting it. It was important that I allow myself to feel this darkness without becoming it.

At first, acceptance felt overwhelming and unachievable. Watching myself approach my grief was like a mother watching her child venture into the ocean alone for the first time. I wanted to call myself back, fearing the surf would be too strong, the tide too severe. Learning to trust that I would be safe was challenging for fear that this current, so much more powerful than I, might grab me and pull me under. Would I be able to surface again and come up for air? I had to be able to be with the pain of wanting to die, knowing it was just an expression of the depth of the pain I was feeling, not a true desire.

There was no book or YouTube video to show me how to grieve. It was mine to figure out. The challenge was to accept the beauty of it, but first I must be willing to experience the primal nature of it. Healing required me to be present with the expression of grief, the wailing so loud I hoped the neighbors wouldn't think someone was in danger. Sometimes, I resorted to grieving in my car, parking in isolated locations to express an anger that was so monstrous I wouldn't dare expose its ugliness to others. On occasion I screamed until I had no voice left, utterly exhausting myself. Other times I sobbed until there were no more tears.

One day, roughly two years after Bart's death, I returned from an errand to an empty house and found myself staring at the memorial shelf we had created for Bart in our living room. There, in a photo, sat Bart in his army regalia in his Abrams tank, his smile full of joy and glory. Surrounding the picture were various items of memorabilia: medals, mementos, and gifts of remembrance. Sadness welled in my throat. *It's time to let it come, Ginny,* I consoled myself, but I resisted, holding back my tears. *Come on, Ginny. You can do this. Let it wail.*

I surrendered, releasing a scream that originated in hell. There were two of me: one watching and one wailing. My watching self felt secure, as if she were stroking the back of my wailing self and soothing her with gentle encouragement. *Be with it, Ginny. You got this.*

Words of sadness, anger, and blame spewed from my wailing self. As I came up for air, I felt a gentle shift, a lightness much like I did when my mother passed. There was a deep beauty and sense of joy amid the grief—nothing I ever expected. My tears were tinged with love—the deep love I felt for Bart—and joy for the journey I'd had with him.

At that moment Jack came bursting through the front door. He saw my face, reddened from screaming, tears and mucus dripping from my chin, and ran to me, hugging me to him as if I were a toddler needing soothing and security after a frightening fall. "Oh, my gosh, Ginny! Oh, my gosh! Are you okay?"

Jack did not let go until I was calm. "I just got home. When I got out of the car, I heard this screaming and, honest to God, I thought it was our neighbor's kids in the back screaming in pain. I thought something terrible had happened. When I came in and saw you screaming, I freaked out! What happened?"

"Oh, honey, I'm so sorry. I didn't know you were coming home. This was one of those moments when I thought I could just let it all go. I needed to do this. It's part of my healing."

"I'm just glad you're okay. You let it go, all you need to. I'll be here if you want, or…not," he said half-jokingly.

"I think I'm done for now. Thank you, sweetheart. I usually do this alone so I don't scare anyone, like I just did you."

I had done it. Feeling the fear and allowing the grief to visit me at a deep, dark level did not destroy me. I had handled it. And after having passed through it, I emerged on the fringe of joy. Grateful for the struggle and the growth that came from it, I was able to turn the tears of fear into tears of love, if only for a nanosecond.

I had accepted my grief, though I knew I was not done and perhaps never would be. But I had committed to working through the pain, knowing that on the other side of it was something true and good. And I was looking forward to the day I could actually embrace the grief with open arms—invite it in and explore it with curiosity.

These healing moments began with explosive releases of the pain that filled every cell in my body. I wanted them—needed them—to pass through me like a thunderstorm on an oppressively humid summer day, revealing as the clouds dissipated a glorious rainbow, the promise of the beauty that follows struggle. Those days of anger at losing Bart and blaming others in my grief would eventually be replaced by tears of joyful memories of the life we had together. When I was present with these tears, I could embrace joy as if it were my best friend.

Grief, I came to learn, is not who I am, but rather the expression of the deep love I have felt every day since losing Bart. Grief has become my badge of courage and honor. Like the stretch marks on my belly, they are not ugly scars to hide but beauty marks of motherhood. It is not something to be afraid of, nor something to resist. It doesn't have to be with me all the time or at any designated time or place. Whenever it bubbles to the surface, which can be at the most unpredictable of times, it's an opportunity to experience the depth of love that I remember with gratitude, not the love I have lost.

Struggle is the gift for growth to blossom. Hold on to this notion! There is a hidden treasure in every struggle. Embrace them, explore them, learn from them. And when you find the gift, healing flourishes and enlightenment prevails. Many believe their mistakes or failures define them as "less than," not enough, not worthy. Quite the contrary; the mistakes, failures, and struggles we experience actually propel us forward.

I am lucky to have had many angels in these times of struggle, including my struggle to write this book. You can recognize an angel by the timing and alignment of their presence in your life. I have learned through both tragedies that my family is not necessarily the one I was born into; it's the people I hold to be true to my heart, the people in my life who are always there for me no matter what. My family of origin were the angels that catapulted me to search for the love inside me.

Your most authentic family, however, is you—all the family you will ever need. You are the one who chooses how to see and be with yourself in every moment. What you offer to yourself you strengthen, whether you are wishing yourself well or wishing yourself hell. And what you offer yourself surely will be projected to others. Your journey is to create experiences that inspire you to find self-worth with unconditional love.

My life has changed and will never be the same. I continue to keep breathing and, with the tiniest bit of willingness and faith, taking a step forward in the face of what at times does not seem fair, hopeful, or even possible. I continue to gain new vision, strength, and deeper wisdom from sharing my story with others. By virtue of my story, these mothers, spouses, and children can rephrase their own stories, giving themselves the strength to hold tighter to their visions of hope. I have met incredible human resilience, and with that comes a deep knowing that all is well.

## Chapter 45

# MEMORIAL DAY 2020

*You can't go back and change the beginning,*
*but you can start where you are and change the ending.*
—*Unknown*[47]

Memorial Day 2020 was the perfect day for me to do what I had been putting off for over 11 years. There was no place to go, nothing to do. We were in the midst of a pandemic, sheltering in place. The tropical paradise we were living in was a ghost town; even the public beaches were closed. And to make this melancholy holiday even bleaker, torrential rain poured throughout the day. So dark were the skies that you couldn't tell what time of day it was without looking at a clock. We kept the lights on in the house all day.

When I awoke in the morning gloom, a little voice reminded me what day it was. Memorial Day: the annual reminder of the sacrifice Bart made for the sake of our freedom. I sat up and threw off the covers, remembering my promise. "Today is the day, Ginny. You are finally going to do it," I declared with confidence. "You can do this!"

It was time. Time to listen to the 911 recording of Bart's murder. I was in the middle of writing this book and had been thinking about the recording. Before I could say Bart's story was complete, I had to *hear* how he died. For one thing, I needed to confirm that the facts as stated in the book were correct, but I was also considering putting a transcript of the recording in the book.

Bart had once told Jack and me that if he were to "die" suddenly, during his military service, not to trust what the army told us because it could be a cover-up for CIA work he might choose to do in the future. Bart's warning was something we did not take lightly. And because the army had told us he was shot in the chest, when we later found out he was shot in the head, we wanted details from a more reliable source. We requested all available records from the Killeen Police Department a few weeks after Bart's death.

The civilian police report had given us more detail than we learned from the army, and Jack was eager to listen to the 911 recording to ease any lingering doubts about Bart's death. I was curious too, but afraid of the emotional impact it would have on me if I listened to it then. The pain was still too raw.

"You don't have to," Jack, always in rescue mode, said. "I'll listen to see if there's anything we don't already know. You'll know when, or if, you are ready to hear it."

Now I was ready. In addition to hearing the details exactly as they happened that day, I wanted to hear my baby's voice—his last words spoken on this Earth.

Jack and I had been searching the house for the past few days for all the records of Bart's murder. We found most everything, except for the newspaper articles and the CD recording of the 911 call. They were all together, packed away safely somewhere, but where?

"Jack, I've looked everywhere. I've gone through every drawer in this house. They're not in his memorial bin. I don't understand where they could be. I know we wouldn't have put that stuff in the garage."

"I don't know either. I can't figure it out, sweetie."

With nowhere else to look, we headed out in the pouring rain to search the garage from top to bottom. I got up on the stepladder and saw a large Ziploc bag stuffed under some other things in the loft.

"Look what I just found!" I sang. There, sitting on top of the articles in the bag, was a CD titled *911 call.*

"Bingo! Now, are you sure you want to do this?"

"Yup, I'm sure. I'm ready now," I said, hoping it was true. "It's a perfect day for it. Just like the sky, I've got all day to cry."

Determined, but scared shitless, I was curious about what I would experience while we listened. I wondered if I would be able to recognize his voice. Would I be plagued by nightmares? I was positive about only one thing: I was no longer afraid to feel my feelings and I invited them in, knowing they were important to my healing. Being able to *watch* myself feel was a compelling challenge for me.

When we went into the house, I paused. "Uh-oh. Jack, I don't think we have a CD player."

"Oh, yes we do. Right here in the kitchen cabinet." Jack pulled it out and fumbled to plug it in.

I had forgotten about the small portable player John had bought for us recently.

"You ready?"

"Yes, but I want you here with me." I took a few deep breaths.

"Absolutely. I'm right here with you." He slipped in the CD and pressed play.

"911. What is your emergency?"

As I observed myself listening in these first moments, it was hard to be still. I paced a bit, stopping several times to listen to my body. I was beginning to feel overwhelmed by what I was hearing. My body was shutting down, going into a survival state. A surge of adrenaline flooded through me. My jaw tightened. My heart raced. *You got this, Ginny,* I reminded myself. *Breathe.*

I focused on Bart's voice. Had the Killeen Police Department sent us the correct CD? "His voice sounds different. It doesn't sound like him," I said to Jack.

"That's him, sweetie. You'll see."

Had I forgotten the sound of my own son's voice?

We were one minute into a six-minute-and-42-second recording of this murder, and it already felt too long. I wanted to fast-forward to get it over with. But the more I listened, the more familiar Bart's voice became until it was fully recognizable. My eyes watered as the mother in me connected with him like the first moment we met, face-to-face, on the day of his birth. How many times had I heard that voice as he had grown up in this house? I was comforted by this connection, but my old friend sadness began to knock on the door.

*Hello, sadness,* I said to myself. Sadness was back, here to remind me not of the loss this time, but of the love.

As the recording progressed, I felt sadness slipping away. *Come on sadness, don't leave me now!* When sadness retreats numbness steps in. Numb seemed to be a deeply patterned go-to response for me when life became fragile and I attempted to protect myself from feeling the real feelings that lie beneath, the ones that would help me heal. The wall of numb was too thick for me to break through in this moment. I knew my focus on the present would slip away. I was shutting down in anticipation of the end of the recording and Bart's final moments of life. It was hard to make out the words in the final 30 seconds. I missed most of it, trying to manage my anxiety, but there would be plenty of time to listen to it again when I transcribed it. I just watched—watched myself with curiosity in my attempt to handle this.

When the recording was done, I paced. No tears. No anger. No sadness. Just agitation. *What the hell is the matter with me? Shouldn't I be devastated, wailing, and sobbing at the unfairness of it all?*

My functional self kicked in. *Just keep moving, Ginny, one foot in front of the other like you did after Bart died. Time to move on and get this done.*

"Okay, now the transcription," I declared to Jack. He retreated to the back bedroom to watch TV while I took on the task.

I plopped myself on the living room couch, putting the CD player on the side table next me. *No need to think, thank goodness. Just focus on the words.* With a deep breath I pushed play and let the CD dictate what I would write.

To make sure every word was transcribed correctly, I had to backtrack after each sentence. On a one-track CD, this meant it returned to the beginning of the call each time. After a minute of transcription, I felt myself becoming extremely irritated. *How am I going to get through this entire thing without losing it if I have to repeat it from the beginning over and over?* I got up and paced, taking deep breaths. Then I had an idea. I picked up the CD player and went to Jack's room.

"Hey, would you do me a humongous favor?"

"Sure." Jack was up for anything to support me in this.

"Would you record the whole thing on my phone so I don't have to keep going back to the beginning every time I want to repeat a sentence? I don't want to listen to the whole thing over and over again. The less I listen to it, the better." I wasn't resisting my emotions each time I heard the recording. What I was resisting was the torture of having to listen to it repeatedly. There is a difference between welcoming feelings and welcoming torture. One felt healing, the other like self-abuse.

Jack took the player and went into the office. He recorded the whole thing on my phone while I paced in the living room.

"Here you go." He handed everything back. "It's done." Once again, he retreated into the back bedroom to finish watching *Naked and Afraid,* his favorite TV reality show. Ironically, "naked and afraid" perfectly described my reality at the moment.

With the recording on my phone, I was able to confirm the dialogue by going back only two to three seconds at a time, reducing my angst significantly. Another hour into my project, I had transcribed about two-and-a-half minutes of the recording when Jack came out to check on me.

"It's time for you to stop. You need a break."

"I'm fine. Really." It was a pathetic attempt to convince him.

"No, you're not fine. I can see it in your face. You're stressed out. Go take a bike ride. The rain has stopped for now. I looked at the weather radar, and you have time."

"No. Really, I'm okay."

"Nope. You're going to stop and go for a bike ride. Now shut it off."

Once on my bike, I rode hard. That damn recording played over and over in my head, like the soundtrack to my out-of-body state, totally hijacking my ride. I hoped I hadn't made the wrong decision in listening to it. But observing my agitated thoughts gave me the power to realign them into something more peaceful, if I chose.

*Are these thoughts accomplishing the outcome I want?*

A clear *No!* resounded in my brain.

*What thoughts will help me right now?*

*I am safe. I can handle this.*

As I rode, echoing this new thought, I forced myself to be present by noticing the now. The saturated ground was covered with puddles that I rode through with sheer delight, like a young child going for the biggest splash ever. The screaming frogs in the marshlands bordering the road drowned out any noise of traffic, and wading egrets and fluorescent roseate spoonbills in the overflowing culverts fought for my attention, bringing me back to the beauty of the moment.

In my mind was Bart's voice, absent of the stress in the recording, encouraging me. "Mom, you can do this! Go big or go home!"

*All is well. I am loved. He was loved. All is well.*

My mind quieted and I was back now, in the present, enjoying my ride and grateful for the break in the rain. I completed my usual 20 miles, and when I rolled into my driveway the skies opened up again like the tears I wanted to shed but couldn't.

After washing up, I went right back to the transcription. The hardest part was anticipating the end because the end meant just that—the *end*. The end of my life with Bart.

When I was done, I cried. It was final. There was no disputing it now. Did he suffer? Was he scared? Did he know those were the last moments of his life? I cried tears of sadness, tears of relief, and tears of joy. Sadness for the recognition of loss. Relief for getting through it without total devastation. And joy for the closure I had wanted so badly at Fort Hood and the funeral home after Bart died, but never got. I was consoled by telling myself that Bart could not have suffered in his moment of death. It had all happened so quickly that he never had a moment to process it.

Some people might think that choosing to listen to your son die is downright crazy. It would have been, years ago, when my wounds of resistance were so raw. But since I have accepted and embraced my grief, the feelings seem to come with less intensity than they did back then. Because I embraced whatever feelings came, without resistance, the intensity of the storm dissipated, and the closure brought me the calm I so desperately sought.

## Chapter 46

# AGAINST THE WIND

*The only condition for love is that there are no conditions.*
—*UNKNOWN*[48]

As I was riding my bike recently, I reflected on how my life's journey parallels a bike ride. The difficulty of my ride is often determined by the direction of the wind and its speed. When I am riding against a strong wind, I struggle to pedal to keep my speed. I push and pant and force myself to get through it until the direction of the wind (or my bike) changes and it comes from behind, relieving me. In life, the wind that comes at me head-on is the fear, anger, and resistance of the struggle in a moment of conflict. When the wind comes from behind it is the acceptance, hope, and gratitude that allow me as the rider to surge forward, pedaling in self-love and interdependence.

In my journey with my children, the ride of parenting varied with each child. What I have discovered in loving all my children is that I do not love them the same. I am equal in the depth of love I feel for each one, yet different in how I connect with my love because each relationship has its own dance.

My ride with Kristy, the oldest in our blended family, has been easy, simply because I did not raise her. She chose to reside with her mom in upstate New York when our families blended and we moved to Florida. She was in an adolescent phase when peers were a primary focus in her life, and we wanted to honor the option that she felt most comfortable with. I have primarily supported her in the raising of her children. We have always maintained a respectfully loving relationship. Even though she was not an integral part of the family as a child, I will always consider her my daughter, and her children will always be my grandchildren.

With John, the wind was a steady, head-on push from the time our families blended when he was 10. He was not ready to accept love from his stepmom until he left home on his adult journey. I could have chosen to ride against him in his resistance, but instead opted to change directions, riding with him in love. Accepting that his resistance might last a lifetime, I chose to love him without expectation, and it paid off. When he left home at age 18, the wind took a dramatic shift in my favor. My choice to love him unconditionally, despite his attempts to push me away, had a positive impact on us both. I am lucky that we share a deep love and that he accepts me as one of his moms today.

Nic, my firstborn, was a smooth ride with the wind mostly at my back. Love was so easy with him. He was a flexible and happy child, always singing or whistling his way through life and looking out for the safety of his brother. He easily entertained himself with puzzles, Legos, and Transformers, rarely demanding my attention. He had his own journey, trying to maintain his balance while weathering the sudden and fierce gusts of crosswinds that came from my tussles with Bart. He never complained, but I know there was fallout. He had to live in Bart's shadow, sacrificing his own emotional needs to avoid the distress and surrendering the connection he so needed and deserved from me. Despite his challenging ride, he has created a beautiful family of his own and is an amazing, loving dad to his two children.

With Bart, the wind started out quiet and still, but in no time built to gale-force. I couldn't pedal against it. The more I resisted, the more exhausted I became. Slowly I began to shift my direction, letting go of what

I couldn't make happen. In choosing to see his behavior as a call for help and shifting from fear of his anger to love and understanding of his needs, I let go, changed my course, and allowed the wind to push me from behind.

All that I learned about myself in the journey with my children didn't guarantee a smooth ride. But I knew that when the wind kicked up, I could ride against it or consciously change my course to ride with it. Love is a choice, but you can't choose love if you don't recognize that it is a choice in the first place.

When my dad died tragically, my ride was upwind in the pitch-black dark on an unpaved road of fear. I couldn't see what direction I was going, much less avoid the potholes. The more I resisted the wind, the more self-abuse endured from bulimia to a failed marriage.

My ride with Bart, and later with my mom, brought me the light of day. I learned to repair two of the most difficult relationships of my life through love and gratitude. When they died within five months of each other, I was in a much better place to deal with my pain than I had been when my dad died. I was able to shift more readily to position the wind behind me, fortified by the love that broke open in both relationships. If I had resisted by lashing out at the world in my sorrow, I honestly think I would be a raging alcoholic today, still stuck in that storm of helplessness and hopelessness. Instead, I chose love and gratitude, even connecting with my mother before she died in a way I once thought wasn't possible.

Along my often-challenging ride I learned that if peace and joy were going to be a part of my world, I had to extend them to others because what I offer to others I strengthen in myself. When I offer love through kindness, helpfulness, respect, and compassion—without any expectation of receiving it back—love miraculously reciprocates, which is what I am seeking in this journey we call life. And then I can be my authentic self.

As a society we must ask ourselves how we want to be with each other. Consider this exercise I sometimes offer in my parenting classes. I give each person in the room of 100 or so a balloon and ask them to blow it up and write their name on it. Then I ask them to close their eyes and throw their balloons into the middle of the room. I tell them I'm going to count to three, and then I want each person to open their eyes and find their own balloon within one minute.

You can imagine the chaos that ensues with everyone scurrying around trying to beat the clock. Most would be unable to find their balloon and lose the challenge. But then I give them a second chance. This time I tell them that instead of looking for their own balloon, grab the first balloon they touch and find that person and give it to them. What do you suppose the outcome is? More people are reunited with their balloon not through competition, but through cooperation. We all win when we work together, rather than just looking out for Number One. Offering helpfulness to others is helpful to you.

We have a choice of how we want to be with one another. Do we want to be "us and them," or do we want to be united? Being right in blame feels good at first but separates and divides in the long run. Choosing cooperation and kindness amid internal chaos is a much more loving approach.

It is difficult to find and be your best self to others when you are stressed from focusing on all the wrongs of the world. You become a part of the struggle and feel helpless to calm yourself. When you consciously relax and align yourself with gratitude and connection, you can find a place within where there is calm. The struggle is still there—it always will be—but you can choose to ride with the wind of it, instead of against it.

END

*Epilogue*

# GOOD LEADERS ARE HARD TO RAISE

*Becoming a leader is synonymous with becoming yourself.*
*It is precisely that simple, and it is also that difficult.*
—*Warren Bennis*[49]

Good leaders are hard to raise. The qualities it takes to make a positive impact on the world are not often compatible with a parent's view of what makes a family run smoothly. Leaders are born with a sense of power that can trigger a parent to want to squelch or control that power in an effort to keep family life more peaceful, but that parent's vision of success for their child can interfere with the child's vision for himself. A child's success is best accomplished by the parent surrendering any plan to direct or control their child in favor of offering them an abundance of choice within a set of boundaries that guide them toward an outcome that satisfies both child and parent. I did not possess that knowledge or that skill in the beginning of my parenting journey.

Regardless of my many semesters of studying early childhood development, my primary concepts of effective discipline came from how I was parented. Although my parents loved me unconditionally, they often disciplined me with conditions. "If you don't do as I say, then I will punish you," or "If you do what I say, I will be happy." That approach led me to believe it is possible to control what others think and do and that it was, in fact, a parent's job to do just that.

Bart was not, by any means, easy to raise, but he did exhibit from the get-go what I eventually recognized as leadership skills. From the time he was seven months old to the end of his life, he was a force of nature. He dared bravely. Yet, I was fearful of where his leadership potential might take him. There is good leadership and there is bad leadership, and I was afraid of him choosing the latter if I didn't guide him on a positive path. My initial attempt was to pull on the reins to slow him down and to get him to conform to what I thought he should do or be. When I found myself threatening him with a wooden spoon and his response was to challenge me, I knew that this was going to be a long journey that would require both of us to change and grow together.

Bart's behavior challenged me to see his need for power as a call for help and to direct him down an altruistic path. I realized his potential from the day I followed that string of Christmas lights to find him beaming in total delight at the other end. He was not cognitively aware of his power at such an early age, of course, but I knew by the joy it brought him that his awareness of it was emerging. It wouldn't be long before he'd be discovering other things that made him feel powerful and creating a vision of where he wanted to go with them. His intuitive pairing of a GI Joe uniform and a tea set was a clue to a positive outcome. His continued love of guns, on the other hand, alarmed me. I eventually came to understand that it was not something I would be able to convince him to give up. Allowing him to play with guns, even though they were obviously unrealistic ones, was my first step toward letting go of controlling his vision for his life.

Good leaders are hard to raise because they must overtly defy. Most parents know that when children are developing a sense of autonomy there are times when defiance is common. Some refer to these stages in the Twos and Teens as terrible or tumultuous and bide their time—or count the minutes and seconds, depending on the intensity of the behavior—until the developmental milestone passes. Those who have leadership potential take it a step further than the norm, however; they are not willing to accept "no" for an answer. They courageously engage in conflict "knowing" at an intuitive level that it is the only way to bring about change. They go to great lengths to manipulate, defy, and wear you down until you give in.

Bart's defiance emerged at 18 months and was exhausting and frightening for me at times. My attempts at controlling it were futile. When adults attempted to control him with an intention of getting him to do things their way, it only encouraged him to double down and fight harder. I had to learn how to pick my battles with him. It was hard to let go of control because I thought I, the adult, knew better than he, the child. I had to learn to let life happen for him, which sometimes might involve failure.

Like most parents, I hated to see him fail. His hurt was my hurt. At all costs I wanted to protect him from the hurt in the world, yet risking and recovering from failure are skills required for good leadership. Every time Bart stepped outside the box and risked failing, he only strengthened his tenacity and resiliency in proceeding forward. In his relentless mission to drive that boat in Centreville Amusement Park, he risked being punished or abandoned. When he persistently pursued his Portugal and West Point goals, he risked failing his mission.

The strongest quality of leadership Bart possessed, and often the hardest to parent, was his tenacity. He was never one to give up on anything he set his mind to accomplish. As a parent I felt at times like I was riding a stallion in an open field when he suddenly realizes his freedom and takes off at a gallop. I eventually had to relinquish control of the reins and hang on for dear life, no matter what the outcome, because the force compelling the horse to experience the freedom of an all-out gallop is too much for him to resist and too much for me to fight. When Bart, at 15, declared he was going to Portugal after meeting all of my conditions, there was no turning back. When he announced he was going to do whatever it took to convince his major to commission him earlier than recommended, I had to let go of the reins.

Doing whatever it takes to reach the goal requires the leadership quality of resourcefulness. When Bart was presented with a struggle head-on, without me to rescue him, his resourcefulness emerged with flying colors. When, exhausted by the "Mommy, Mommy, Mommy!" hurled at me after a long day at work, I abruptly changed my name to George, and Bart called me out simply by using my "new name" when he addressed me, as if to say, "You want to be called George? Whatever. Just get out here, now. We need you."

That day he forgot to take his lunch to school, he was able to get his fill of the junk food I refused to buy him, and he dared bravely to ask my clientele for sponsorship for his exchange program in Portugal. He created a new path to accomplish his educational and military goals so that he could be with Katie. The struggle for me was to let go and let him grow in resourcefulness and resiliency. It was hard to know what was important to hold onto for his own safety and what was acceptable to let go of so that I could help build his leadership skills. I was taking a risk every time I let go: risk of him getting hurt, which I would never forgive myself for, and risk of being a bad parent and potentially sacrificing my livelihood.

Good leaders are self-driven and do not depend on what other people think about their goals or their methods. They don't worry that people won't like them. They know that there will always be people who disagree. They believe in their endeavors despite what people think because they are confident of the outcome and their intent to benefit others. As a parent, I was not always as confident as Bart, especially when he had to complete two years of academics in just one year and apply to West Point after spending his exchange year in Portugal. When he returned from Portugal as a "man," he felt no shame in asking me if he could have sex with his girlfriend at our house, but his drive to accomplish his goal and disregard for my boundaries almost cost him the security of his home life.

Good leaders are courageous. Like all of us they have fears, but their intent is to overcome them. Very few knew that Bart was petrified of heights. He hated going over bridges or venturing to the top of famously tall buildings. Yet he took a paratrooper course one summer that was not a requirement for his tank commander training to overcome his fear. Days before he was deployed, I could see underneath his "warrior" exterior that Bart harbored a silent fear of going off to the front lines of war that others, perhaps, wouldn't let show. Yet despite his understandable fear, there is no way he would have missed that opportunity to serve his country.

Finally, good leaders lead with their heart in service to others. Their self-worth does not come from what they achieve for themselves as much as the difference they may make in someone else's life. They often sacrifice their own needs to support another's success. Bart's letters from Iraq were humble, compassionate, and caring in his sacrifice to the soldiers he led. He took the time, when they returned from Iraq, to honor and acknowledge them for the service they gave to our country. He stepped up to support me when his oma was dying, taking time from the one and only—and very brief—break he'd had since his return from Iraq. And he got more pleasure from giving Katie and me our spa day in Killeen than taking much needed personal time for himself.

None of these qualities and skills by themselves defines a good leader. It is the integration of them that fosters altruism. For the short life he lived, Bart inspired many, but most especially me. More than any of the education I pursued, my struggle parenting a child with these qualities became the growth in me, helping me to shift my beliefs to understanding that discipline with connection is a more powerful motivator than discipline with control. He was the mirror I gazed into to examine my own struggles in childhood, reflecting to me my own unconditional self-worth. It was difficult, but we helped grow each other up. It's hard to know which came first, the chicken or the egg, but during the most trying times with him, as I began to see the best in him, I was able to see the best in myself.

In 2010 Jack and Ginny Luther created Bart's Blue Star Foundation, a nonprofit that supports social-emotional learning programs for the families of children like Bart and like Jody, the man who killed their son.

# ACKNOWLEDGEMENTS

I first and foremost want to thank the person who was the wind beneath my wings in making this book happen. Cindy Rothstein was by my side every step of the way from pulling all the pieces together to announce there was a book in the making, to seeing my capability to accomplish this beyond what I ever thought possible and encouraging me daily. The editing we did together seemed endless but divine. The book would never have come to fruition without her. I feel forever blessed by her being in the right place at the right time and dedicating her life to this book during the pandemic. She will always be considered one of my angels.

Second, I want to acknowledge my husband Jack for being the soulmate in my life that opened the doors for me to begin my personal journey in healing. He has always been there to hold me up, encourage me and acknowledge my accomplishments often by introducing himself to my peeps as "Mr. Ginny"

To all the mentors in my life, Dr. Becky Bailey, Dr. Tim and Ann Jordan, Kath Kvols, Paul Wrubel, and Norm Christensen who in my journey of transformation believed in me from the get-go. They saw potential in me that I was not able to see and never gave up in their support.

Fourth, I want to thank all the angels in the midst, Amy Speidel, Chris Mooney, Tim Malloy, and my high school girlfriends: Kate Thomson, Liz Christensen, Tory Christian, Kim Pitcher and Helen Huff who were there for me through this entire process. I am grateful for the life I have shared with them.

To those who supported me during the several stages of creation: Julie Rath, Eve Porinchak, Susan Duncan, Marla Murphy, Jackie Barnett, Susan Jones, Lindy DiPietro, Teresa Salvatore-Fuller, Ginny Beagan, Arthie Shedhak, Ann Crary and John & Wanda Fedorek and the many who participated in reading various edits of the manuscript (you know who you are.) Thank you for your honest feedback and encouragement.

Lastly and not least, I'd like to thank my children Nic, John and Kristy for their unyielding, consistent, and unconditional love they have held in the journey of healing our family loss. It has been hard for each of us and I feel grateful that we were able to hold each other up and stay connected as a family.

# ENDNOTES

1 Unknown.

2 "A Quote by Bob Marley," Goodreads (Goodreads), accessed November 2, 2022, https://www.goodreads.com/quotes/884474-you-never-know-how-strong-you-are-until-being-strong.

3 Unknown.

4 Goodreads (Goodreads), accessed November 2, 2022, https://www.goodreads.com/quotes/9335958-how-lucky-i-am-to-have-something-that-makes-saying.

5 "History of the Patriot Guard Riders," New Hampshire Patriot Guard Riders, accessed November 2, https://nhpatriotguard.org/who_we_are/history-of-the-pgr/.

6 Scott-Holland, Henry. "Death Is Nothing at All." *Death Is Nothing at All.* (London: Souvenir Press Limited, 1987).

7 Goodreads (Goodreads), accessed November 2, 2022, https://www.goodreads.com/quotes/6603842-we-are-not-given-a-good-life-or-a-bad.

8 Unknown.

9 Versey, Jason. *A Walk With Prudence* (Raleigh, North Carolina: LuLu.com, 2013), 46.

10 Pausch, Randy. *The Last Lecture* (London: Hachette, 2008).

11 Ziegler, Maseena. "7 Famous Quotes You Definitely Didn't Know Were From Women." Forbes. September 1, 2014. https://www.forbes.com/sites/maseenaziegler/2014/09/01/how-we-all-got-it-wrong-women-were-behind-these-7-famously-inspiring-quotes/?sh=676a929c1016.

12 Bennett, Roy T., *The Light In The Heart* (Roy Bennett, 2020).

13 Palmieri, Tuchy. *Oprah, in Her Words: Our American Princess* (BookSurge Publishing, 2008).

14 Unknown.

15 Bailey, Becky. *Easy to Love, Difficult to Discipline: The 7 Basic Skills for Turning Conflict into Cooperation* (William Morrow Paperbacks, 2001).

16 Lee, Harper. *To Kill a Mockingbird.* (New York: Harper Perennial Modern Classics, 2006).

17 Goodreads (Goodreads), accessed November 2, 2022, https://www.goodreads.com/quotes/649802-a-leader-is-one-who-knows-the-way-goes-the.

18 Karen Drucker. "Relax and Let Go," Karendrucker.com https://www.karendrucker.com/wp-content/uploads/Relax-And-Let-Go.pdf.

19 Clark, Bob, director. 1983. *A Christmas Story.* Metro-Goldwyn-Mayer. 94 minutes.

20 Ralph Waldo Emerson. *Ralph Waldo Emerson on Self Reliance*, Illustrated edition (Kessinger Publishing, LLC, 2005 edition).

21 Alfie Kohn. *Unconditional Parenting: Moving from Rewards and Punishments to Love and Reason* (Atria Books, 2005).

22 Unknown.

23 Goodreads (Goodreads), accessed November 2, 2022, https://www.goodreads.com/quotes/433293-imperfections-are-not-inadequacies-they-are-reminders-that-we-re-all.

24 Unknown.

25 Joseph P. Lash, *Helen and Teacher: The Story of Helen Keller and Anne Sullivan Macy* (New York: Delacorte Press, 1980) 498.

26 Fred Rogers. *You Are Special: Neighborly Wit And Wisdom From Mister Rogers.* (Philadelphia: Running Press, 1981).

27 Unknown.

28 Goodreads (Goodreads), accessed November 2, 2022, https://www.goodreads.com/quotes/83433-the-face-is-the-mirror-of-the-mind-and-eyes.

29 Susan Jeffers. *Feel the Fear…and Do It Anyway.* (New York: Ballantine Books, 2006).

30 "Supraventricular tachycardia (SVT)," NHS.uk, April 2021. https://www.nhs.uk/conditions/supraventricular-tachycardia-svt/.

31 Unknown.

32 Goodreads (Goodreads), accessed November 2, 2022, https://www.goodreads.com/quotes/525386-the-truth-is-of-course-that-there-is-no-journey.

33 Munsch, Robert. *Love You Forever.* (Firefly Books, Limited. 1995).

34 The Editors of TIME-LIFE. *TIME-LIFE World War II: 1945: The Final Victories.* (United Kingdom: TI Incorporated Books, 2015).

35 Harrison, George. "Here Comes the Sun." Genius. Accessed Nov. 2, 2022, https://genius.com/The-beatles-here-comes-the-sun-lyrics.

36 Unknown.

37 "911 Police Dispatch." Audio recording. Killeen Police Department. Killeen, Texas, Sept. 8, 2008.

38 L. Frank Baum, *The Wonderful Wizard of Oz* (London: Puffin Classics, 2008).

39 Guy Finley, *The Secret of Letting Go* (Llewellyn Worldwide, 1990).

40 "JodyWirawan.com", accessed Nov. 2, 2022, http://jodywirawan.com/biographies/the-life-story-of-jody-michael-wirawan/.

41 Goodreads (Goodreads), accessed November 2, 2022, https://www.goodreads.com/quotes/278812-as-i-walked-out-the-door-toward-the-gate-that.

42 Klein, Joey. *Inner Matrix System.* (Balboa Press, 2014).

43 John Lennon. "Imagine." Genius. Accessed Nov. 2, 2022, https://genius.com/John-lennon-imagine-lyrics.

44 John F. Kennedy, U.S. President, Proclamation, "Proclamation 3560—Thanksgiving Day, 1963," *U.S. Government Publishing Office. Accessed Nov. 2, 2022,* https://www.govinfo.gov/content/pkg/STATUTE-77/pdf/STATUTE-77-Pg1030.pdf.

45 Hourly History, *King George VI: A Life From Beginning to End* (Hourly History, 2017).

46 Goodreads (Goodreads), accessed November 2, 2022, https://www.goodreads.com/quotes/7907646-you-either-get-bitter-or-you-get-better-it-s-that.

47 Unknown.

48 Unknown.

49 Warren G. Bennis. *On Becoming a Leader* (New York: Basic Books, 2009).

CPSIA information can be obtained
at www.ICGtesting.com
Printed in the USA
LVHW101246140623
749396LV00002B/16